BRITAIN'S BEST DISH

over **100** delicious dishes from across the nation

London, New York, Munich, Melbourne, Delhi

Editor Daniel Mills
Art Editor Saskia Janssen
Executive Managing Editor Adèle Hayward
Managing Art Editor Kat Mead
Senior Production Editor Jennifer Murray
Production Editor Kelly Salih
Production Controller Man Fai Lau
Creative Technical Support Sonia Charbonnier
Art Director Peter Luff
Publisher Stephanie Jackson

Produced for DK by Siobhan O'Connor (Project Editor),
Lucy Bannell (Editor) and Jim Smith (Designer)

Photography by Clive Streeter

First published in Great Britain in 2009
by Dorling Kindersley Limited
80 Strand, London WC2R 0RL
First paperback published by Dorling Kindersley in 2010

Penguin Group (UK)

Copyright © 2009 Dorling Kindersley Limited

A CIP catalogue record for this book
is available from the British Library

ISBN 978-1-4053-5915-3

Colour reproduction by MDP, Bath, UK
Printed and bound in Singapore by Tien Wah Press

Discover more at **www.dk.com**

Contents

Introduction

It all started in 2007 as ITV began a search for the very best British dish, not in the professional world of the restaurant kitchen, but in the home kitchens of keen amateur cooks from around the country. Under the watchful eyes – and tastebuds – of three expert judges, hundreds of hopeful chefs presented their best starter, main course, or dessert.

Over weeks of competition, the judges tasted family favourites, dinner-party classics and innovative experiments, with the very finest progressing to the competition finals. These last tense few days saw fifteen cooks pull out all the stops to impress the judges and the viewing audience, and culminated in a public vote to select the very best dish.

Every year since then, Britain's most original home cooks have been lining up to present their signature dishes on the show, and this book is a compilation of the tastiest, most exciting recipes from the first three series, broadcast in 2007, 2008 and

2009. The recipes are divided into three chapters, arranged by course into starters, mains and puddings.

Alongside every recipe you will find helpful advice on preparation and cooking times, and a difficulty rating so you can see at a glance how much you are taking on. All of the recipes are designed to serve four people. Many recipes also include the contestants' suggestions for plating up, so you can be sure your dish will look as good as it tastes. Some of the recipes are quick and easy family favourites, while others are more elaborate, ideal for dinner parties and entertaining.

A great part of what makes British cuisine so exciting is the incredible variety it offers, as traditional ingredients rub shoulders with flavours from around the globe. The food in this book is no exception, and the recipes here reflect the fantastic diversity of cultural and culinary influences across the country, ranging from great British classics such as Bangers and Mash, to Italian-inspired Pork Tortellini, Austrian-style Spaetzle, Jamaican Jerk Chicken and Sri Lankan Chicken Curry.

Equally, the food in these pages reflects the tremendous diversity of Britain's own natural larder. Regional British produce from small-scale local farmers is increasingly recognized as some of the finest in the world, including unique cheeses such as Lanark Blue, prime livestock such as Welsh lamb and Angus beef, and specialist ingredients such as beremeal, a flour used for making bannocks, milled from an ancient variety of barley grown on Orkney, the Shetlands and the Western Isles.

Local ingredients like these are integral to many of the dishes in this book, from Ayrshire Ham and Cheese Tart, to English Apple Strudel with East Anglian White Wine Mousse. Some of the most successful combine British produce with more exotic traditions to create exciting fusion food, from a luxurious paella made

with Cornish seafood, to the Scots–
Indian blend of Blade Steak with
Tandoori Tatties.

There are also a few experimental
recipes so that more adventurous
chefs can test their skills and
palettes. You will find unusual
combinations such as Chocolate
Stout Ice-cream and a jam made
from rhubarb and Earl Grey tea.
Some dishes use ingredients you
might never have considered before:
Squirrel Pie introduces you to a
tasty variation on British game meat,
and Christmas Tree Granita offers a
novel use for seasonal decorations.

Whatever their origins and
ingredients, and however unusual
their flavours, every recipe here has
received the seal of approval from
the fiercely critical panel of expert
judges. This means that, whatever
your tastes and cooking abilities, and
whatever the occasion, you can be
sure to find something in these pages
to impress family and friends.

Time to get cooking!

Starters

Tasty morsels

So what goes to make a great British starter? The key seems to be using a combination of choice ingredients to produce strong, exciting flavours. After all, the aim is to tempt your guests' palates without overwhelming their appetites, so you need to ensure that whatever you choose provides maximum flavour in a small serving.

And what is it that makes a starter particularly British? One answer might be that it uses great British ingredients, and there are plenty of those in evidence in this chapter. Fish make a star appearance in many of these recipes, along with crab, scallops and brown shrimp.

Great British cheeses such as Stilton and Lancashire are also given a chance to shine in dishes such as Warm Savoury Stilton Cheesecake. And with the addition of flavourful tomatoes, freshly-picked asparagus, garden-fresh peas, juicy apples and pears, and succulent ham and bacon, this chapter is a true celebration of regional and home-grown produce.

Regional produce inevitably gives rise to regional specialities, and some of these starters are longstanding favourites. Cullen Skink originated in the Scottish fishing village of Cullen, with its fine smoked haddock. Somerset Tiddy Oggy takes its name from the West Country term for a Cornish pasty, a parcel of flavour commonly carried to work by the region's miners.

Of course, not all the starters are based in tradition and some of them have their roots outside these shores. In this chapter you can also find inventive interpretations of classic dishes from other countries, such as Austrian-style dumplings, and representatives from ethnic cuisines that are now very much part of Britain's culinary landscape, such as Caribbean Spicy Vegetable Soup. And there are one or two surprises on the menu, such as Vegetarian Haggis Pakoras, a truly magical melding of Scottish ingredients and Punjabi cooking.

Langoustine and spicy pumpkin soup

A colourful soup, with flavourful pumpkin and a good kick of chilli and Thai spices

Prep time 20 minutes
Cooking time 1 hour
Difficulty Medium

450g (1lb) pumpkin (prepared weight), deseeded and chopped
2 tbsp olive oil
sea salt
1kg (2¼lb) fresh langoustines (preferably Scottish)
1 onion, finely chopped
1 red pepper, deseeded and finely chopped
1 fresh red chilli, finely chopped
4 garlic cloves, finely chopped
1 tbsp Thai red curry paste
1kg (2¼lb) ripe tomatoes, blanched, skinned and chopped
1 small bunch of fresh coriander, leaves picked and chopped
handful of toasted pumpkin seeds, to garnish

1 Put the pumpkin in a baking tray, drizzle with half the oil and sprinkle with sea salt. Roast in the oven at 200°C (400°F/Gas 6) for 30 minutes or until tender. Leave until cool enough to handle, then peel (discard the rind) and chop the flesh into cubes. Set aside.

2 Bring a deep heavy saucepan of salted water (enough just to cover the shellfish) to the boil over a medium-high heat, then add the langoustines. Reduce the heat and poach for 4 minutes. Plunge the langoustines into cold water for a couple of minutes to stop the cooking process, then drain and peel, reserving both the cooking water and the shells (discard the heads and thoraxes). Set aside the langoustine tails.

3 In another saucepan, heat the remaining oil over a medium heat and add the onion, pepper, chilli and garlic. Sauté for 5 minutes until soft but not coloured, then add the curry paste and pumpkin and stir until everything is well coated. Add the reserved langoustine shells and their cooking water, then tip in the tomatoes. Top up with water to cover, if needed and leave to simmer for 20 minutes.

4 Remove from the heat, allow to cool slightly, then process in batches in a blender or food processor, until the shells have broken into very small pieces. Push the soup through a sieve back into the rinsed-out pan, using the back of a spoon to press out as much flavour as possible. Discard the contents of the sieve and gently reheat the soup until piping hot. Check the seasoning.

5 Divide the soup among 4 warm bowls, adding the langoustine tails and coriander equally to each serving, then sprinkle with the pumpkin seeds. Serve hot, with warm naan bread.

Sparkling fish risotto

A unique sparkle and a flourish of seared scallops make this a truly special dish

Prep time 30 minutes
Cooking time 40 minutes
Difficulty Medium

900ml (1½ pints) good-quality fresh fish stock
50g (1¾oz) butter
1 small red onion, finely chopped
a few saffron threads, soaked in a little hot water
6–8 baby leeks, finely chopped
handful of fresh shiitake mushrooms, finely sliced
300g (10oz) Vialone Nano risotto rice
2 glasses of Camel Valley sparkling wine
280g (10oz) Loch Duart salmon fillets, skinned and cubed
280g (10oz) cod fillet, skinned and cubed
8 large prawns, peeled and de-veined
8 fresh asparagus spears, trimmed
100g (3½oz) English goat's cheddar, grated
a squeeze or two of lemon juice, plus 2 lemons, halved, to serve
8–12 large hand-dived Loch Fyne scallops
olive oil
4 slices smoked salmon such as Bleiker's Apple Wood Smoked Romanov
sea salt and freshly ground black pepper

1 Pour the stock into a saucepan, place over a medium heat, and bring to a simmer.

2 Melt the butter in a large frying pan and add the onion and the saffron and its soaking liquid. Gently sweat for 10 minutes until soft but not coloured, then add the leeks, mushrooms and rice. Cook, stirring, for a few minutes until the rice grains are well coated and the vegetables have softened. Pour in the wine and stir until it has all been soaked up and the alcohol has evaporated.

3 Add the hot stock to the rice a little at a time, stirring constantly and allowing the liquid to be absorbed each time before adding more. Cook for 15 minutes or until the rice is nearly tender. Add the cubed salmon fillets and cook for 3 minutes, stirring gently. Now add the cod and prawns and cook for a further 2 minutes.

4 Meanwhile, bring a pan of water to the boil. Add the asparagus and cook for 3 minutes, then quickly refresh the spears in cold water and drain.

5 When the rice is tender but still retains some bite, remove from the heat, add the cheese and a squeeze of lemon juice and season with salt and black pepper. Stir very well, then cover the pan and leave to stand.

6 Working quickly, heat a ridged cast-iron grill pan over a high heat until searing hot, then lightly brush the scallops with oil, squeeze over a little lemon juice (if liked) and sear for 3 minutes, turning once. Sear the asparagus spears in the same pan, turning until coloured slightly.

7 Spoon the risotto onto warm plates and arrange 2 or 3 scallops on top of each serving, along with a roll of smoked salmon and 2 asparagus spears. Serve each plate with a lemon half, wrapped in muslin, for squeezing over.

Smoked mackerel soufflé tart

A light, fluffy tart with a punchy flavour and enough for seconds

1 Preheat the oven to 180°C (350°F/Gas 4). To make the pastry, either rub the flour and butter together with your fingertips, or whizz together in a food processor, until the mixture resembles fine breadcrumbs. Gradually add the iced water, a very little at a time, until the mixture just comes together to form a dough. Wrap in cling film and leave to rest in the refrigerator for 30 minutes.

2 On a floured work surface, roll out the pastry and use it to line a non-stick 18cm (7in) or 20cm (8in) fluted tart tin. Line the pastry case with greaseproof paper, fill with baking beans and blind-bake in the oven for 7 minutes. Remove the beans and paper and return the pastry case to the oven for a further 3 minutes. Leave to cool. Do not turn off the oven.

3 Flake the mackerel into a bowl and gently stir in the horseradish sauce until well combined. Spread the mixture evenly over the bottom of the cooled pastry case.

4 Melt the butter in a saucepan, stir in the flour and cook for a minute or two. Slowly add the milk, a little at a time, stirring well to prevent lumps. Simmer until thickened and smooth. Remove from the heat and add the cheese and the 2 egg yolks. Whisk the 3 egg whites to firm peaks, then gently fold them into the cheese mixture. Spoon the cheese sauce on top of the mackerel in the pastry case, making sure that it covers this filling completely. Bake in the oven for 20 minutes.

5 Mix together the orange and watercress and serve a slice of the warm tart on each plate, with the salad on the side.

Prep time 1 hour
Cooking time 30 minutes
Difficulty Medium

For the pastry
200g (7oz) plain flour
100g (3½oz) butter or hard margarine, diced
about 50ml (1¾fl oz) iced water

For the filling
200g (7oz) smoked mackerel fillet, skinned
1 tbsp mild horseradish sauce
25g (scant 1oz) butter
25g (scant 1oz) plain flour
300ml (10fl oz) whole milk
50g (1¾oz) Wensleydale cheese, crumbled
2 eggs, separated, plus 1 extra egg white
sea salt and freshly ground black pepper

To serve
2 oranges, segmented
a large bunch of watercress

"It's like eating smoked air. It is very, very light and the mackerel is delicious."
— Ed Baines

Ham and asparagus flan

A springtime flan using prime seasonal ingredients and fine Northumbrian cheese

Prep time **10 minutes**
Cooking time **50 minutes**
Difficulty **Easy–medium**

For the pastry
240g (9oz) plain flour
pinch of salt
60g (2oz) hard margarine, diced
60g (2oz) lard, diced
about 60ml (2fl oz) iced water

For the filling
10 fresh asparagus spears
knob of butter
1 small onion, finely chopped
60g (2oz) Northumberland Nettle cheese, grated
60g (2oz) Snowdonia Black Bomber cheese, grated
120g (4½oz) cooked ham, finely sliced
5 whole eggs, plus 1 egg yolk
140ml (4½fl oz) double cream
½ red pepper, deseeded and sliced
freshly ground black pepper

1 To make the pastry, either rub the flour, salt and fat together with your fingertips, or whizz together in a food processor, until the mixture resembles breadcrumbs. Gradually add iced water, a very little at a time, until the mixture comes together to form a dough. Wrap the pastry in cling film and leave to rest in the refrigerator for 30 minutes. Meanwhile, preheat the oven to 190°C (375°F/Gas 5).

2 Remove the pastry from the refrigerator, roll it out on a floured work surface and use to line a 20cm (8in) flan or pie dish. Line the pastry case with greaseproof paper, fill with baking beans and bake for 15 minutes. Take out of the oven, remove the beans and paper and return the pastry case to the oven for 5 minutes until the pastry is cooked and golden. Leave to cool for 10 minutes. Do not turn off the oven.

3 Meanwhile, to make the filling, bring a large pan of water to the boil, tip in the asparagus and cook for 2 minutes, then refresh in iced water. Drain, then cut each spear in half. Melt the butter in a small pan and sweat the onions for a few minutes, stirring, until soft and translucent.

4 Arrange the cheese, onion, asparagus and ham in the pastry case. Beat the eggs with the cream and season generously with black pepper. Carefully pour half the egg mixture into the flan, then arrange the red pepper evenly over the filling. Pour over the remaining egg mixture.

5 Bake the flan in the oven for 25 minutes and serve hot, with a salad of lettuce, tomatoes and cucumber.

Red lentil soup with lentil vadai

Full of authentic South Indian flavour, with savoury, doughnut-like vadai

1 Soak the lentils and rice for the vadai in warm water to cover for 30 minutes.

2 To make the soup, heat the 1 tsbp sunflower oil in a frying pan over a medium heat. Gently fry the curry leaves, dried chillies, and mustard and cumin seeds for 2 minutes until the mustard seeds start to pop. Add the onion and fry for a few minutes until softened. Now add the garlic, fresh chillies, tomatoes and ginger and stir for 2 minutes. Add the sambar and chilli powders and the turmeric. Stir through, then add the red lentils and 2 litres (3½ pints) water. Bring to the boil and simmer, uncovered, for 20–25 minutes until the soup has thickened a little and the lentils are soft but not too mushy.

3 To make the vadai, drain the lentils and rice well, then whizz in a food processor or blender until a thick batter forms. Add the bicarbonate of soda, baking powder, asafoetida powder and salt to taste. Working quickly, take ladlefuls of the mixture and shape into small patties on a sheet of cling film, then use your finger to make a hole in the centre of each one, like a doughnut.

4 Meanwhile, half-fill a large pan with oil and place over a medium-high heat until the temperature reaches 170°C (338°F) on a cook's thermometer. Gently slip the vadai into the hot oil, and deep-fry for about 10 minutes until golden on all sides, turning over about halfway through cooking. Remove with a slotted spoon and drain on kitchen paper.

5 Spoon the soup into 4 warm bowls, sprinkle with the coriander leaves and serve with the hot, crispy vadai on the side.

Prep time 35 minutes
Cooking time 1 hour
Difficulty Medium

For the vadai
175g (6oz) urad dal (black gram lentils), picked and rinsed
1 tbsp basmati rice
pinch of bicarbonate of soda
pinch of baking powder
1 tsp asafoetida powder
salt
sunflower oil for deep-frying

For the soup
1 tbsp sunflower oil
2 sprigs of fresh curry leaves
2 dried red chillies
1 tsp mustard seeds
1 tsp cumin seeds
1 red onion, chopped
2 garlic cloves, finely chopped
2 fresh green chillies, finely chopped
4–5 vine-ripened tomatoes, chopped
3cm (1¼in) piece of fresh root ginger, finely chopped
2 tsp sambar powder
1 tsp chilli powder
1 tsp ground turmeric
200g (7oz) red lentils, picked and rinsed
1 bunch of fresh coriander, leaves picked and chopped

"I'm blown away by this delicious lentil soup. The flavours are fabulous. There's a bit of fire in there, but I love that."

— Jilly Goolden

Smoked Arctic char pâté with bannocks

A wonderful pâté, scooped up with an old
Orkney speciality, beremeal bannocks

Prep time 15 minutes, plus
1 hour's marinating
Cooking time 45 minutes
Difficulty Easy–medium

For smoking the char
2 whole Arctic char, scaled,
   gutted and gilled (if you
   can't get hold of char, use
   good-quality salmon)
1 tbsp soft brown sugar
1 tbsp sea salt
1 small glass of medium-
   sweet sherry

For the pâté
1 medium onion, diced
a little salted butter
smoked fillets of char
   (see above)
1 tbsp freshly squeezed
   lemon juice
2 tbsp crème fraîche
small handful of fresh chives,
   to taste, roughly chopped
salt and freshly ground
   black pepper

For the bannocks
230g (8oz) beremeal
   (a type of barley flour)
115g (4oz) plain flour
½ tsp baking powder
½ tsp cream of tartar
pinch of salt
100ml (3½fl oz) whole milk

To serve
fresh chives, to garnish
lemon wedges

1 To smoke the char, first fillet the fish and marinate in the sugar, salt and sherry for 1 hour. Using a smoker, hot-smoke the char over oak chips for 45 minutes. Keep in the refrigerator until needed.

2 To make the pâté, sweat the onion in a little butter for about 5 minutes until soft but not coloured.

3 Carefully remove the skin from the smoked char and debone. Flake the fish and put it in a food processor. Add the lemon juice, crème fraîche and chives to taste, along with the cooked onion. Season with salt and black pepper and blend until smooth.

4 To make the bannocks, in a bowl, mix together the beremeal, plain flour, baking powder, cream of tartar and pinch of salt. Add the milk and mix to a stiff but soft dough. Divide into 2 or 3 pieces and roll out each on a floured board to form a long oval.

5 Heat an unoiled griddle or cast-iron grill pan until fairly hot. Cook the bannocks for 5 minutes on each side, until both sides are browned and the middle is cooked. Practice will make perfect.

6 To serve, place a quenelle of pâté on one side of each serving plate. Cut the bannocks into small circles using a pastry cutter. Serve 5 or 6 of these mini bannocks with each serving of pâté, and garnish each plate with some chives and a wedge of lemon.

Scottish baked pear cheesecake

Sharp blue cheese, creamy mascarpone and luscious pears – culinary alchemy

Prep time 20 minutes
Cooking time 30 minutes
Difficulty Medium–easy

1 To make the oatcakes, preheat the oven to 220°C (425°F/Gas 7). Grease a baking tray. Sift together the flour, bicarbonate of soda and salt into a bowl. Mix the oatmeal into the dry ingredients, then add the melted butter with a round-bladed knife. Pour in just enough boiling water, a little at a time, to form a stiff dough. Roll out the dough thinly, cut into rounds with a pastry cutter, and arrange on the baking tray. Bake in the oven for 15 minutes, then leave to cool for 10 minutes. Do not turn off the oven.

2 Peel, core and chop the pears into small pieces. Put in a pan with a little water and gently poach over a low heat until the pears have softened and are starting to break down into a purée.

3 Meanwhile, melt the butter in a pan. Crush the oatcakes with a rolling pin and put in a bowl. When the butter has melted, pour over the crushed oatcakes and mix together until well coated. Sit four 10cm (4in) or 12cm (5in) metal food rings on a baking tray lined with silicone paper and press the oatcake mixture down into the bottom of the rings. Evenly spread about 2 tsp of the mixture across the bottom of each one to make a thin base.

4 Once the pears have softened, add the Poire William liqueur and reduce a little. Using a hand-held blender, purée until smooth. Spread some of the pear purée on top of the oatcakes in the food rings, again making sure to spread the mixture evenly.

5 Next, put the cream cheese and mascarpone in a bowl and mix until combined. Crumble in the Lanark Blue in smallish bits and mix through. Mix in the chopped chives and beaten egg, season with salt and black pepper and mix again until well combined. Spoon the cheese mixture on top of the pear purée, filling right up to the top. Bake in the oven for 10–15 minutes until the cheesecakes have browned slightly on top, but the mixture still wobbles a little when nudged. Allow to cool slightly.

6 To make the salad, whisk together the mustard, vinegar and oil, season with salt and pepper and use to dress the lamb's lettuce. Put a cheesecake, in its ring, on each of 4 plates. Run a knife around the edges to loosen the rings and gently lift off. Garnish with a couple of chive stalks and serve with a small pile of salad.

3 ripe Conference pears
80g (3oz) butter
110g (4oz) oatcakes
 (see below)
2 tbsp Poire William liqueur
100g (3½oz) cream cheese
50g (1¾oz) mascarpone
 cheese
150g (5½oz) Lanark Blue
 cheese
1 small bunch of fresh chives,
 chopped, plus a few extra
 stalks, to garnish
1 egg, lightly beaten
salt and freshly ground black
 pepper

For the oatcakes
45g (1½oz) plain flour
¼ tsp bicarbonate of soda
pinch of salt
110g (4oz) medium oatmeal
30g (1oz) butter, melted
about 90ml (3fl oz) boiling
 water

For the salad
1 tbsp Dijon mustard
1 tbsp white wine vinegar
4–6 tbsp walnut oil
4 handfuls of lamb's lettuce
Salt and freshly ground black
 pepper

Aromatic green chicken curry

Fresh fenugreek leaves add an authentic, slightly bitter taste to this fragrant dish

Prep time 10 minutes
Cooking time 25 minutes
Difficulty Medium

100g (3½oz) fresh coriander, including stalks, chopped
100g (3½oz) fresh fenugreek leaves, chopped
6 spring onions, chopped, plus more to garnish
4 garlic cloves, chopped
2 tsp chopped fresh root ginger
5 fresh hot green chillies, chopped
1 tsp cumin seeds
30g (1oz) butter
3 tbsp Greek-style yogurt
4 skinless chicken breast fillets, diced
1 tsp garam masala
1 tsp ground turmeric
1 tsp salt
2 tbsp single cream
200g (7oz) peeled and de-veined cooked king prawns

1 Put the fresh coriander, fenugreek, spring onions, garlic, ginger and chillies in a blender and whizz to a purée.

2 In a large saucepan over a medium heat, dry-toast the cumin seeds, stirring, for a couple of minutes until they become aromatic, then add the butter. Once the butter has melted, tip in the herb purée and 1 tablespoon of the yogurt and continue cooking until the fat separates and starts to float on top.

3 Add the chicken, garam marsala, turmeric and salt. Stir in the remaining yogurt and the cream and simmer gently for 12 minutes. Lastly, add the prawns and cook for a further 2–3 minutes until the prawns are just heated through.

4 Serve sprinkled with chopped spring onions.

"The sauce is fresh, gorgeous, with a little piquance going on with it, but it's made that chicken so tender that it really melts."

— Jilly Goolden

Prep time 30 minutes, plus
30 minutes' resting time
Cooking time 35–40 minutes
Difficulty Medium–easy

STARTERS • SPINACH, MUSHROOM AND CHUTNEY TART

For the pastry
225g (8oz) plain flour
pinch of salt
100g (3½oz) good-quality
   butter
3 sprigs of fresh thyme,
   leaves picked

For the chutney
3 tbsp extra virgin olive oil
4 red onions, finely sliced
4 garlic cloves, finely sliced
1 tsp coriander seeds
2 tbsp organic red wine
   vinegar such as Aspall
2 tbsp soft dark brown sugar
sea salt and freshly ground
   black pepper

For the filling
3 field mushrooms, sliced
150g (5½oz) butter
5 garlic cloves, crushed
squeeze of lemon juice
handful of fresh flat-leaf
   parsley, roughly chopped
1 large free-range egg
130ml (4½fl oz) single cream
1 tbsp extra virgin olive oil
4 handfuls fresh spinach
   leaves
2 handfuls of fresh thyme,
   leaves picked
1 small round of goat's
   cheese, finely sliced
salt and freshly ground black
   pepper

To serve
2 handfuls of fresh spinach
4 leafy sprigs of fresh flat-leaf
   parsley
squeeze of lemon juice
extra virgin olive oil

Spinach, mushroom and chutney tart

This simple and delicious tart is lifted by tangy red onion chutney and goat's cheese

1 To make the pastry, sift the flour and salt into a large bowl and, using your fingertips, rub in the butter until the mixture resembles breadcrumbs. Stir in the thyme leaves, then gradually trickle in iced water, a very little at a time, until the mixture just comes together into a dough. Form into a ball, wrap in cling film, and leave to chill in the refrigerator for 30 minutes.

2 Meanwhile, preheat the oven to 190°C (375°F/Gas 5). Grease four 10 (4in) or 12cm (5in) individual tart tins.

3 On a floured work surface, roll out the pastry and use it to line the tart tins. Prick the bases with a fork and bake in the oven for 5–8 minutes. Allow to cool. Do not turn off the oven.

4 To make the chutney, heat the oil in a saucepan over a low heat and add the onion, garlic and coriander. Cook gently for 10 minutes, then add the vinegar and sugar and cook for a further 5–10 minutes, stirring occasionally. Remove from the heat, taste and season with salt and black pepper.

5 Meanwhile, make the filling. Lay the mushrooms in a baking tray. In a small bowl, mix together the butter, 3 of the garlic cloves, lemon juice and parsley and dot over the mushrooms. Bake in the oven for 15 minutes, then remove and allow to cool. Beat together the egg and cream in a small bowl and season with salt and black pepper.

6 Heat the oil in a large saucepan over a medium heat. Tip in the spinach, thyme and remaining garlic. Cook for 3–4 minutes until the spinach has wilted. Drain very well in a sieve, pressing the spinach with the back of a spoon to remove excess moisture.

7 Brush the pastry cases with a little of the cream and egg mixture. Add a little chutney to each, then divide the spinach among them, then the mushrooms. Pour the egg mixture over the top. Lay some cheese slices over the top of each tart and cook in the oven for 15 minutes or until lightly browned.

8 Dress the fresh spinach and parsley leaves with a little squeeze of lemon and a drizzle of olive oil. Lay the dressed leaves on each of 4 plates and top with a warm tart. Serve immediately.

Austrian-style spaetzle

Hearty spaetzle dumplings with a cheesy sauce and a crisp, fresh bacon coleslaw

1 To start the coleslaw, place a small dry frying pan over a medium heat and add the caraway seeds. Cook, stirring, for 2–3 minutes until they become aromatic. Put the cabbage in a large bowl and tip in the toasted caraway seeds. Season well and set aside.

2 For the spaetzle, in another large bowl, beat the flour and a large pinch of salt with the eggs, milk and 50ml (2fl oz) water until everything is smoothly blended.

3 Bring a large pan of salted water to the boil over a high heat. Take a "Spatzlhobel" – or use a colander pierced with quite big holes – and press the spaetzle dough through it into the water. When the dumplings float to the top of the water, drain, refresh in cold water and drain again.

4 Slice half of the white onion into rings and chop the remaining onions. Melt a knob of the butter in a small frying pan over a low to medium heat, add the onion slices and fry, stirring occasionally, until golden brown. Set aside to keep warm. Melt the remaining butter in a large frying pan or sauté pan over a medium heat. Sauté the chopped onion for 5 minutes until soft and translucent.

5 Add the spaetzle to the chopped onions and sauté for another minute, then add the cheese and stir until melted.

6 At the same time, in another frying pan over a medium heat, slowly fry the speck in the oil until crisp. Add the vinegar to the coleslaw, then tip in the speck with its fat. Toss the coleslaw together and check the seasoning.

7 To serve, divide the spaetzle among 4 warm plates. Top with the golden brown onion slices and sprinkle with the chives. Serve the coleslaw on the side.

Prep time 30 minutes
Cooking time 10 minutes
Difficulty Medium

For the coleslaw
1 tsp caraway seeds
½ pointed green cabbage, shredded
100g (3½oz) speck, or fatty smoked pancetta or bacon, chopped into lardons
1 tbsp extra virgin olive oil
1 tbsp white wine vinegar
sea salt and freshly ground black pepper

For the spaetzle
200g (7oz) plain flour
large pinch of salt
2 eggs
50ml (2fl oz) whole milk
1 large white onion
1 large red onion
60g (2oz) butter
150g (5½oz) strong hard cow's milk cheese, such as Wrekin White from Shropshire, grated
1 small bunch of fresh chives, snipped

Orange-infused North Sea fish soup

Full of clean, fresh flavours, this soup benefits from a good, home-made stock

Prep time **30 minutes**
Cooking time **2½ hours**
Difficulty **Medium**

For the stock
120ml (4fl oz) dry white wine
3 white fish carcasses,
   including heads
generous knob of butter
4 or 5 raw prawns with heads
   and shells
1 tbsp Calvados
2 onions, chopped
2 celery sticks, chopped
1 carrot, chopped

For the soup
200g (7oz) mussels
200g (7oz) clams
1 medium-large onion
5 garlic cloves
2 celery sticks
1 bulb of fennel
1 large leek
1 dried red chilli
1 small orange
olive oil
pinch of saffron threads,
   crumbled
1.2 litres (2 pints) fish stock
   (see above)
3 sprigs of fresh lemon thyme
2 sprigs of fresh lemon balm
1 small bunch of fresh
   flat-leaf parsley, plus extra,
   chopped, to garnish
2 fresh bay leaves
2 sprigs of fresh marjoram
2 tbsp dry vermouth, to taste
juice of 1 lemon
1 small squid with tentacles,
   cleaned and sliced
400g (14oz) monkfish tail,
   chopped into chunks
200g (7oz) halibut, chopped
   into chunks
salt and freshly ground
   black pepper

1 To make the stock, put the white wine in a large saucepan over a medium heat and bring to the boil. Add the fish carcasses, reduce the heat and simmer for 3–4 minutes.

2 Add 1.5 litres (2¾ pints) water, bring back to the boil and simmer for 20 minutes.

3 In a small frying pan over a medium-high heat, melt the butter and add the prawns. Stir, then add the Calvados. Tip the prawns into the stockpot and simmer for a further 20 minutes.

4 Sieve the stock, pushing it through with the back of a spoon to extract the maximum flavour from the bones and shells, then add the chopped vegetables and discard the fishy detritus.

5 Bring the liquor back to the boil and simmer for 45 minutes, then sieve once more through a very fine sieve lined with muslin. Refrigerate for up to 24 hours or until needed.

6 Prepare the mussels. Pour them into a clean sink, then pull away the frond of hairs protruding from each shell. This is called the "beard". Scrub each mussel well to remove as many barnacles as possible, then rinse very well. Remove and discard any mussels that are cracked, or any which do not close when firmly tapped on the side of the sink. Scrub the clams well and again discard any that have broken shells or do not close when firmly tapped. Set aside.

7 Finely chop the onion, garlic, celery, fennel and leek. Deseed and chop the chilli. Using a vegetable peeler, pare the orange zest away from the fruit.

8 Add a little olive oil to a large pan and sweat the vegetables, chilli and orange zest with the saffron, stirring, for 5 minutes until starting to soften. Add the stock, herbs and vermouth and simmer for 12 minutes. Taste and add lemon and more vermouth, if liked. Season with salt and black pepper.

9 Remove the herbs, whizz to a purée in a food processor or blender – you may need to do this in batches – then sieve, return to the rinsed-out pan and bring to a simmer, adding more stock if necessary to achieve the consistency you prefer.

10 Add the squid, monkfish and halibut and cook for 5 minutes. It is very important to ensure that the fish is just cooked and remains moist. Do not allow it to overcook and dry out.

11 Add the shellfish and simmer for another 5 minutes. Discard any shellfish that remain closed at the end of the cooking time, as they should not be eaten.

12 Pour the soup into 4 warm bowls, evenly distributing the fish and shellfish between each serving and sprinkle with the parsley.

"Phenomenal flavour ... It's very, very good. You'd be pleased to eat this anywhere. Absolutely beautiful."

— Ed Baines

Trout mousse with beetroot and wasabi

Balsamic beetroot is a mellow, sweet foil to hot wasabi cream and smooth fish mousse

STARTERS • TROUT MOUSSE WITH BEETROOT AND WASABI

Prep time 20 minutes
Cooking time 1 hour
Difficulty Medium

For the mousse
1 large sea trout or farmed
  trout, about 1kg (2¼lb),
  or 2 smaller ones
2 bay leaves
2 free-range egg yolks
200g (7oz) cream cheese
1 x 284ml carton single
  cream
juice of 2 lemons
sea salt and freshly ground
  white pepper

For the beetroot
1 large beetroot, julienned
generous drizzle of balsamic
  vinegar
drizzle of extra virgin olive oil

To serve
500ml (16fl oz) crème fraîche
wasabi paste, to taste
6–8 slices good crusty white
  bread
2 garlic cloves, halved

1 Preheat the oven to 180°C (350°F/Gas 4). Place the trout in a lightly oiled baking tray, season with salt and white pepper, then put the bay leaves on top. Loosely cover with foil and bake in the oven for 30 minutes. Remove and, when cool enough to handle, flake the fish, discarding the skin and bones.

2 Put the egg yolks, cream cheese, cream and lemon juice in a blender and season with salt and white pepper. Whizz the mixture until smooth. Add the trout and pulse until combined. Liberally grease 6–8 ramekins with butter, then spoon the mousse evenly into each one. Wrap each ramekin in foil and place them in a deep baking tray. Carefully pour enough water into the baking tray to come about halfway up the sides of the ramekins and cook in the oven for 15–20 minutes until just set.

3 Meanwhile, bring a small pan of water to the boil and add the beetroot. Return to the boil and cook for 3–4 minutes until soft. Drain, return to the pan and add the balsamic vinegar and a drizzle of extra virgin olive oil, then reduce over a medium-high heat until the juices are syrupy.

4 To make the wasabi cream, mix together the crème fraîche and wasabi paste, to taste. (Add the wasabi sparingly and with care, as it is very hot and pungent.)

5 Carefully remove the trout ramekins from the oven and allow to cool for 15 minutes. Meanwhile, toast the bread and rub each slice with the cut side of a garlic clove.

6 Turn the mousse out onto individual serving plates and spoon the wasabi cream around. Arrange a small pile balsamic beetroot on top of each mousse and serve with the garlic toast for scooping up the delicate mousse.

Lime-chilli prawn and scallop skewers

With a fantastic mint hummus, this is a feast of flavours to make your palate sing

Prep time 1 hour, plus overnight soaking
Cooking time 1 hour 40 minutes
Difficulty Medium

1 The night before, put the chickpeas in a bowl and cover with water to soak. The next morning, drain and rinse the chickpeas and put in a saucepan of fresh cold water. Bring to the boil and simmer for 1 hour or until tender. If using bamboo skewers, soak in cold water for at least 30 minutes.

2 To make the dressing, put the balsamic vinegar and sugar in a saucepan over a medium-high heat and reduce until syrupy.

3 To make the hummus, process the garlic with a little of the oil in a blender. Add the chickpeas, lemon juice, tahini and mustard, blend together, then taste and add more tahini if liked. Pour in the remaining oil, blend until smooth and transfer to a bowl. Stir in the mint and paprika, season well with black pepper and set aside.

4 For the marinade, pour the lime juice into a large bowl, grate in the ginger, add the chilli and garlic and stir. Reserve a little of the marinade in a separate small bowl. Add the prawns and scallops to the large bowl and toss in the marinade. Put both bowls in the refrigerator and leave the seafood to marinate for 15 minutes.

5 Meanwhile, preheat the grill to its highest setting. Brush the vegetables with olive oil and cook under the hot grill for 5 minutes or until golden brown, turning once. Set aside and keep warm.

6 Heat a ridged cast-iron grill pan until very hot and brush with a little oil. Thread the marinated prawns and scallops alternately onto 4 skewers, allowing 4 prawns and 3 scallops for each skewer. Quickly sear the skewers for a minute on each side, brushing with a little extra marinade.

7 To serve, place a skewer on each of 4 serving plates and dress with the reserved marinade. Assemble the vegetables on top of the salad leaves and drizzle with the dressing. Spoon some hummus on the side of each plate, sprinkle it with paprika and garnish with a mint leaf. Serve immediately.

For the mint hummus
300g (10oz) dried chickpeas
1 garlic clove
150ml (5fl oz) olive oil
juice of 1 lemon
3 tbsp tahini paste, or to taste
1 tbsp Dijon wholegrain mustard
1 bunch of fresh mint, leaves picked and chopped, plus extra, to garnish
1 tsp paprika, plus extra, to garnish
salt and black pepper

For the dressing
300ml (10fl oz) balsamic vinegar
300g (10oz) caster sugar

For the marinade
juice of 3 limes
thumb-sized piece of fresh root ginger
1 red chilli, finely chopped
1 garlic clove, finely chopped
salt and pepper

For the skewers
16 raw king prawns, peeled and de-veined
12 raw king scallops

For the vegetables
4 baby aubergines, sliced
2 courgettes, sliced
2 yellow peppers, sliced
olive oil

For the salad
handful of young rocket
1 cos lettuce, chopped
1 oak leaf lettuce, chopped

Prep time 30 minutes, plus
up to 6 hours' freezing time
Cooking time 1½ hours
Difficulty Medium–hard

For the soup
knob of butter
1 onion, chopped
1 garlic clove, finely chopped
800g (1¾lb) ripe tomatoes,
  chopped
400ml (14fl oz) chicken stock
pinch of caster sugar
1–2 tbsp double cream
salt and freshly ground
  black pepper

For the tomato sorbet
olive oil
½ small onion, chopped
750g (1lb 10oz) tomatoes,
  chopped
1 tbsp chopped basil
1 tbsp tomato paste
juice of ½ lemon
caster sugar, to taste

For the salad
450g (1lb) cherry tomatoes,
  halved
½ red onion, finely chopped
½ fresh green chilli, finely
  chopped
150ml (5fl oz) extra virgin
  olive oil
60ml (2fl oz) white wine
  vinegar
pinch of sugar

For the flat breads
125g (4½oz) strong white
  flour
½ tsp sugar
½ tsp dried yeast
pinch of salt

For the cheese basket
4 handfuls of Lancashire
  cheese, grated

Tomato medley

Smooth soup, fresh-tasting sorbet, tangy salad – a culinary ode to the tomato

1 To make the soup, melt the butter in a large saucepan over a medium heat, then add the onion and garlic. Sweat, stirring, until softened. Add the tomatoes and simmer for 10 minutes. Pour in the stock and cook for 30 minutes or until soft and pulpy. Whizz in a blender or food processor until smooth, then push the soup through a sieve back into the rinsed-out pan. Reduce the soup over a medium heat until it is as thick as you want it. Add the sugar and cream, season with salt and black pepper and set aside.

2 To make the sorbet, put a little oil in a saucepan over a medium heat, add the onion and sweat, stirring, until softened. Add the tomatoes, basil, tomato paste and lemon juice and season well. Cook for 30 minutes or until soft, then add a little sugar. Remove from the heat and push the mixture through a sieve into a clean bowl. Allow to cool completely, then freeze for 3–6 hours. Halfway through freezing, remove the sorbet from the freezer, break up with a fork and put in a blender. Blend until smooth and re-freeze.

3 To make the salad, mix together all the ingredients and adjust the seasoning. Set aside to marinate for at least 1 hour.

4 Preheat the oven to 220°C (425°F/Gas 7). To make the flat breads, mix together the flour, sugar, yeast and salt, add a little water – no more than 150ml (5fl oz) – until the dough comes together, then knead for 2 minutes on a floured work surface. Roll out to 1cm (½in) thick, cut into 10cm (4in) rounds, place on a baking sheet, cover with a clean tea towel and leave in a warm place to rise for 15 minutes. Bake for 15 minutes until risen and golden.

5 Put a handful of cheese into a dry frying pan over a very low heat and spread it out. Warm until the fat starts to run, then turn off the heat. Invert a small bowl and cover with cling film. Place the melting cheese sheet over the bowl and gently push it down over the sides. Leave to cool, then repeat for the remaining baskets.

6 Gently reheat the soup. Scoop a little salad onto a flat bread and put one on each of 4 serving plates. Pour the soup into 4 small warm bowls and add one to each plate, along with a cheese basket. Scoop a little tomato sorbet into each basket and serve.

Pan-fried scallops with Noilly Prat

Sensational scallop dish with asparagus wrapped in bacon and a vermouth sauce

Prep time **10 minutes**
Cooking time **40 minutes**
Difficulty **Medium**

For the fish stock

1 onion, chopped
1 head of fennel, chopped
3 celery sticks, chopped
1 leek, chopped
2 garlic cloves, roughly
  chopped
2 or 3 sprigs of fresh thyme
2 or 3 sprigs of fresh
  rosemary
2 or 3 bay leaves
good pinch or two of herbes
  de Provence
good pinch of salt
2 white peppercorns
turbot and monkfish bones
½ x 75cl bottle of dry
  white wine

For the Noilly Prat sauce

250g (9oz) finely sliced
  shallots
275ml (9fl oz) fish stock
  (see above)
275ml (9fl oz) Noilly Prat
whipping cream, to taste
knob of butter

12 freshly picked British
  green asparagus spears
fresh chicken stock, to steam
  asparagus
a little cream
12 Wiltshire smoke-cured
  streaky bacon rashers
12 Scottish hand-dived
  scallops
a little olive oil
salt and freshly ground
  black pepper
pea shoots, to garnish

1 To make the stock, sweat all the vegetables until soft, then add the garlic, herbs, salt and peppercorns. Cut up and break open your fish bones, then add them to the pot and allow to sweat for a few minutes. Pour in the wine and add water until the bones are almost covered. Bring to the boil as fast as possible, then reduce the heat and simmer gently for 20 minutes. Remove from the heat. Set aside for 20–30 minutes to infuse. Strain through a fine sieve.

2 To make the Noilly Prat sauce, in a heavy pan, gently sweat the shallots until they are as soft as possible without colouring. Pour in equal amounts of the fish stock you have just made and the Noilly Prat. Reduce until there is no liquid left. Add the cream, to taste and whizz in a blender until smooth, then pass through a sieve if needed. Keep warm. Just before serving, whisk in a little butter.

3 Cut off about 5cm (2in) from the top of the asparagus spears and set aside. Chop the remainder and steam over the stock until tender. Drain and refresh in iced water. Using a hand-held blender, purée, then push through a fine sieve. When needed, gently reheat, season with salt and pepper and whisk in a little cream.

4 Put the reserved asparagus tops in a pan with some fresh chicken stock and cook until tender but still with a bite. Drain. Using your fingers, stretch the bacon on a chopping board until it lies flat, then wrap the asparagus in the bacon, from the bottom until just below the tip. Fry in a hot pan until the bacon is golden.

5 Break the muscle of the scallop shells, open and remove the contents. Separate out the firm white meat (you can reserve the coral for another use if you like), clean and pat dry with kitchen paper. Pour a little olive oil into a hot (preferably cast-iron) pan. Season the scallops with salt and black pepper and add to the pan, moving them back and forth in the pan initially to prevent them sticking. Cook for 1½–2 minutes on each side, depending on thickness. Allow to rest for a few minutes.

6 To serve, arrange 3 scallops and 3 bacon-wrapped asparagus tips on of each of 4 warm plates. Garnish with pea shoots. Add a quenelle of asparagus purée to each and drizzle around the warm Noilly Prat sauce. Serve immediately.

Full English risotto

All the flavours of the iconic breakfast transformed into an Italian classic

Prep time 20 minutes
Cooking time 40 minutes
Difficulty Easy

1 Preheat the oven to 180°C (350°F/Gas 4). In a large saucepan over a low heat, gently warm the stock.

2 Split the sausage skins and remove the filling; discard the skins. Roll the sausagemeat into little balls, each slightly smaller than the size of a Malteser.

3 Arrange the tomatoes over a baking tray. Season with salt and black pepper, drizzle with a little olive oil and roast in the oven for 10–15 minutes until spotted with brown and starting to collapse. Set aside to keep warm.

4 Heat a splash of olive oil in a large saucepan and gently sweat the onion and garlic for a few minutes until soft and translucent. Tip in the rice and cook, stirring, for 2 minutes, making sure that each grain is well coated. Add the wine and keep stirring until the liquid has been absorbed and the alcohol has evaporated.

5 Start adding the warm stock, a ladleful at a time, stirring continuously and making sure that the stock is absorbed between each addition. Continue in this way for 15–20 minutes until the rice is almost cooked, but still with a bite. Add the spring onions and cook for 1 minute more.

6 In a frying pan over a medium heat, fry the sausage balls and lardons, stirring, for 5 minutes or until cooked. Remove from the pan with a slotted spoon and add to the risotto pan. Add the bread to the bacon pan and fry, turning once, until golden and crisp. Cut into quarters, keep warm and set aside.

7 Add a little more oil to the frying pan and fry the quail's eggs until the whites are cooked and the yolks are runny.

8 Stir the crème fraîche into the risotto, taste and season with salt and black pepper. Leave to stand for 5 minutes.

9 To serve, spoon a portion of risotto into a small bowl, then invert a bowl of the risotto onto each of 4 warm plates. Place the tomatoes on one side, the fried bread on the other and top each risotto mould with a fried quail's egg. Serve immediately.

1.5 litres (2¾ pints) vegetable stock
3 Yorkshire sausages
16 cherry tomatoes
olive oil
1 onion, finely chopped
2 garlic cloves, finely chopped
350g (12oz) Arborio rice
150ml (5fl oz) dry white wine
3–4 spring onions, finely chopped
4 dry-cured streaky bacon rashers with black treacle, chopped into lardons
1 slice white bread
4 quail's eggs
75–90ml (2½–3fl oz) crème fraîche
salt and freshly ground black pepper

Smokie in a pokie

An elegant, full-flavoured starter using wonderful smoked Finnan haddock

Prep time **20 minutes**
Cooking time **40 minutes**
Difficulty **Easy**

350g (12oz) Finnan smoked
   haddock
300ml (10fl oz) milk
45g (1½oz) butter
35g (1¼oz) plain flour
1 small carrot, grated
100g (3½oz) fresh salmon,
   diced
8 large slices Scottish
   smoked salmon, cut
   in half lengthways
salt and freshly ground
   black pepper

For the sauce
50g (1¾oz) shallots, finely
   chopped
2 tbsp white wine vinegar
3 tbsp dry white wine
2 tbsp good-quality fresh
   fish stock
50g (1¾oz) butter, diced
juice of ½ lemon, or to taste
1 tbsp finely chopped dill,
   plus 4 extra sprigs, to
   garnish
salt and freshly ground
   black pepper

1 Preheat the oven to 180°C (350°F/Gas 4).

2 Put the haddock in a deep frying pan, add the milk and a knob of the butter and place over a medium heat until very gently simmering. Poach the fish for 6 minutes, then strain, reserving the milk. Remove and discard the skin and bones and flake the fish.

3 Melt the remaining butter in a saucepan over a medium heat, then add the flour, stirring for 1–2 minutes. Gradually add the fish poaching liquor, stirring constantly to prevent lumps and simmer for 2 minutes, then add the carrot. Remove from the heat, add the fresh salmon and haddock and season with salt and black pepper, going easy on the salt.

4 To make the sauce, put the shallots, vinegar and wine into a separate small saucepan over a medium heat and simmer until reduced to about 1 tablespoon. Add the fish stock, then whisk in the butter, bit by bit, until the sauce is slightly thickened. Season with salt and black pepper and add a squeeze of lemon juice and the chopped dill.

5 Make pokes, or cornets, from the smoked salmon slices and fill with the haddock mixture. Place on a baking tray. Transfer to the oven and bake for 2–3 minutes.

6 To serve, coat the bottom of 4 warm plates with a little of the sauce and place 2 pokes on each. Pour the remaining sauce over and garnish each plate with a sprig of dill. Serve immediately.

Crab, prawn, and leek pasty

A great pasty of rich seafood and pastry lifted by a tangy salad

Prep time **10 minutes**
Cooking time **40 minutes**
Difficulty **Medium**

1 For the pastry, put the flour in a large bowl, cut in the butter and fat in small pieces and rub together with your fingertips until the mixture resembles breadcrumbs. Add iced water, a very little at a time, mixing first with a knife, then with your hands, until the mixture just comes together into a dough. Wrap in cling film and leave to chill in the refrigerator for 30 minutes or until ready to use.

2 To make the filling, melt the butter in a frying pan over a low heat. Add the leeks and cook for 4–5 minutes until soft but not coloured. Leave to cool. Lift into a bowl with a slotted spoon and mix in the dill, soured cream, prawns and crab. Set aside.

3 Preheat the oven to 180°C (350°F/Gas 4). Butter four 10cm (4in) mini quiche tins. Remove the pastry from the refrigerator and roll it out on a floured work surface. Place a quiche tin onto the pastry and cut out four rounds 5cm (2in) larger than the tin. Carefully line the tins with the pastry, taking care not to make any holes, then fill each with the filling mixture. Using a pair of kitchen scissors, make small snips around the edge of the pastry, then fold the pastry over the mixture and pleat together the edges, pasty-style, leaving a small hole in the centre. Beat together the egg and milk and use this to brush the pastry. Put the pasties on a baking sheet, in their tins and bake for 20–25 minutes. Leave to cool for 5 minutes.

4 To make the salad, put the lime juice in a bowl, whisk in the olive oil and season with black pepper. Carefully remove the pasties from the tins and decorate each with a prawn and sprig of dill. Toss the salad leaves with the dressing, and put a warm pasty and a small pile of salad on each of 4 plates.

For the pastry
450g (1lb) self-raising flour
115g (4oz) salted butter, at room temperature
115g (4oz) white vegetable fat, at room temperature
a little iced water
1 egg
2 tbsp milk

For the filling
80g (2¾oz) salted butter
250g (9oz) leeks (trimmed weight), finely chopped
2 heaped tsp chopped fresh dill, plus 4 extra sprigs, to garnish
100g (3½oz) soured cream
100g (3½oz) peeled and de-veined cooked prawns (preferably Icelandic), plus 4 extra, to garnish
200g (7oz) fresh Cromer crabmeat (use both white and brown meat)

For the salad
juice of ½ lime
25g (1oz) olive oil
handful of watercress, rocket and radicchio
freshly ground black pepper

"The pastry is phenomenal. And that lovely leek, with the cream and the dill, sort of brings it all together. All in all, it's a fabulous thing."
— John Burton Race

Potato and ham cake

Crispy potato cakes lovingly served with a vegetable liquor and a pork and cider jus

Prep time 10 minutes
Cooking time 1¾ hours
Difficulty Medium

For the potato cakes

4 unsmoked rindless
   streaky bacon rashers
115g (4oz) butter
½ onion, finely chopped
½ leek, finely chopped
700g (1½lb) Maris Piper
   potatoes
570ml (18fl oz) whole milk
450g (1lb) cooked ham
1 small bunch of fresh parsley
1 small bunch of fresh chives
1 tbsp plain flour
2 eggs, beaten
175g (6oz) toasted fine
   breadcrumbs
vegetable oil for deep-frying
salt and black pepper

For the liquor

150g (5½oz) peas
150g (5½oz) broad beans
15g (½oz) butter
15g (½oz) plain flour
150ml (5fl oz) vegetable stock
150ml (5fl oz) whole milk
1 small bunch of fresh curly
   parsley, chopped
salt and black pepper

For the jus

1 onion, roughly chopped
1 carrot, roughly chopped
1 leek, roughly chopped
1 tomato, roughly chopped
400g (14oz) belly pork
600ml (1 pint) cider
150ml (5fl oz) vegetable stock
½ tsp mustard powder
1 tsp tomato purée
1 tsp redcurrant jelly
1 tbsp butter
1 tbsp plain flour
salt and black pepper

1 To make the potato cakes, preheat the oven to 180°C (350°F/ Gas 4). Put the bacon on a baking sheet and cook in the oven until crisp. Set aside, retaining the rendered fat.

2 Melt a knob of the butter in a small pan over a medium heat, tip in the onion and leek and sauté, stirring, until the onion is soft and golden. Set aside.

3 Bring a large saucepan of water to the boil over a medium-high heat. Peel and roughly chop the potatoes, add to the pan and simmer until tender. Drain and leave for 2 minutes, uncovered, to dry out, then mash with the remaining butter and the milk and season with salt and black pepper. Chill for 30 minutes.

4 When the mash has cooled, shred the ham and combine with the potato, onion and leek. Finely chop the herbs and add them, along with the rendered bacon fat, to the potato mixture. Mix together. Form the mixture into small apple-sized balls, then slightly flatten each one and smooth the edges.

5 Put the flour, egg and breadcrumbs into 3 separate bowls. Coat each potato cake first in flour, then in egg and lastly with the breadcrumbs. Repeat the process for each cake to get an extra-crispy double-crumb coating. Set aside in the refrigerator.

6 To make the liquor, bring a large pan of water to the boil. Add the peas for 2 minutes, then remove and refresh in cold water. Repeat the process for the broad beans. Peel each bean and set aside. Melt the butter in a saucepan over a medium heat, then sprinkle in the flour, stirring for 1–2 minutes. Add the stock and the milk gradually, stirring constantly to prevent lumps. Season, then add the parsley, beans and peas. Set aside.

7 For the jus, evenly spread the vegetables over a roasting tin and place the pork on top. Roast in the oven for 1–1½ hours. Remove the pork from the roasting tin and put away for another time. Strain the juices into a jug, remove the fat, then return the juices to the roasting tin. Pour the cider into the tin, mixing with the browned vegetables and scraping at all the sticky bits below, to deglaze the tin. Add the vegetable stock, then strain the jus into a bowl.

8 Mix the mustard powder, tomato purée and redcurrant jelly to a paste. Melt the butter in a small pan over a medium heat, sprinkle in the flour and cook, stirring, for 1–2 minutes. Gradually stir in the pork jus until you reach the consistency of thin gravy. Stir in the mustard paste and season with salt and black pepper. Keep warm.

9 Heat the vegetable oil into a large pan or deep-fryer until it reaches 170°C (340°F) on a cook's thermometer. Deep-fry the potato cakes until golden, turning once, taking care not to crowd the pan (you may need to do this in batches). Drain on kitchen paper and keep warm while you fry the remaining cakes.

10 Gently reheat the broad bean and pea liquor, then serve each potato cake on a bed of liquor, surrounded with the roast pork and cider jus and garnished with a rasher of the reserved streaky bacon.

Prep time 20 minutes,
plus overnight chilling
Cooking time 30–35 minutes
Difficulty Easy

For the potted shrimp
75g (2½oz) salted butter
6 blades mace
1 tsp ground mace
pinch of cayenne pepper or
   freshly ground black pepper
125g (4½oz) peeled brown
   shrimps

For the mackerel pâté
2 smoked mackerel fillets
125g (4½oz) cream cheese
grated zest of 1 lemon
1 tbsp horseradish sauce,
   or to taste
1 tbsp capers, rinsed and
   drained, or to taste
salt and black pepper

For the potted crab
1 banana shallot, finely
   chopped
4 tbsp sherry vinegar
pinch of cayenne pepper
pinch of grated nutmeg
140g (5oz) unsalted butter
2 dressed crabs
1 tsp anchovy essence
1 tsp lemon juice
salt and black pepper

For the walnut and
sunflower seed bread
450g (1lb) wholemeal flour
125g (4½oz) plain flour
35g (1¼oz) sunflower seeds
50g (1¾oz) walnuts, chopped
1 tsp salt
1 tsp bicarbonate of soda
450ml (15fl oz) buttermilk

1 lemon, cut into 4 wedges,
   to serve

Trio of Norfolk seafood pots

Delectable ramekins packed with punchy flavours, with warm, oven-fresh soda bread

1 Make the potted shrimp. Gently melt the butter in a saucepan over a low heat with both types of mace and the cayenne or black pepper. Remove from the heat and leave to infuse for 5 minutes. Strain the butter to remove the mace.

2 Put the shrimps in a bowl, add two-thirds of the melted butter and combine. Pack the shrimp into 4 small ramekins, then seal the tops with a thin layer of the melted butter. Leave to chill in the refrigerator overnight.

3 To make the pâté, flake the fish into a bowl. Add the cream cheese, lemon zest, horseradish and capers. Taste and season with salt and black pepper, adding more horseradish or capers if needed. Divide the mixture evenly among 4 ramekins and leave to chill in the refrigerator overnight.

4 For the potted crab, tip the shallot, vinegar, cayenne and nutmeg into a saucepan. Bring to the boil over a high heat and reduce until only 4 teaspoons of liquid remain. Strain into a clean bowl and whisk in the butter. Allow to cool slightly, then add the crabmeat, anchovy essence, lemon juice, salt and black pepper. Pack into 4 ramekins and leave to chill in the refrigerator overnight.

5 To make the walnut and sunflower seed bread, preheat the oven to 220°C (425°F/Gas 7).

6 In a bowl, mix together all the dry ingredients for the bread, then add enough of the buttermilk to form a soft dough. Turn out of the bowl and knead very gently until smooth and satiny.

7 Shape into a loaf, cut a deep cross on top and place on a greased baking sheet. Bake in the oven for 15 minutes, then reduce the temperature to 200°C (400°F/Gas 6). Bake for a further 15–20 minutes until the bottom of the bread sounds hollow when tapped. Remove from the oven and turn out onto a wire rack.

8 Place a ramekin of each seafood on each of 4 serving plates, and serve with slices of the warm soda bread and a lemon wedge.

Caribbean spicy vegetable soup

The sunny flavours of chilli, coconut and sweet potato, with bacon dough balls

1 Put the chicken and vegetables for the stock in a large saucepan. Pour in enough water to cover and bring to a simmer over a low heat. Simmer for 1 hour. Remove from the heat, strain and leave to cool for 1 hour. Skim off and reserve the fat. Meanwhile, put the rinsed lentils in another pan. Pour in enough water to cover. Bring to a simmer over a medium heat. Simmer for 1 hour, then drain.

2 Chop the potato, yam, sweet potato, green banana and carrots into small, equal-sized pieces and put in a large bowl, adding very cold water and a splash of oil. Finely chop the onion, chilli, leek and garlic and mix with the sugar. Place a heavy saucepan over a high heat, add the remaining sunflower oil, and heat until quite hot. Add the onion mixture and stir briskly.

3 Drain the vegetables and pat dry with kitchen paper. Add to the saucepan with the onion, leek and chilli. Cook for 1 minute, stirring continuously. Add 400ml (14fl oz) of the stock, the milk and the cooked lentils and season with the salt and pepper. Bring the soup to the boil and simmer for 30 minutes. Stir in the cream and coconut milk, taste and adjust the seasoning. Cook for a further 10 minutes. Liquidize with a stick blender, adding a little more stock to achieve a smooth consistency. Set aside and keep warm.

4 To make the dough balls, sift the flour and salt into a bowl. Add a little pepper and the yeast. Dice in the butter and rub with your fingertips until the mixture resembles breadcrumbs. Stir in the egg white. In a small bowl, add the vinegar to 100ml (3½fl oz) water, and slowly pour this into the flour until it forms a dough. Knead for 5–10 minutes, then leave to rise in a warm place for 30 minutes.

5 Preheat the oven to 200°C (400°F/Gas 6). Put the unsmoked bacon into a frying pan over a high heat, stirring, until crispy. Add to the dough, mix well, shape into balls and coat in the bacon fat. Leave to rise for a further 30 minutes, then bake for 15–20 minutes.

6 In another small frying pan, heat the reserved chicken fat with the smoked bacon until crisp. Add the callaloo and stir until wilted.

7 Pour the soup into 4 warm soup bowls, sprinkle over the callaloo and serve the dough balls on the side.

Prep time 50 minutes, plus 1 hour's proving for dough
Cooking time 1 hour 40 minutes, plus 1 hour's cooling for the stock
Difficulty Medium

For the stock
2 chicken legs
2 chicken thighs
2 chicken wings
2 carrots, roughly chopped
1 onion, roughly chopped
3 garlic cloves, halved

For the soup
60g (2oz) green lentils, picked and rinsed
1 large potato
200g (7oz) yam
200g (7oz) white sweet potato
1 green (unripe) banana
3 organic carrots
4 tbsp sunflower oil
1 large Spanish onion
1 fresh green chilli
1 leek
1 garlic clove
1 tbsp granulated sugar
200ml (7fl oz) skimmed milk
1 tbsp fine sea salt
1 tsp coarsely ground black pepper
100ml (3½fl oz) single cream
150ml (5fl oz) coconut milk
2 smoked back bacon rashers, finely chopped
handful of fresh callaloo or spinach, very finely sliced

For the dough balls
170g (6oz) plain flour
pinch of salt
2 tbsp dried yeast
50g (1¾oz) butter
1 egg white
1 tbsp vinegar
2 unsmoked bacon rashers, very finely chopped
freshly ground black pepper

Somerset tiddy oggy

Marvellous cheesy pork and apple bites,
with crab apple jelly and apple chutney

Prep time 25 minutes
Cooking time 40 minutes
Difficulty Medium–easy

1 Put the lard, butter, flour and salt in a food processor and whizz until the mixture resembles breadcrumbs. Gradually add the iced water, a very little at a time, until the mixture just comes together into a ball. Remove from the dough from the food processor, wrap in cling film and leave to rest in the refrigerator for 30 minutes.

2 To make the filling, peel, core and finely chop the apple. Melt the butter in a small saucepan over a medium heat and fry the onion, celery and apple until the onion is soft and translucent. Transfer to a bowl. Put the mince in the same pan and fry it in its own fat, stirring frequently, until lightly browned. Add to the onion with the parsley, season well with salt and black pepper and stir well. Allow to cool, then chill in the refrigerator until needed.

3 Preheat the oven to 180°C (350°F/Gas 4). Remove the pastry from the refrigerator and allow it to come almost back to room temperature (this helps to avoid cracking). Roll out the pastry on a floured work surface and cut into 15cm (6in) rounds.

4 Place a spoonful of the mince mixture in the centre of each pastry round, brush the edges with water, then pull up the sides and press together, leaving a hole at the top. Fill the holes with the cheese and top with breadcrumbs. Brush each of the pastries with a little beaten egg to glaze.

5 Place the tiddy oggys on a baking tray and bake in the oven for 30 minutes until the pastry is cooked and golden. Serve warm or cold with crab apple jelly and apple chutney.

For the pastry
100g (3½oz) lard
100g (3½oz) butter
450g (1lb) plain flour
pinch of salt
about 6 tbsp iced water

For the filling
1 medium cooking apple
  such as Bramley
knob of butter
1 onion, finely chopped
50g (1¾oz) celery, finely
  chopped
225g (8oz) pork mince
1–2 tbsp chopped parsley
2 tbsp grated mature
  Cheddar cheese
4 tbsp toasted breadcrumbs
1 free-range egg, beaten
salt and freshly ground black
  pepper

To serve
crab apple jelly (home-made
  if possible)
apple chutney (home-made
  if possible)

"Delicious, light as a feather
and still very crumbly
inside. Lovely. Very herby.
Very good little dish."
— Jilly Goolden

Trio of polenta crostini

Imaginative and moreish toppings on grilled polenta make fine finger food

Prep time 10–15 minutes, plus overnight soaking
Cooking time 2¼ hours
Difficulty Medium

For the cod topping
500g (1lb 2oz) salt cod
500ml (16fl oz) milk
1 garlic clove, crushed
2 tbsp chopped parsley
150ml (5fl oz) mild olive oil

For the bean, sausage and scallop topping
300g (10oz) dried borlotti beans
3 garlic cloves
a few sprigs of fresh thyme
sprig of fresh rosemary, plus extra 8–10 sprigs
3 bay leaves
1 small potato, halved
3 cherry tomatoes
1 celery stick
extra virgin olive oil
balsamic or red wine vinegar
handful of flat-leaf parsley
8–10 thin slices pancetta
8–10 king scallops
4 or 5 Italian sausages
salt and black pepper

For the crostini
500g (1lb 2oz) quick-cook white polenta
250g (9oz) quick-cook yellow polenta
15g (½oz) dried porcini mushrooms, finely chopped
a few drops of truffle oil

For the mushroom topping
a little extra virgin olive oil
handful of fresh porcini mushrooms, sliced
2 garlic cloves, chopped
1 dried chilli (optional)
1 tbsp chopped parsley

1 Soak the cod in cold water for at least 24 hours, changing the water at least four times. Taste a small piece before you begin cooking – if it's too salty, it will need longer soaking. At the same time, soak the beans overnight in a large bowl of cold water.

2 To make the bean topping, drain and rinse the beans, put in a large pot, cover with fresh water and throw in the garlic, thyme, 1 sprig of rosemary, bay leaves, potato, tomatoes and celery. Bring slowly to the boil over a low heat, cover and simmer gently for 1 hour until the beans are soft. Skim and top up with boiling water if needed. Drain, reserving enough liquid to come halfway up the beans. Discard the herbs and celery. Put the tomatoes, potato and garlic on a plate, remove the potato skin and mash together. Stir into the beans with the reserved cooking liquid and season with salt and black pepper. Mix in a few generous glugs of oil and a few splashes of vinegar, then chop and add the parsley. Set aside.

3 Remove the skin and bones from the salt cod and break the fish into strips with your fingers, following the fibres of the cod (do not use a knife). Put in a large pan and add the milk and just enough water to cover. Bring to the boil, then simmer for 30 minutes. Drain and transfer to a food processor. Blend at high speed for 1 minute or until the fish is shredded. Add the garlic and parsley, then pour in the olive oil a drop at a time, as if making mayonnaise.

4 For the crostini, bring 1 litre (1¾ pints) well-salted water to the boil over a medium-high heat. Sprinkle in half the white polenta, slowly stirring with a whisk to prevent lumps. Reduce the heat to low and stir constantly to prevent sticking. It should be soft; if it's too dry, add a little more water. Pour onto a baking sheet, spread out to about 1.5cm (⅝in) thick and allow to cool. Cook the yellow polenta in the same way. Repeat with the remaining white polenta, adding the porcini to the boiling water before stirring in the grains and stirring through a few drops of truffle oil before cooling.

5 When ready to serve, make the mushroom topping. Heat a little oil in a frying pan over a medium heat. Sauté the mushrooms and garlic, adding the dried chilli (if using), then remove from the heat. Stir through the parsley, season to taste and keep warm.

6 Cut all the polenta into small round, diamond, or triangular shapes. Grill them in a lightly oiled hot ridged cast-iron grill pan until warmed through and with good char lines.

7 Meanwhile, working quickly, wrap a slice of the pancetta in a ring around the side of each scallop and skewer in place with the extra sprigs of rosemary. Cut each sausage into 4 slices and fry the scallops and sausages in a little olive oil until golden.

8 Arrange the crostini on a large serving platter. Spoon some beans onto the white slices, then arrange 2 slices of sausage and a scallop on top of each one. Generously spread the yellow slices with the salt cod mixture and serve the mushrooms on the truffle polenta crostini. Drizzle all the crostini with olive oil and serve.

"Every single part of it is executed beautifully ... The salt cod is done brilliantly. What a beautiful starter."

— Ed Baines

Prep time 10 minutes, plus
30 minutes' chilling time
Cooking time 25 minutes
Difficulty Easy–medium

For the pastry
125g (4½oz) organic
  plain flour
pinch of Maldon sea salt
60g (2oz) organic butter,
  diced
1 organic egg yolk
1 tbsp iced water

For the filling
2 organic garlic cloves,
  crushed
knob of organic butter
180g (6oz) organic smoked
  salmon, sliced into large
  strips
1 organic egg
150ml (5fl oz) organic double
  cream
2 tbsp chopped organic
  flat-leaf parsley
4 tbsp freshly grated organic
  Parmesan cheese

For the salad
juice of ½ organic lemon
2 tbsp organic olive oil
handful of rocket and
  watercress
handful of smoked prawns

Organic smoked salmon tart

Deceptively simple ingredients go to make a sophisticated and elegant starter

1 To make the pastry, sift the flour and salt into a bowl and rub in the butter with your fingertips until the mixture resembles breadcrumbs. Make a well in the centre and add the egg yolk, then the iced water, a very little at a time, until the mixture just comes together into a ball. (Alternatively, use a food processor. Whizz the butter for a few seconds. Add the egg yolk and whizz again. With the motor running, add the salt and flour, then add the iced water, a little at a time, until the dough just comes together.) Remove the pastry from the bowl, wrap in cling film, and leave to chill for 30 minutes.

2 Meanwhile, in a frying pan over a medium heat, fry the garlic in butter for 1 minute until softened, taking care that it does not brown. Add the smoked salmon and remove from the heat. In a small bowl, beat the egg and mix in the double cream and parsley.

3 Preheat the oven to 190°C (375°F/Gas 5). Remove the pastry from the refrigerator and roll out on a floured work surface until it is about 1cm (just under ½in) thick. Cut out 4 circles with a pastry cutter to fit into 10cm (4in) non-stick individual tart tins. Press the pastry into the tins and divide the smoked salmon mixture evenly among them. Spoon over the egg mixture and sprinkle with the Parmesan. Bake in the oven for 25 minutes or until nicely browned. Lift out and cool on a wire rack for 1 minute.

4 To make the salad, whisk together the lemon juice and oil, then turn the salad leaves over in this dressing until coated. Serve a warm tart on each of 4 serving plates, with a little salad on the side and a scattering of smoked prawns.

Magic crab gratin with Swiss chard

A simple and delectable dish, packed with succulent greens and tasty crab

Prep time **10 minutes**
Cooking time **30 minutes**
Difficulty **Easy**

1 Preheat the oven to 180°C (350°F/Gas 4). In a small frying pan over a low heat, gently sweat the garlic in the oil and butter for 1 minute or so. Stir in the breadcrumbs and fry for a few minutes, then remove from the heat.

2 Separate the chard leaves from the stalks. Chop the stalks and slice the leaves. In a large frying pan over a medium heat, gently sweat the shallot in the oil. Add the chard stalks and chilli and continue to sweat gently for 5–10 minutes. Add the vermouth and allow to reduce until it has nearly all disappeared and the alcohol has evaporated. Add the butter and sprinkle in the flour, stirring constantly for 1–2 minutes. Remove the frying pan from the heat and gradually add the evaporated milk and enough semi-skimmed milk to form a thick sauce, stirring constantly to prevent lumps. Season with salt and black pepper.

3 Return the frying pan to the heat, add the chard leaves and most of the parsley and cook for 5–10 minutes, stirring constantly. Add more milk if it gets too thick. Add the cheese, crab and the remaining parsley.

4 Pour the crab mixture into 4 small ovenproof serving dishes, and sprinkle over the topping. Bake in the oven for 10 minutes until golden and serve hot and bubbling.

For the topping
1 garlic clove, chopped
1½ tbsp olive oil
25g (scant 1oz) butter
4 tbsp panko breadcrumbs

For the filling
200g (7oz) Swiss chard
1 large shallot, finely chopped
1 tbsp olive oil
large pinch of red chilli flakes
2 tbsp extra-dry vermouth
50g (1¾oz) butter
30g (1oz) plain flour
2 tbsp evaporated milk
200ml (7fl oz) semi-skimmed milk
small handful of fresh parsley leaves, chopped
3 tbsp English Parmesan-style cheese, finely grated
150g (5½oz) picked white crabmeat
Maldon sea salt and freshly ground pepper

"**Absolutely stunning. It's really lovely. I haven't had a hot crab dish in ages. This is a really good one… it's a delightful dish.**"
— John Burton Race

Avocado and goat's cheese tartlets

Home-made red chilli sauce adds zing
to creamy tartlets served with guacamole

Prep time 25 minutes, plus
1 hour's cooling and resting
Cooking time 25 minutes
Difficulty Medium

For the pastry
250g (9oz) plain flour
pinch of Maldon sea salt
180g (6oz) unsalted butter,
  diced
a little iced water

For the guacamole
1 large Hass avocado
1 lime
4 spring onions, finely
  chopped
1–2 medium vine-ripened
  tomatoes, finely diced
2 tsp mayonnaise
salt and a pinch of cracked
  black pepper

For the chilli sauce
2 fresh red chillies, deseeded
  and finely diced
1 fat garlic clove, finely diced
3 tbsp Japanese rice vinegar
1 tbsp red wine vinegar such
  as Aspall organic
3 tbsp golden caster sugar

For the tart filling
1 large Hass avocado
1 lime
2 mild goat's cheese logs,
  about 100g (3½oz) each

For the salad
2 tbsp light, fruity extra virgin
  olive oil
1 tbsp red wine vinegar
¼ fat garlic clove, crushed
large pinch of golden caster
  sugar
100g (3½oz) mixed leaves,
  such as rocket, baby
  spinach and watercress
salt and black pepper

1 Make sure that all the ingredients for the pastry are very cold. Put the flour, salt and cubed butter in a food processor. Pulse until the mixture resembles breadcrumbs. Trickle in iced water, little by little, until the dough just comes together into a ball. Wrap in cling film and leave to rest in the refrigerator for 30 minutes.

2 Remove the pastry from the refrigerator and roll out on a floured work surface until 5mm (¼in) thick. Press the pastry gently into four 10cm (4in) individual tartlet tins, making sure that there are no holes. Trim the tartlets neatly, prick the bottoms of the pastry cases with a fork and return to the refrigerator to rest again for at least 20 minutes, preferably longer.

3 Preheat the oven to 180°C (350°F/Gas 4). Put a baking sheet into the oven to heat up. Cut out circles of baking parchment slightly bigger than the pastry cases and use them to line the tartlet tins. Fill the lined cases with baking beans and place on the hot baking sheet in the oven. Blind-bake for 20 minutes or until just light golden in colour, but cooked through.

4 Remove the tartlet tins from the oven and take out the beans and paper. Carefully remove the pastry cases from their tins, then place them back on the baking sheet and return to the oven for another 2–3 minutes until slightly golden, watching closely to avoid them burning. Remove from the oven and place on a wire rack to cool completely. Do not turn off the oven.

5 Make the guacamole. Peel and roughly chop the avocado, squeezing over a little lime juice to avoid discoloration. Put in a small bowl and mash with a fork, leaving some pieces chunky. Add the spring onion and tomato, then stir in the mayonnaise. Season with salt and cracked black pepper. Taste and adjust the seasoning, adding more salt or lime if you prefer. Cover with cling film, making sure that the cling film touches the surface of the guacamole to avoid discoloration. Leave in the refrigerator until needed.

6 To make the chilli sauce, put all the ingredients in a small saucepan and add 1–2 tablespoons water. If you prefer a hot sauce, leave in some or all of the seeds, but warn your guests before

serving! Bring to a boil over a medium heat, reduce the heat slightly and simmer for 10–15 minutes until syrupy, stirring from time to time. Decant into a small bowl and set aside.

7 To make the tart filling, peel the avocado, discard the stone, and slice the flesh into long strips lengthways. Squeeze over a little lime juice to prevent discoloration and set aside.

8 Slice the cheeses into 8 cylindrical portions.

9 Place the cooled pastry cases on a baking sheet. Put a few dollops of the guacamole into the bottom of each one, add a few avocado slices and place 2 circles of cheese on top. Bake in the oven for 2–3 minutes until the cheese is just starting to melt.

10 Make the vinaigrette for the salad by whisking together the olive oil, vinegar, garlic and sugar and season with salt and black pepper. Toss with the salad leaves.

11 To serve, place a pile of salad on each of 4 plates, top with a tartlet and drizzle with the chilli sauce.

STARTERS • AVOCADO AND GOAT'S CHEESE TARTLETS

Crisp-fried whitebait

A new twist on an old favourite, served with crusty home-made breadsticks

Prep time 5 minutes
Cooking time 10 minutes
Difficulty Easy

1 Preheat the oven to 240°C (475°F/Gas 9). Mix the yeast with 120ml (4fl oz) of tepid water. Put the flour and ½ tsp salt in a large bowl, add the yeast mixture and stir until combined. Knead this dough on a floured board until smooth, then roll 12 small pieces into thin sticks and lay on a baking sheet. Plait into 4 slightly larger breadsticks, if you like. Drizzle the sticks with olive oil and sprinkle with extra sea salt. Bake for 10 minutes until golden. Set aside.

2 To make the salad dressing, put the garlic (if using) in a sieve, then juice the lemons through the sieve into a bowl, to remove the lemon pips and pick up some garlic flavour. Discard the contents of the sieve, add the oil to the bowl and season with salt and cracked black pepper. Whisk until well combined, then set aside in the refrigerator until needed.

3 Arrange the rocket, cherry tomatoes and cucumber neatly on 4 serving plates and set aside.

4 Heat enough oil for deep-frying in a deep-fat fryer until the temperature of the oil measures 170°C (340°C) on a cook's thermometer. Meanwhile, wipe the whitebait dry with kitchen paper, place in a shallow dish, toss over the flour and season with salt and black pepper. Lift out the fish, shaking off any excess flour, then deep-fry in batches for 3–4 minutes until golden and crisp. Remove with a slotted spoon. Drain on kitchen paper to absorb the excess oil and keep warm while you cook the rest of the whitebait.

5 Take the dressing out of the refrigerator and drizzle lightly over the salad on each plate. Place 6 fish on top of each salad and serve immediately, with the breadsticks.

For the breadsticks
1 x 3g sachet dried yeast
200g (7oz) strong white flour
½ tsp sea salt, plus extra for
  sprinkling
olive oil

For the salad
1 garlic clove (optional)
4 lemons
75ml (2½fl oz) extra virgin
  olive oil
4 handfuls of rocket leaves
12 cherry tomatoes
½ cucumber, diced
sea salt and cracked black
  pepper

For the fish
vegetable oil for deep-frying
24 whitebait, preferably fresh
  not frozen
100g (3½oz) plain flour
salt and black pepper

Cullen skink

Prep time **5–10 minutes**
Cooking time **35 minutes**
Difficulty **Easy**

60g (2oz) slightly salted
   butter
1 onion, finely chopped
1 garlic clove, finely chopped
2 medium fillets of undyed
   smoked haddock, diced
5 Scottish Rooster potatoes,
   peeled and cubed
285ml (9fl oz) whole milk
300ml (10fl oz) double cream
sea salt and freshly ground
   black pepper
handful of chives, chopped,
   to garnish

A classic from the Scottish Highlands,
this easy soup packs a flavour punch

1 Melt the butter in a large saucepan over a medium heat. Add
the onion and gently sweat for 5–10 minutes until soft. Add the
garlic and smoked haddock. Cook for 2 minutes.

2 Meanwhile, in another saucepan, add the potatoes to the milk.
Bring to a simmer and cook slowly for 15 minutes or until tender.
Add the double cream.

3 Pour the potatoes, milk and cream into the saucepan containing
the smoked haddock and cook everything over a medium heat for
a further 3 minutes. Season with salt and black pepper and serve
in 4 warm soup bowls, sprinkled with chopped chives.

Pea, ham and watermelon verrine

Layered in a glass, this summery dish is impressive to look at and very refreshing

Prep time 45 minutes
Cooking time 3 hours
Difficulty Medium

1 Fill a large saucepan with enough water to completely submerge the green ham and bring to the boil over a high heat. Add the cubed ham, reduce the heat and simmer for 2–2½ hours.

2 Preheat the oven to 180°C (350°F/Gas 4).

3 Using a melon baller, ball the honeydew melon and leave in the refrigerator to chill.

4 Juice the watermelon flesh in a juicer or blender and sieve out the seeds. In a bowl, soak the gelatine in 200ml (7fl oz) of the watermelon juice for about 10 minutes. Put the gelatine mixture in a small saucepan over a low heat. Gently heat until the gelatine has dissolved, then add the remaining watermelon juice. Stir well and set aside to cool but not set.

5 Bring a saucepan of water to the boil and add the sugarsnap peas. Cook for 5 minutes, then drain.

6 Pat the cooked ham dry with kitchen paper, then shred the meat using 2 forks. Add the mustard seeds and peas. Season with salt and fold together. Divide the ham mixture among 4 glasses, so that each is a quarter full.

7 Cover these ham rillettes evenly with the watermelon mixture and leave in the refrigerator to set for 30 minutes.

8 Using the same-sized glass as the verrines as a guide, cut a disc from each slice of black ham. Set aside.

9 Put the bacon on a baking sheet and cook in the oven for 5 minutes or until crispy. Cool, then chop. Meanwhile, bring a saucepan of water to the boil, add the egg and boil for 8 minutes. Drain, shell the egg and chop. Mix together the egg and bacon.

10 Once the verrines are set, place a disc of black ham on top of each one, then a layer of honeydew melon balls and baby tomatoes. Add another disc of black ham with a scattering of the chopped bacon and egg and scatter each verrine with wild rocket.

400g (14oz) green ham,
  cut into 2.5cm (1in) cubes
1 honeydew melon, halved
  and deseeded
1 watermelon, halved
4 leaves gelatine
200g (7oz) sugarsnap peas
  or garden peas
1 tsp mustard seeds
8 thin slices black ham
6 thin streaky bacon rashers
1 egg
20 baby tomatoes
sea salt
wild rocket, to garnish

Chicken tikka roll with coconut sauce

Fantastic, slightly bitter fenugreek, or methi, adds a special touch to this dish

Prep time 30 minutes, plus cooling time
Cooking time 10 minutes
Difficulty Easy–medium

For the chicken tikka roll
500g (1lb 2oz) skinless chicken breast fillets, thinly sliced
1 bunch of fresh fenugreek leaves
1 bunch of fresh spinach
1 white onion, chopped
6 garlic cloves
5cm (2in) piece of fresh root ginger
2 tsp red chilli powder
2 tsp garam masala
2 tbsp sunflower oil
50g (1¾oz) plain yogurt
1 tbsp tandoori masala
salt

For the coconut sauce
1 tbsp sunflower oil
1 bunch of spring onions, chopped
5–6 fresh green chillies, sliced
1 bunch of fresh coriander, leaves picked and chopped
1 x 400ml can coconut milk
juice of 4 lemons
salt

To garnish
2 handfuls of rocket
2 red radishes, grated

1 Preheat the oven to 220°C (425°F/Gas 7).

2 Rinse the chicken slices, dry them on kitchen paper, sprinkle with salt and set aside.

3 Pick the fenugreek and spinach leaves off the stems and clean them thoroughly in four or five changes of cold water. Drain, then leave on kitchen paper to dry.

4 Put the onion, garlic and ginger in a food processor and whizz to a paste, adding a pinch of salt, the red chilli powder and the garam masala. Rub this paste onto the chicken and set aside.

5 Heat the oil in a saucepan over a low heat, and cook the fenugreek and spinach for 1–2 minutes, adding a pinch of salt. Remove from the heat and allow to cool.

6 Spread the chicken slices on a baking sheet. Stir the yogurt, and paint it onto the chicken. Sprinkle with the tandoori masala and cover each chicken slice with a layer of fenugreek and spinach. Roll up each chicken slice and push a cocktail stick through to hold it together. Put the chicken rolls on a greased baking sheet, cover with foil and leave to marinate for 10 minutes. Preheat the grill to its highest setting.

7 To make the sauce, heat the oil in a saucepan over a medium heat. Add the spring onions and cook, stirring from time to time, for 1–2 minutes. Add the green chillies and coriander and cook for a further 1–2 minutes. Remove the pan from the heat, cool the mixture for 5 minutes, then blend to a paste with a stick blender. Add the coconut milk, return the mixture to the rinsed-out pan and simmer for 5 minutes. Remove from the heat, add the lemon juice and a little salt, stir and leave to cool.

8 Put the chicken in the hot oven and cook for 10 minutes, then remove the foil and place the sheet under the hot grill until the chicken is browned, turning so that it is evenly coloured. Carefully cut each roll into small slices, taking care that they do not split.

9 Put the chicken slices on a plate. Garnish with a few leaves of rocket and some radish and serve the coconut sauce on the side.

Creamy cauliflower and Stilton soup

With truly exceptional three-cheese scones, this soup is a comforting winter warmer

Prep time **25 minutes**
Cooking time **2 hours**
Difficulty **Easy**

1 To make the stock, put the vegetables in a large pan. Pour in 1.2 litres (2 pints) water, bring to the boil and simmer for 1 hour. Strain into a bowl.

2 To make the soup, melt the butter in a large saucepan over a medium heat. Add the onion and sweat, stirring, for about 5 minutes until soft and translucent. Pour in the cider and gently simmer for 10 minutes.

3 Put the leek, celery and 600ml (1 pint) of the vegetable stock in another pan over a medium heat. Bring to a simmer and cook until the liquid is reduced by a third, then add the cauliflower and cook until soft. Crumble in the Stilton, then pour in the onions and cider. Stir through. Using a stick blender, purée the mixture until smooth, taste and season with salt and black pepper. Remove the pan from the heat, stir in the cream and set aside.

4 To make the scones, preheat the oven to 190°C (375°F/Gas 5). Put the potatoes in a large pan of boiling water and simmer until just cooked. Drain, then dice and set aside. Sift together the flour and baking powder into a bowl and season with salt and black pepper. Add the butter and rub together with your fingertips until the mixture resembles breadcrumbs. Mix in most of the cheeses, the cooked diced potato and the herbs.

5 In a small bowl, beat together the milk, egg and mustard, then add most of this to the flour mixture, stirring with a knife until the dough comes together. Roll out the dough on a floured work surface until 2cm (¾in) thick, then cut out triangles for the scones. Brush the scones with the reserved milk mixture, sprinkle with the remaining cheese and bake in the oven for 15–20 minutes.

6 To serve, gently reheat the soup over a medium heat, then serve in warm bowls, accompanied by the scones and some butter.

For the stock
1 onion, roughly chopped
5 celery sticks, roughly chopped
1 leek, roughly chopped
3 carrots, roughly chopped

For the creamy cauliflower soup
50g (1¾oz) butter
1 onion, finely chopped
600ml (1 pint) scrumpy cider
1 leek, chopped
3 celery sticks, chopped
1 cauliflower, cut into florets
225g (8oz) Stilton cheese
300ml (10fl oz) single cream
salt and freshly ground black pepper

For the three-cheese scones
5 new potatoes, peeled and halved
150g (5½oz) self-raising flour
1 tsp baking powder
50g (1¾oz) butter
50g (1¾oz) Red Leicester cheese, grated
50g (1¾oz) double Gloucester cheese, grated
50g (1¾oz) mature Cheddar cheese, grated
1 tsp finely chopped fresh sage leaves
1 tbsp finely chopped basil leaves
300ml (10fl oz) whole milk
1 free-range egg
2 tsp grainy mustard
salt and black pepper

Prep time 10–15 minutes
Cooking time 1 hour
45 minutes
Difficulty Medium

For the pastry
100g (3½oz) butter
200g (7oz) wholemeal flour
1 egg, beaten
salt and black pepper

For the beetroot
4 uncooked baby beetroot
2 tbsp sour cream
2–3 tsp fresh horseradish,
   finely grated
4 sprigs of fresh lemon
   thyme
salt

For the filling
75g (2½oz) butter
2 onions, chopped
2 garlic cloves, crushed
200g (7oz) watercress
200g (7oz) hot-smoked
   trout, flaked
large bunch of chives,
   chopped
3 eggs
200ml (7fl oz) double cream
1 tbsp soured cream
4 tsp garlic and horseradish
   mustard
Maldon sea salt and crushed
   black peppercorns

For the salad
1 shallot, finely chopped
4 tbsp white wine vinegar
large pinch of caster sugar
4 sprigs of fresh tarragon,
   finely chopped
½ garlic clove, crushed
1 tsp honey mustard
90ml (3fl oz) rapeseed oil,
   plus extra for the leaves
1 bunch of watercress

Smoked trout and watercress tart

Showcasing the best Hampshire produce, this is a gorgeous marriage of flavours

1 To make the pastry, rub the butter into the flour with your fingertips until it resembles fine breadcrumbs, then season with a pinch of salt and a little black pepper. Add just enough iced water until the mixture comes together as a dough. Wrap in cling film and rest in the refrigerator for 30 minutes. Meanwhile, preheat the oven to 180°C (350°F/Gas 4).

2 Roll the pastry out on a floured work surface and use it to line a 20cm (8in) fluted tart tin. Prick the base all over with a fork, brush with the egg and bake in the oven for 30–35 minutes. Leave to cool. Reduce the oven temperature to 150°C (300°F/Gas 2).

3 Meanwhile, bring a small pan of water to the boil with a pinch of salt, add the beetroot, reduce the heat and simmer for 30 minutes.

4 To make the filling, melt the butter in a frying pan, add the onions and sauté over a medium heat for about 5 minutes until golden. Add the garlic and sauté for a further 30 seconds until the garlic turns white and opaque. Turn off the heat.

5 Bring a saucepan of water to the boil, drop in the watercress for 1 minute, then plunge into iced water. Squeeze well and blot on kitchen paper, then chop and add to the cooling onions. Gently mix in the trout and chives and season with salt and black pepper.

6 Gently whisk together the eggs, cream, soured cream and mustard. Season with salt and lots of pepper, then add the trout mixture, mix and gently pour into the tart case. Bake in the oven for 55–60 minutes until the centre is just set, but still has a slight wobble to it. Remove from the oven and leave to cool a little.

7 To make the salad, in a small bowl, whisk together the shallot, vinegar, sugar, tarragon, garlic, mustard and 90ml (3fl oz) oil. Toss the watercress in a little more oil to coat.

8 To serve, cut the warm tart into wedges. Serve a wedge on each plate and place a beetroot next to it. Top the beetroot with a spoon of the vinaigrette, a little soured cream, some grated horseradish and a sprig of lemon thyme. Arrange the watercress next to it and drizzle more vinaigrette around each plate. Serve.

West Country pork tortellini

Pasta is given a West Country twist with fine local ingredients – including scrumpy!

1 Pile the flour onto a clean work surface and form into a volcano shape, with a central hole. Beat the eggs together, then pour into the well. Gradually incorporate the eggs into the flour until a dough forms. Knead for at least 10 minutes until it becomes silky to the touch. Chill for 30 minutes, before rolling out, passing through a pasta machine and cutting into discs 4–5cm (1¾–2in) across.

2 Meanwhile, to make the tortellini filling, remove and discard any fat from the pork and cut the meat into cubes. Heat the oil in a pan over a medium-high heat and brown the pork on all sides for about 10 minutes. Peel, core and chop the apple and add to the pork for the last 2 minutes of the cooking time.

3 Put the pork and apple into a food processor and add the goat's cheese to taste. Process the mixture for about 30 seconds. Be careful not to process to a paste; you want the mixture to remain slightly coarse. Set aside to cool.

4 To make the sauce, pour the scrumpy or cider into a pan and bring to the boil. Reduce by one-third. Add the cream, stir through and season with salt and black pepper. Set aside in a warm place.

5 Working as quickly as you can, put a small amount of filling in the centre of each of the pasta disc (don't use too much filling – you need to be able to fold the pasta without breaking it). Take one and wet the edge of the pasta with a little warm water. Fold the pasta over the filling so that the edges almost meet and press together firmly to seal, ensuring that no air is trapped inside. Hold the filled pasta between your thumb and index finger and fold it around your finger to bring the two ends together. Press the two ends together, then fold the sealed edge down. Sit the shaped pasta, or tortellini, on a clean tea towel and continue in the same way until you have filled and shaped all the tortellini. (You can cook them at once, or leave to dry for 40 minutes, turning once or twice so that they dry evenly.)

6 Bring a large, deep pan of salted water to the boil and cook the tortellini for 2 minutes; drain. Serve on a bed of the mixed leaves, with the scrumpy sauce drizzled over the top.

Prep time 15 minutes
Cooking time 25 minutes
Difficulty Medium–hard

For the pasta
200g (7oz) '00' flour, plus more, to dust
2 free-range eggs

For the filling
1 Gloucester Old Spot pork chop
1 tbsp olive oil
1 Bramley apple
200g (7oz) Somerset goat's cheese

For the scrumpy sauce
285ml (9fl oz) farmhouse scrumpy or cider
200ml (7fl oz) double cream
salt and freshly ground black pepper

seasonal mixed leaves, to serve

Prep time **30 minutes, plus chilling time**
Cooking time **45 minutes**
Difficulty **Easy–medium**

For the cannelloni
2 roasted red peppers
8 tbsp soft goat's cheese
4 handfuls of wild rocket
grated zest and juice of
   1 lemon
pinch of salt
4 fresh asparagus spears
1 tbsp olive oil
4 slices Parma ham

For the tarts
125g (4½oz) plain flour
pinch of salt
60g (2oz) hard margarine
½ tsp dried mixed herbs
a little iced water
3 shallots, finely chopped
1 garlic clove, crushed
about 2 tbsp olive oil
175ml (6fl oz) double cream
4 free-range egg yolks
4 tbsp soft goat's cheese
4 asparagus spears
½ roasted red pepper,
   deseeded and finely sliced
4 thin slices Parma ham,
   chopped
freshly ground black pepper

For the stack
olive oil
12 fresh asparagus tips
handful of lemon thyme
1 block soft goat's cheese,
   plus extra 4 tbsp, to serve
4 slices Parma ham
1 red pepper, quartered
   and roasted in olive oil

Asparagus, ham and goat's cheese trio

A beautiful springtime dish filled with the flavours of the season

1 To make the cannelloni, blend the red pepper, goat's cheese, rocket, lemon juice and zest and salt in a food processor until smooth. In a small frying pan, fry the asparagus in the olive oil until al dente. Lay each ham slice on a small piece of cling film. Spoon 2 tablespoons of the cheese mixture on each. Place an asparagus spear on top. Roll each ham slice lengthways over the filling, wrap tightly and chill for as long as possible, ideally a couple of hours.

2 To make the tarts, mix together the flour and salt, dice in the margarine and rub with your fingertips until the mixture resembles breadcrumbs. Season with black pepper and the herbs. Stir in iced water, a very little at a time, until the dough comes together. Knead lightly, then roll out on a floured work surface. Use to line four 10cm (4in) individual tart tins. Cover each with cling film, then leave to chill for 30 minutes. Preheat the oven to 190°C (375°F/Gas 5).

3 Remove the tart cases from the refrigerator and take off the cling film. Line the cases with greaseproof paper and fill them with baking beans. Bake them for 10–15 minutes, remove the beans and paper and allow to cool. In a small frying pan over a medium heat, gently sweat the shallot and garlic in 1 tbsp oil for 10 minutes. Mix in the cream, egg yolks and goat's cheese and season. Cook, stirring, for 5 minutes. Fry the asparagus spears for a couple of minutes in olive oil over a medium heat. Finely slice half of each spear (keep the tips whole). Layer the asparagus slices, red peppers and ham in the pastry cases, top with the asparagus tips and cover with the cream mixture. Bake for 12 minutes.

4 For the stack, heat a little olive oil in a small frying pan over a medium heat. Gently sauté the asparagus tips and lemon thyme. Preheat the grill to its highest setting. To make the cheese crisps, cut 4 thick slices of goat's cheese and place under the hot grill for 5–6 minutes until melted and turning brown. Fry the ham in a hot pan until brown and crisp, then cool.

5 Place a tart and a cannelloni, sitting on a cheese crisp, on each of 4 plates. Make a stack of the Parma ham, red pepper and asparagus tips. Form 4 quenelles by shaping the remaining goat's cheese between two spoons and place one on top of each stack.

Prep time 10 minutes
Cooking time 4½ hours
Difficulty Medium

For the jelly
1 raw pork hock, split
2 pig's trotters, split

For the filling
450g (1lb) shoulder or belly
    pork, coarsely minced
1½ tsp salt
½ tsp freshly ground black
    pepper

For the pastry
150g (5oz) lard
400g (14oz) plain flour
1½ tsp salt
1 egg, beaten

For the chutney
½ onion, roughly chopped
1 fresh red chilli, finely
    chopped
1 tbsp vegetable oil
400g (14oz) vine-ripened
    tomatoes, chopped
1 beef tomato, chopped
85ml (3fl oz) red wine vinegar
30g (1oz) sugar
pinch of salt
½ tsp ground black pepper
60g (2oz) baby gherkins,
    chopped

The porkie pig pie

A hugely satisfying version of a classic, with a piquant home-made chutney

1 To make the jelly, pour 1.7 litres (3 pints) water into a very large saucepan. Add the hock and trotters, bring to the boil and simmer for 2 hours. Strain and set aside.

2 To make the filling, put the pork mince in a large bowl, add the salt, pepper and 3 tbsp water and mix well. Set aside.

3 Warm the lard with 150ml (5fl oz) water in a small pan over a low heat until melted; do not boil. Remove from the heat, add the flour and salt and mix together. Tip out and knead gently on a floured work surface. Leave to cool slightly, but do not allow to go cold.

4 Cut the pastry into three sections, one for each pie, then cut out and set aside a small piece of each for the lids. Roll out on a floured work surface until about 5mm (¼in) thick and drape over the bottom of an upturned jam jar. Mould the pastry around the jar and trim the edges straight. Refrigerate for a maximum of 30 seconds to allow the mould to set a little. Using a sharp knife, very carefully lift the pastry from the jar, turn over and stand on a baking sheet greased with a little lard. Preheat the oven to 220°C (425°F/Gas 7). Roll out the pastry pieces set aside for the lids into circles and cut a hole in the centre of each one.

5 Dvide the meat filling evenly among the pastry cases, ensuring that they are full almost to the brim. Wet the edges of the pastry lids with water and place on top. Pinch together the edges all around to seal. Brush the pies with beaten egg. Make a double-thickness band from foil and wrap it around each pie to help to keep their shape in the oven. Cover each pie with more foil. Bake for 20 minutes, then remove from the oven, brush again with egg and re-cover with foil. Return to the oven for a further 20 minutes.

6 Reduce the oven temperature to 200°C (400°F/Gas 6) and cook for a further 30 minutes, checking at intervals to avoid any burning to the crusts. The pies are cooked when the filling bubbles up well through the top. Remove from the oven and allow to cool slightly.

7 Using a funnel and the hole on top of the pies, pour the hot jelly into the pies until each is three-quarters full. Never add hot jelly to cold pies; instead, top up with cool gravy the next day to seal.

8 Freeze the pies for 20–25 minutes, then refrigerate.

9 To make the chutney, in a large pan over a medium heat, fry the onion and chilli in the oil for 1 minute or until softened. Add the tomatoes and red wine vinegar and stir through. Do not allow to boil. Add the sugar, season with salt and black pepper and simmer for 25–30 minutes until reduced to a jam-like consistency.

10 Finally add the chopped gherkins, mix in well and remove from the heat. Decant the chutney into a hot sterilized jar with a tight-fitting lid, seal and leave to cool on a wire rack. Store in the refrigerator until needed.

11 Serve the pies with lots of the chutney.

Monkfish, fennel and tomato soup

Vibrant Mediterranean tastes fill this soup,
served with a rustic home-made bread

Prep time 10–15 minutes
Cooking time 2 hours
Difficulty Easy

For the olive oil bread
375g (13oz) strong white
  bread flour
1 tsp sea salt
2 tsp dried yeast
3 tsp olive oil

For the soup
2 tbsp olive oil
120g (4¼oz) monkfish,
  trimmed, deboned,
  and sliced
4 scallops, cut in half
  crossways
8 vine-ripened tomatoes
¼ fennel bulb, sliced
1 small onion, sliced
6 garlic cloves, crushed
250ml (8fl oz) white wine
250ml (8fl oz) chicken stock
75ml (2½fl oz) sweet sherry
2 tbsp fish sauce
2 tbsp sun-dried tomato
  paste
pinch of saffron threads
8 fresh mussels, scrubbed
  and beards removed
8 raw tiger prawns, peeled
  and de-veined
1 lemon, quartered
1 tbsp capers, drained,
  rinsed and gently squeezed
  dry
sprig of fresh marjoram,
  chopped

1 To make the bread, sift the flour and half the salt into a bowl. Stir the yeast into 250ml (8fl oz) lukewarm water and mix this into the flour, stirring until the dough starts to come together. Knead on a floured work surface for 15 minutes, then put into another, lightly oiled bowl, cover and leave to rise for 1 hour in a warm place. Preheat the oven to 220°C (425°F/Gas 7).

2 Knead the dough again on a floured work surface for a further 2 minutes. Roll out into a 1cm (½in) thick circle and transfer to an oiled baking sheet. Brush the bread with the olive oil and sprinkle with the remaining salt. Bake in the hot oven for 25 minutes or until golden brown.

3 To make the soup, heat half the oil in a heavy pan over a medium-high heat and fry the monkfish and scallops until browned. Remove from the heat and set aside. Put the tomatoes in a large bowl and cover with boiling water. Leave to stand for 1–2 minutes, then slip off the skins and discard. Slice the flesh.

4 Heat the remaining oil in a large pan over a medium heat. Add the fennel and onion and sweat for 5 minutes or until soft but not coloured. Add the garlic and sweat for a further 5 minutes. Add the white wine, stock, sherry, fish sauce, tomatoes, tomato paste and saffron and bring to the boil. Simmer for 15 minutes, then purée in a food processor or blender until smooth.

5 Return the soup to a clean pan and add all the fish and shellfish, along with the lemon, capers and marjoram. Simmer over a medium heat for 30 seconds or until the mussels have opened (discard any that do not) and the prawns are pink and cooked.

6 Serve the soup in 4 warm bowls, with the bread on the side.

Smoked trout and salami risotto

Unusual flavours provide a great hit of flavour in this punchy risotto

Prep time **20 minutes**
Cooking time **25 minutes**
Difficulty **Easy–medium**

1 Pour the stock into a saucepan, place over a low heat and bring to a slow simmer.

2 In a heavy saucepan, heat the oil and butter. When foaming, add the leek and salami and sweat for 2 minutes. Add the rice and stir until each grain is well coated in the butter mixture. Pour in the cider and keep stirring until it has all been absorbed and the alcohol has evaporated.

3 Add the stock, one ladleful at a time, stirring constantly and ensuring that the liquid is absorbed before adding more. Continue in this way for 15–18 minutes until the rice is swollen and soft, but still al dente and the risotto looks creamy.

4 Remove from the heat and stir in the trout. Taste and season with salt and black pepper, then cover and leave for 2 minutes for the trout to warm through and its flavour to infuse the risotto.

5 Meanwhile, bring a saucepan of water to a simmer over a high heat, then reduce the heat to medium. Swirl the water and crack the eggs into the eddy, one at a time. Poach the eggs for 1 minute, then remove with an egg slice. Drain on kitchen paper.

6 Mix together the salad leaves, tomatoes and capers in a bowl. In another small bowl, whisk together the oil, vinegar and mustard, then toss with the salad.

7 Arrange a circle of leaves on each of 4 serving plates. Place a mound of risotto on top of the leaves, top with a poached quail's egg and serve immediately.

For the risotto
300ml (10fl oz) good-quality vegetable stock
1 tbsp extra virgin olive oil
50g (1¾oz) unsalted butter
150g (5½oz) organic leeks, finely diced
100g (3½oz) salami, diced into 5mm (¼in) cubes
200g (7oz) Carnaroli rice
4 tbsp dry cider
2 smoked trout fillets, flaked
4 quail's eggs
Halen Môn sea salt and freshly ground black pepper

For the salad
selection of leaves, such as rocket or baby spinach
4 vine-ripened tomatoes, chopped
2 tsp capers, rinsed, gently squeezed dry and diced
2 tsp olive oil
4 tsp white wine vinegar
1 tsp Dijon mustard

Prep time 20 minutes, plus
20 minutes' cooling
Cooking time 40 minutes
Difficulty Easy

For the soda bread
110g (4oz) plain flour
110g (4oz) wholemeal flour
50g (1¾oz) muesli
25g (scant 1 oz) wheatgerm
1½ tsp bicarbonate of soda
1 tsp sugar
1½ tsp salt
175ml (6fl oz) buttermilk
100ml (3½fl oz) plain yogurt
1 large egg

For the tartare
350g (12oz) royal fillet of
    smoked salmon, cut into
    1cm (½in) cubes
1 large bunch of fresh dill,
    finely chopped
2–3 tbsp finely chopped
    chives
3–4 tbsp Hendricks gin,
    to taste
1–2 tbsp horseradish cream,
    to taste
150g (5½oz) soured cream
pinch of sugar
1 cucumber
3 tsp white wine vinegar
1 tsp freshly squeezed
    lemon juice
salt and freshly ground
    black pepper

To garnish
lumpfish caviar
chive flowers
sprigs of fresh dill

Salmon tartare with dill and horseradish

A very simple dish, with beautiful fish balanced by a sharp sauce

1 To make the soda bread, preheat the oven to 200°C (400°F/Gas 6). Mix together all the dry ingredients in a large bowl and make a well in the centre. In a separate bowl, whisk together the buttermilk, yogurt and egg and add to the dry ingredients. Mix until well combined.

2 Divide the dough into 4 equal-sized portions and form into balls. Using a pair of kitchen scissors, chop into the top of each one to make crosses. Sit the balls of dough on a tray and bake in the oven for 8 minutes. Reduce the oven temperature to 190°C (375°F/Gas 5) and bake for a further 7 minutes until golden. Remove from the oven and leave to cool slightly on a wire rack.

3 To make the tartare, mix together the salmon, dill and chives. Season with black pepper, then add the gin, to taste. It should not be prominent, but still give a kick along with the horseradish. In a separate bowl, mix together the horseradish cream, soured cream and a pinch of sugar. Season to taste. Leave both mixtures to chill in the refrigerator for 20 minutes, to allow the flavours to develop. Taste and adjust the seasoning once more as needed.

4 Peel, halve and deseed the cucumber. Sprinkle all over with salt and leave to stand for 30–40 minutes. Rinse off the salt, pat dry the cucumber with kitchen paper and cut into fine slices. Put in a small dish and sprinkle over the vinegar and lemon juice. Leave to stand until ready to serve.

5 To serve, oil a 10cm (4in) or 12cm (5in) metal food ring. Use to layer the salmon and horseradish mixture on each of 4 serving plates, carefully removing the ring each time. Arrange the cucumber in a ring around the bottom of the salmon and top each salmon tartare with a spoonful of lumpfish caviar. Garnish with chive flowers and a sprig of dill. Serve with the warm soda bread.

Pea and shrimp ravioli

The delicate flavours in this ravioli are perfectly set off by rich parsley butter

1 Pile the flour onto a clean work surface and form into a volcano shape, with a central hole. Add the salt, 2 of the whole eggs and the egg yolks to the well. Mix well until all the flour is incorporated, adding light sprinkles of water if the dough becomes too firm. Form into a ball, wrap in damp muslin and rest for 1 hour.

2 Split the ball into two. On a floured work surface, roll out the dough until it is just less than 1cm (½in) thick.

3 Pass the rolled dough through a pasta machine several times, at ever decreasing gauges: at each gauge, pass the pasta sheet through the roller 3 times, then fold it over itself and turn the sheet 90 degrees. You will end up passing the pasta through the roller about 12 times in total.

4 Using a pastry cutter, cut out discs 4cm (1¾in) in diameter from the sheets of pasta. You should be able to get 40–48 discs.

5 Bring a saucepan of water to the boil, add the peas and cook for 2 minutes, then drain and pulverize in a food processor, with seasoning, until smooth.

6 Melt the butter in a frying pan, increase the heat to high, and tip in the shrimps and nutmeg. Fry, stirring, for 1 minute.

7 To make each ravioli, put 1 teaspoon of the pea purée onto a pasta disc and add 1 teaspoon of shrimp. Beat the remaining egg and use this to moisten the edge of each disc. Place a second disc on top of each, sealing the edges and ensuring that no air is trapped inside.

8 Bring a very large saucepan of salted water to the boil over a high heat, then drop in the ravioli for 3–5 minutes.

9 Meanwhile, melt the butter for the parsley butter in a small frying pan. Add the parsley, then the vinegar and sugar, to taste.

10 To serve, arrange 5 or 6 ravioli, slightly overlapping, on each of 4 warm plates. Drizzle over the parsley butter, garnishing with the pea shoots and radishes.

Prep time 50 minutes, plus 1 hour's resting time
Cooking time 10 minutes
Difficulty Medium–hard

For the pasta
250g (9oz) '00' flour
pinch of salt
3 whole eggs, plus 2 egg yolks

For the filling
200g (7oz) peas
25g (scant 1oz) butter, slightly salted
200g (7oz) brown shrimps
pinch of freshly grated nutmeg
sea salt and freshly ground black pepper

For the parsley butter
50g (1¾oz) butter
75g (2½oz) flat-leaf parsley, finely sliced
3 tbsp cider vinegar
pinch of granulated sugar

To serve
50g (1¾oz) pea shoots
2 radishes, finely sliced

Vegetarian haggis pakoras

With a duo of chutneys, this is an enticing blend of Scottish and Punjabi cuisines

Prep time 10 minutes
Cooking time 1 hour
20 minutes
Difficulty Medium

For the rhubarb chutney
2–3 sticks rhubarb, chopped
1 tsp nigella seeds
½ tsp freshly ground black pepper
½ tsp red chilli powder
½ tsp ground cumin
¼ tsp salt
½ tsp garam masala
2–3 tbsp granulated sugar
6 cloves

For the fresh mint and apple chutney
1 large cooking apple
1 large onion
1 tbsp oil (optional)
1 bunch of fresh mint
1 bunch of fresh coriander
juice of 1 lemon
3 fresh green chillies, chopped
2 tomatoes, chopped
1 tsp freshly ground black pepper
½ tsp salt
½ tsp garam masala

For the pakoras
250g (9oz) gram flour
1 tbsp garam masala
1 tbsp dried fenugreek leaves
pinch of salt
1 tsp ajwan seeds
chilli powder, to taste
3 tbsp plain yogurt
1 small vegetarian haggis
3 fresh green chillies
2–3 green cabbage leaves
2 large potatoes, grated
1 large onion, sliced
sunflower oil for deep-frying

1 To make the rhubarb chutney, put all the ingredients in a large pan with 2–4 tbsp water. Bring to the boil, reduce the heat slightly and simmer for 5–6 minutes. Remove the pan from the heat and leave the chutney to cool for 15–20 minutes, then decant into a sterilized jar. Set aside.

2 For the mint and apple chutney, peel and chop the apple and the onion. (If you like, heat the oil in a frying pan over a medium heat and gently sweat the apple and onion for about 5 minutes until soft; otherwise, omit both this step and the oil to make a really fresh chutney.) Roughly chop the herbs. Put the apple, onion and herbs in a blender with the remaining ingredients and blend well. Decant into a sterilized jar and put in the refrigerator.

3 To make the pakora batter, put all the dry ingredients in a large bowl and mix. Add the yogurt and stir, drizzling in water gradually, until the batter is smooth but not thick. Set aside for 5–10 minutes.

4 Steam the haggis for 20 minutes, then leave to cool a little.

5 Finely chop the chillies and cabbage. Mix these into the batter with the grated potatoes and onion slices.

6 Heat enough oil in a deep heavy pan to come halfway up the sides, until the temperature of the oil reaches 170°C (340F) on a cook's thermometer. Scoop out a small spoonful of haggis and drop it in the pakora batter to coat. Carefully lower the haggis pakora into the hot oil (the oil should sizzle straight away) and deep-fry for 2–3 minutes until golden brown, turning repeatedly to ensure even frying. Remove from the pan and leave to drain on kitchen paper. Keep warm while you fry the remaining pakoras.

7 Serve the hot, crispy pakoras on a bed of fresh salad made with finely shredded carrot, cucumber, red onion and Iceberg lettuce, with the chutneys in small bowls as accompaniments.

Prep time 10 minutes
Cooking time 3 hours
Difficulty Medium

For the stock

1 whole roasted chicken
    carcass (meat removed)
5 cooked bacon rashers
1 small roasted onion
1–2 roasted carrots
a few bits sprigs of fresh
    flat-leaf parsley
sprig of fresh rosemary
sprig of fresh thyme
1 bay leaf

4 oven-ready quails
about 60g (2oz) very soft
    salted butter or good
    olive oil
16 rashers of streaky bacon
10 large garlic cloves, left
    whole and unpeeled
a few sprigs of fresh thyme
a few sprigs of fresh
    rosemary
about 1.2 litres (2 pints)
    chicken stock (see above)
several glugs of whisky,
    to taste
juice of 10 limes
1½–2 tbsp clear honey
    (preferably Scottish
    heather honey)
freshly ground black pepper

To serve

handful of watercress
vegetable oil for frying
red pepper, to garnish
chopped spring onions,
    to garnish

Whisky MacQuail

Gorgeous quail dish with a rich sauce
and stir-fried watercress

1 To make the stock, put all the stock ingredients in a large
saucepan, cover with water and gently simmer for a 2–3 hours.
Skim off any scum that rises to the surface. Strain the stock,
and leave to cool.

2 Preheat the oven to 240°C (475°F/Gas 9).

3 Smear the quails liberally with the softened butter or oil, season
with black pepper and wrap tightly in the bacon rashers, especially
over the legs.

4 Put the whole garlic cloves into a heavy lidded casserole. Crowd
the bacon-wrapped quails into the casserole, then add the thyme
and rosemary. Pour in enough of the stock to just cover the bottom
of the casserole by about 4cm (¾in), then pour in several good
glugs of whisky and the juice of 4–5 limes. Cover tightly and cook
in the oven for about 20 minutes.

5 When the quails go into the oven, begin to boil the rest of the
stock and add some more lime juice and honey to taste. Take care
that the stock does not burn or boil dry.

6 Check the quails. When they are tender and the bacon looks
cooked but still soggy, remove the pot from the oven and reduce
the oven temperature to 220°C (425°F/Gas 7). Transfer the quails
and garlic into an ovenproof dish and return them to the oven for
15–25 minutes until brown. Check them regularly to ensure that
they do not overcook.

7 Skim the excess oil off the juices left in the pot and add the
stock that has already been boiling. Adjust the sauce with more
whisky, honey and lime juice to taste. Boil briskly until the sauce
has reduced and thickened. Check the seasoning.

8 To serve, quickly stir-fry the watercress in a little oil for about
1 minute, then divide between 4 warm plates and garnish with
some red pepper and spring onion. Add a cooked quail to each
plate, pour a little sauce over the quails to glaze and serve the rest
of the sauce in a jug on the side.

Pigeon with sweet chilli butterbeans

A fabulous dish which melds Asian flavours with succulent pigeon

1 Soak the butterbeans overnight in a large bowl of cold water.

2 At the same time, marinate the pigeon. Mix together the garlic, ginger, five-spice, soy sauce and honey in a bowl. Add the pigeon breasts and leave in the refrigerator to marinate overnight.

3 Bring a pan of salted water to the boil over a medium heat, add the drained butterbeans and simmer for 30–40 minutes untl tender. Drain, then mix together the garlic, sweet chilli sauce, sesame oil, soy sauce and lime juice. Pour over the beans. Set aside to soak up the flavours.

4 To make the mayonnaise, take a tall, narrow mixing jar and add, in order, the egg, mustard powder, salt, lemon juice and vinegar. Blend together, then slowly drop in the sunflower oil, still whisking, until the mixture emulsifies. Add the mint and chilli and set aside for 30–45 minutes.

5 To make the Melba toasts, preheat the oven to 140°C (275°F/ Gas 1). Toast the bread, cut the pieces in half diagonally, then slice laterally to give four very thin triangles. Brush a little olive oil on to each side, then put the slices in the oven for 30 minutes or until very crispy and dry.

6 To cook the pigeon, heat the sunflower oil in a frying pan over a medium heat. When the oil is hot, pan-fry the pigeon breasts for 2–3 minutes on each side, depending on their size. Leave to rest for 5 minutes

7 Add the red pepper, spring onion, coriander, mint and chilli to the butterbeans.

8 To serve, pile a mound of the beans on each of 4 warm plates and place a pigeon breast on top of each. Serve with the mayonnaise and Melba toasts.

Prep time 15 minutes, plus overnight soaking and marinating
Cooking time 1 hour 10 minutes
Difficulty Easy–medium

For the butterbeans
200g (7oz) dried butterbeans
1 garlic clove, crushed
1 tbsp sweet chilli sauce
¼ tbsp sesame oil
¾ tbsp soy sauce
¾ tbsp freshly squeezed lime juice
½ red pepper, deseeded and cubed
1 spring onion, sliced
1 small bunch of fresh coriander, finely chopped
1 small bunch of fresh mint, finely chopped
½ chilli, deseeded and finely chopped

For the pigeon
1 garlic clove, crushed
2.5cm (1in) fresh root ginger, grated
½ tsp five-spice powder
2 tbsp soy sauce
1 tbsp clear honey
4 pigeon breasts
2 tbsp sunflower oil

For the mayonnaise
1 egg, at room temperature
1 tsp mustard powder
½ tsp salt
1 tsp freshly squeezed lemon juice
1 tsp white wine vinegar
300ml (10fl oz) sunflower oil
large handful of fresh mint
1 green chilli

For the Melba toasts
1 slice of stale white bread
olive oil

Prep time 1 hour, plus
overnight for the bread
Cooking time 45 minutes
Difficulty Medium–hard

For the ciabatta
22g (¾oz) fresh yeast
350g (12oz) unbleached
   plain flour
60ml (2fl oz) lukewarm milk
500g (1lb 2oz) unbleached
   white bread flour
2 tsp salt
3 tbsp extra virgin olive oil

For the potted shrimp
150g (5½oz) unsalted butter
½ tsp mace
½ tsp nutmeg
pinch of cayenne pepper
200g (7oz) brown shrimps
sea salt
a few sprigs of dill, to garnish

For the monkfish
4 sprigs of fresh oregano
1 garlic clove
120ml (4fl oz) single-estate
   olive oil
2 monkfish tails, 2.5cm (1in)
   thick and 15cm (6in) long,
   boned and skinned
4 rashers of smoked streaky
   bacon
4 cherry tomatoes, halved
splash of balsamic vinegar
1 thick slice white bread,
   crust removed
juice of ½ lime

For the haddock
900g (2lb) Maris Piper
   potatoes, in even pieces
100g (3½oz) olive oil spread
2 tbsp double cream
1½ tsp English mustard
450g (1lb) undyed smoked
   haddock fillet
4 quail's eggs

Medley of seafood

Flavours of monkfish, brown shrimps and
smoked haddock with fresh ciabatta

1 Make the starter dough, or *biga*, the day before. Mix 7g (¼oz) of the yeast with a very little lukewarm water until it forms a cream. Sift the plain flour into a large bowl. Gradually mix in the yeast mixture and enough blood-temperature water to make a firm dough. Turn out on to a lightly floured surface and knead for 5–10 minutes, or until smooth and elastic. Return the dough to the bowl, cover with lightly oiled cling film and leave in a warm place for 12–15 hours until the dough has risen and is starting to collapse.

2 Sprinkle 3 baking sheets with plain flour. Mix the remaining yeast with a very little lukewarm water until it forms a cream, then mix in 400ml (14fl oz) more water. Add this to the biga and gradually mix in, then add the milk. Using your hands, gradually beat in the bread flour, lifting the dough as you mix. Mixing the dough will take 15 minutes or more. You will have a very wet mix. Beat in the salt and olive oil. Cover with lightly oiled cling film, and leave to rise in a warm place for 1½–2 hours or until doubled in bulk.

3 With a spoon, carefully tip one third of the dough at a time onto baking sheets, without knocking back the dough in the process. With floured hands, shape into rough oblong loaf shapes about 2.5cm (1in) thick. Flatten slightly with splayed fingers. Sprinkle with flour and leave to rise in a warm place for 30 minutes. Meanwhile, preheat the oven to 220°C (425°F/Gas 7).

4 Bake the loaves for 25–30 minutes until golden brown and sounding hollow when tapped on the bottom. Transfer to a wire rack to cool.

5 Make the potted shrimp. Warm the butter gently in a pan over a low heat and add the spices and a little sea salt. Add the shrimps and let them mix with the butter, still ensuring that it does not boil. Spoon the shrimps into 4 small ramekins, leaving some butter in the pan and put in the refrigerator for 30 minutes. Remove, seal each pot with the remaining melted butter and place a sprig of dill on top. Store in the refrigerator for up to 48 hours.

6 Start the monkfish. Crush the oregano and garlic and mix with 2 tbsp of the oil. Add the monkfish and refrigerate for 30 minutes.

7 Preheat the oven to 140°C (275°F/Gas 1). Drain the monkfish, reserving the marinade and wrap each piece of fish in the bacon. Pour the marinade into a hot frying pan and add the monkfish, searing until the bacon browns. Place on a baking tray and put in the oven for 15–20 minutes until cooked but still moist, adding the cherry tomatoes, sprinkled with the balsamic vinegar, halfway through the cooking time.

8 Meanwhile, start the haddock. Place the potatoes in a pan of lightly salted water and boil for 25 minutes or until tender. Drain, add the olive spread and cream and mash. Gently mix in the mustard and keep warm.

9 Set up a steamer and bring the water underneath to the boil; fill a saucepan with water and bring this to the boil as well. Place the haddock skin-side down on a piece of foil. Place in the steamer, cover and steam for 5 minutes. Swirl around the boiling water in the saucepan and crack the quail's eggs into the eddy. Poach for 1 minute or until the white has set, but the yolk is still runny.

10 Finish the monkfish: heat 4 tsp of the oil in a frying pan over very high heat. When the oil is smoking-hot, fry the bread until golden brown on both sides, then remove from the pan. Mix the lime juice with the remaining olive oil and spread this on one side of the bread. Cut the bread into quarters.

11 Divide the mash equally among 4 ramekins, flake over the haddock and top each with a poached quail's egg. Cut the monkfish into pieces 2.5cm (1in) long and divide equally among the bread quarters, placing the cherry tomatoes on top.

12 Serve each of your guests with a ramekin of smoked haddock, a ramekin of shrimps and a portion of monkfish, placing the sliced ciabatta on the side.

Spicy chicken flautas

A traditional Mexican dish, with a traditional chilli kick

Prep time 10 minutes
Cooking time 30–35 minutes
Difficulty Easy–medium

For the tortillas
250g (9oz) masa harina
  or fine maize meal

For the chicken
1 tbsp olive oil
2 red onions, finely chopped
4 garlic cloves, chopped
2 organic chicken breasts
handful of fresh coriander,
  chopped
3 tomatoes, chopped
2–3 tbsp tequila
salt and freshly ground black
  pepper

For the salsa
1 tbsp olive oil
1–2 onions, chopped
3 garlic cloves, finely
  chopped
3 tomatoes, chopped
1 chipotle chilli
1 morita chilli
3 tbsp red wine

For the guacamole
1 avocado, finely chopped
1 tomato, finely chopped
1 onion, finely chopped
1 fresh red chilli, finely
  chopped
1 bunch of fresh coriander,
  leaves picked and finely
  chopped
freshly squeezed lime juice,
  to taste

To serve
olive oil for shallow-frying
soured cream
lettuce leaves, sliced

1 Mix the masa harina or maize meal with enough water to create a smooth dough. Make sure that it is not too dry, otherwise the tortillas will break. Roll the dough into 8 small balls. Take a clean plastic bag and insert a ball of dough. Roll the dough through the bag into a very thin round. Repeat with the remaining dough.

2 Place each tortilla gently into a hot, dry frying pan, cooking for a few minutes on both sides, or until browned. Set aside.

3 Heat the oil in a large frying pan over a medium heat and add half the onion. Cook for a few minutes until soft, then add half the garlic and the chicken. Stir for 10–15 minutes until cooked through, then add the coriander. Season with salt and black pepper. Remove the chicken from the pan and leave until cool enough to handle. Shred the meat and return to the pan. Put the tomato and the remaining onion and garlic in a blender and season. Blend until smooth, transfer to a frying pan and cook for 5–8 minutes until thick. Add the chicken mixture and cook for 5 minutes more, then add the tequila and simmer for another 5 minutes.

4 To make the salsa, heat the oil in a saucepan over a medium heat. Add the onions and sweat for a few minutes until soft, then add the garlic, tomatoes, onions and the chillies and cook for 10 minutes. Once all is soft and very slightly burnt, pour into a blender and process until mixed together. Add the red wine, taste and adjust the seasoning.

5 To make the guacamole, mix together all the ingredients.

6 Put some of the chicken on a tortilla and roll it up, making sure that the tortilla does not break. Repeat with the remaining chicken and tortillas. Heat enough oil for shallow-frying in a frying pan over a medium-high heat. When the oil is hot, carefully add the chicken-filled tortillas, or flautas, and fry for 3–5 minutes until golden and crisp.

7 Divide the hot flautas between 4 warm serving plates. Spoon on a little soured cream and salsa, garnish with lettuce and serve immediately, with guacamole on the side.

Warm savoury Stilton cheesecake

A Dorset blueberry relish adds bite to this wonderful late-summer dish

Prep time 30 minutes
Cooking time 30 minutes
Difficulty Medium

For the base
100g (3½oz) wholemeal flour
1 tbsp chopped parsley
25g (scant 1oz) caster sugar
¼ tsp baking powder
¼ tsp poppy seeds
2 tbsp vegetable oil
75g (2½oz) butter
salt and freshly ground
   black pepper

For the relish
150g (5½oz) sugar
juice of 2 lemons
400g (14oz) Dorset
   blueberries
small slice of fresh root
   ginger
sprig of fresh rosemary

For the filling
400g (14oz) full-fat cream
   cheese
1 x 142ml pot soured cream
1 tbsp freshly squeezed
   lemon juice
2 eggs
1 tbsp chopped fresh chives
1 tbsp chopped parsley
175g (6oz) Stilton cheese,
   cubed
1½ tbsp plain flour

1 Preheat the oven to 180°C (350°F/Gas 4).

2 First, make the base. Mix all the dry ingredients in a large bowl, add the oil and a little water, as needed, to form a thick dough. Roll out on a floured work surface until less than 5mm (¼in) thick, then cut into pieces and place on a baking sheet lined with baking parchment. Bake in the oven for 15 minutes or until golden and crispy. Allow to cool, then crush and season well with salt and black pepper. Melt the butter in a small saucepan and mix with the crushed biscuits, combining well. Do not turn off the oven.

3 Tip the mixture into four 10cm (4in) individual tart tins, pressing down firmly with the back of a spoon and refrigerate.

4 Meanwhile, put all the ingredients for the relish in a heavy pan over a medium heat, add 50ml (2fl oz) water and simmer for 15 minutes or until syrupy. Remove the ginger and rosemary.

5 To make the filling, whisk the cream cheese and stir in the soured cream, lemon juice and eggs. Add the herbs, Stilton and flour, mixing again to combine thoroughly. Pour over the biscuit bases and drizzle a spoonful of blueberry relish over the top of each one. Bake in the oven for 15 minutes or until set, then leave to stand for a few minutes before removing from the tins.

6 Place a warm cheesecake on each of 4 plates and spoon over a good dollop more of the blueberry relish. A crunchy fresh salad makes a good accompaniment.

Trio of jack crab verrines

Layers of crab hide a myriad of goodies in this palate-enlivening starter

1 Kill the crabs, then scrub them under a running tap and place in a large pan. Cover with water, bring to the boil over a medium heat and add sea salt. Simmer for 15–20 minutes, depending on size, then remove from the pan and allow to cool for 1 hour. Remove all the meat, keeping the brown meat, white meat and claw meat on 3 separate dishes.

2 Preheat the oven to 220°C (425°F/Gas 7). Rub the red peppers and tomatoes with a little olive oil and roast in the hot oven for 15–20 minutes, then chop, season and add lime juice to taste. In a separate dish, crush the avocado flesh with a little lemon juice. Add a dash of Tabasco and season to taste. Set aside.

3 Heat the butter in a small frying pan, then sauté the cashew nuts with salt, pepper and a pinch of cayenne. Leave to cool.

4 Beat the whipping cream with the juice of ½ lemon. Beat in the soured cream to lighten the texture. Add the milk to the soft cheese, stir, add a dash of Tabasco and season to taste.

5 To make the granary straws, sandwich each slice of bread between sheets of cling film and use a rolling pin to roll out even more thinly. Take a drinking straw and roll the bread around the straw. Remove the straw and place the bread on a baking tray. Bake in the oven for 15–20 minutes until crisp and golden. Allow to cool, then pipe the butter down the middle of the straws and leave to set in the refrigerator.

6 Take 12 small glasses. Put a layer of lemon cream in 4 of the glasses, then a layer of brown crabmeat, a layer of avocado, a layer of white crabmeat, another layer of avocado, a layer of claw meat and top with a spoonful of lemon cream. Put a layer of red peppers and tomatoes in 4 more of the glasses, then a layer of brown crabmeat, a layer of chopped basil, a layer of claw crabmeat and a spoonful of lemon cream. Top with basil leaves and a grinding of black pepper. Put a layer of soft cheese in the remaining glasses, then a layer of brown crabmeat, a layer of cashew nuts and a layer of claw crabmeat. Top with a spoonful of soft cheese and a sprig of rosemary. Serve the verrines with the granary straws.

Prep time 1 hour, plus 1 hour for cooling the crabs
Cooking time 40 minutes
Difficulty Medium

For the verrines
4 fresh jack (cock) crabs
2 red peppers
4 tomatoes
2 tbsp olive oil
juice of 1 lime
2 ripe avocados
juice of 2 lemons
dash of Tabasco sauce
100g (3½oz) unsalted butter
100g (3½oz) cashew nuts, chopped
pinch of cayenne pepper
200ml (7fl oz) whipping cream
200ml (7fl oz) soured cream
4 tbsp whole milk
200g (7oz) soft cheese
1 small bunch of fresh basil, chopped
sea salt and freshly ground black pepper

For the granary straws
4 very thin slices granary bread
butter, softened

For the garnish
4 leaves of fresh basil
4 sprigs of fresh rosemary

STARTERS • TRIO OF JACK CRAB VERRINES

Prep time 1 hour, plus
overnight cooling
Cooking time 1 hour, plus
4 hours the day before
Difficulty Easy

For the boiled ham
1.8kg (4lb) Ayrshire ham
500ml (16fl oz) extra-dry
　cider or apple juice
1 bay leaf
2 or 3 black peppercorns
1 tbsp clear honey

For the pastry
225g (8oz) organic plain
　flour such as Doves Farm
120g (4¼oz) very cold
　unsalted butter, grated,
　plus more for the tin
1 free-range egg, beaten

For the filling
175g (6oz) boiled Ayrshire
　ham, finely chopped
　(see above)
3 free-range eggs, beaten
85ml (2¾fl oz) milk
55ml (2fl oz) double cream
2 shallots, finely sliced
85g (3oz) soft goat's cheese,
　sliced
85g (3oz) mature Dunlop
　cheese, grated
1 tsp Arran grain mustard
sea salt and freshly ground
　black pepper
a dash of chilli oil

For the salad
2 handfuls of mixed rocket,
　lamb's lettuce and
　watercress
strawberry vinegar

Ayrshire ham and cheese tart

A delicious homely tart, with second helpings of both tart and ham for the cook

1 To cook the ham, soak it in cold water for up to an hour to remove the excess salt. It will turn pale when ready.

2 Find a pan just large enough to fit the ham. Add the ham and cider with a little water to just cover the meat. Add the bay leaf, peppercorns and honey and bring to a very gentle simmer over a low heat. Simmer for 4 hours, turning every so often. Turn off the heat and leave the ham in the cooking liquor to cool overnight. The next day, drain and discard the liquor.

3 Put the flour in a food processor and add the butter. Process, adding just enough water, a very little at a time, until the mixture comes together as a dough. Wrap the dough in cling film and leave to rest in the refrigerator for 30 minutes. Preheat the oven to 200°C (400°F/Gas 6).

4 Grease a 30cm (12in) fluted flan tin with butter. Roll out the pastry out on a floured work surface and use it to line the flan tin. Prick the bottom of the pastry case with a fork. Line with greaseproof paper and fill with baking beans, then blind-bake in the oven for 15 minutes. Once cooked, remove the beans and paper and brush the bottom of the pastry case with the egg. Do not turn off the oven.

5 To make the filling, mix together all the ingredients and pour into the pastry case. Bake in the oven for 30 minutes, then leave to stand in the tin for 5 minutes.

6 To serve, drizzle the leaves with just enough strawberry vinegar to coat. Serve a slice of tart on each of 4 plates, with a small pile of the salad on the side.

Harira with herb flat breads

Hearty and spice-laden North African soup designed to satisfy the keenest appetite

Prep time **20 minutes**
Cooking time **1½ hours**
Difficulty **Easy**

1 First soak the chickpeas in a small bowl of cold water overnight.

2 The next day, put the oil in a heavy saucepan over a medium heat and add the onion, celery, ras el hanout, black pepper, salt, paprika, cayenne and ginger and sauté, stirring, for 5 minutes.

3 Add the chunk of lamb, reduce the heat and continue to sauté for another 5 minutes. Next, add the drained chickpeas and the lamb bone, pour in enough water to cover, put the lid on and leave to simmer for 30 minutes.

4 Add the carrot, turnip, courgette, potato, tomatoes and lentils and top up with more water if needed. Simmer for 30 minutes.

5 Meanwhile, make the flat breads. Chop all the herbs very finely and mix them with all the other ingredients.

6 Work the mixture together, adding enough water, a little at a time, until it comes together as a dough. Shape into small balls and roll each one out on a floured work surface, then flatten with your fingers into a small circle.

7 Heat a heavy cast-iron grill pan or griddle over a high heat. Cook the bread on one side until well browned, then turn and cook the other side. Finally, brush the breads with olive oil and keep warm.

8 Return to the soup: put the flour in a small bowl and add water, whisking, until you have a smooth paste. Add to the soup with the coriander, mint, garlic and tomato purée. Cook for 10 minutes, stirring, then remove the lamb bone from the soup.

9 Serve in 4 warm soup bowls, sprinkled with the remaining mint, with the lemon wedges and warm flat breads on the side.

For the soup
3 tbsp dried chickpeas
3 tbsp vegetable oil
1 large onion, finely chopped
2 celery stalks, finely diced
1 tsp ras el hanout
½ tsp ground black pepper
1 tsp salt
½ tsp paprika
½ tsp of cayenne pepper
½ tsp of ground ginger
400g (14oz) lamb, chunk cut from the leg, plus the bone
1 small carrot, finely diced
1 small turnip, finely diced
1 small courgette, finely diced
1 small potato, finely diced
4 tomatoes, skinned and finely chopped
3 tbsp lentils
2 tbsp of flour
1 tsp chopped fresh coriander
1 tsp of chopped fresh mint, plus 1 tsp to garnish
1 garlic clove, crushed
1 tbsp tomato purée
1 lemon, cut into wedges

For the flat breads
1 small bunch each of fresh mint, basil, coriander, flat-leaf parsley and chives
2 spring onions, chopped
150ml (5fl oz) olive oil, plus a little extra for brushing
500g (1lb 2oz) medium semolina flour
½ tsp salt
1 tsp ras el hanout
1 fresh red chilli, chopped

Mains

The main feature

The recipes in this chapter are proof that British main courses, once a byword for the hearty but hopelessly bland meat and three veg, are now fit to compete on the world culinary stage. The classic British roast does make an appearance, but in forms to make us proud: Slow-roasted Pork Belly comes with spiced roast apple and crunchy crackling; the perfect Roast Chicken is enhanced by hearty Scots bread sauce; and succulent Beef Wellington is deliciously accompanied by red wine gravy.

If you want to try something a little special to impress your guests, game – another great British tradition – also features prominently in recipes ranging from Slow-cooked Pheasant Casserole to Wild Norfolk Venison Nelson. For less grand occasions, our favourite comfort foods are represented in first-rate examples of classics such as Bangers and Mash, Toad in the Hole, and that constant favourite, Fish and Chips with Minty Mushy Peas.

As always, Britain's island status makes itself known in the form of fine seafood. Craster Smoked Fish Pie is an explosion of smoky flavour, bringing life to an old British classic. Luxurious Cornish Paella combines Spanish cooking techniques with the very best local produce, brimming with lobster, mussels, prawns and squid. Traditional Stargazy pie, with its curious arrangement of fish heads peeking through the pastry crust, is given an extra West Country stamp with the addition of Cornish Yarg cheese for extra richness.

All these traditional favourites have to work hard to compete with exciting crosscultural dishes, such as a spicy Lamb Biryani, a truly superb Chicken Tandoori Masala and Jamaican Jerk Chicken with Rice and Peas that is vibrant with spice and zest. Even goat makes an appearance in a truly wonderful curry that uses slow cooking and carefully blended spices to bring out the best of this under-used meat.

Slow-roasted pork belly

A succulent, juicy roast with spiced roast apple and crunchy crackling

Prep time 35 minutes
Cooking time 3 hours, plus 4 hours for the stock
Difficulty Medium

For the stock
2kg (4½lb) chicken wings
2 carrots, roughly chopped
1 leek, roughly chopped
1 onion, roughly chopped
2 celery sticks, halved
4 garlic cloves
1 small bunch of fresh thyme
1 bay leaf
1 tbsp tomato purée
small handful of peppercorns

For the pork
1 boneless belly pork joint, about 1.8kg (4lb)
1 banana shallot, finely chopped
300ml (10fl oz) Norfolk dry cider
300ml (10fl oz) home-made chicken stock (see above)

For the apples
2 large knobs of butter
1 tbsp soft brown sugar
4 Cox's apples
4 pinches of ground cinnamon

For the mash
1.3kg (3lb) Maris Piper potatoes
60ml (2fl oz) milk
60g (2oz) butter, or to taste
salt and freshly ground black pepper

For the vegetables
4 large carrots, cut into batons
1 tsp white sugar
50g (1¾oz) butter
1 spring or Savoy cabbage, trimmed and shredded

1 Preheat the oven to 220°C (425°F/Gas 7). Make the stock: put the chicken wings in a baking tray and roast for 45 minutes, turning occasionally, or until brown. Remove from the oven and put them in a stockpot. Add 4 litres (7 pints) water and bring to the boil over a low heat, skimming off any scum that rises to the surface. Add all the remaining stock ingredients and bring back to the boil. Skim again and simmer gently for 3–4 hours.

2 For the pork, trim off and discard the excess fat. Roll neatly, tie with kitchen string and place on a rack over a roasting tin containing a little water. Roast for 20–30 minutes until it starts to crisp up, then reduce the heat to 160°C (325°F/Gas 3) and slow-roast for a further 2 hours. Remove from the oven and leave to rest in a warm place for 30 minutes.

3 Meanwhile, put the shallot in a saucepan with the cider, bring to the boil over a medium heat and reduce for 15 minutes. Pour in the stock and return to a simmer to reduce further. Keep warm until needed.

4 To make the spiced roast apples, melt the butter with the brown sugar in a frying pan. Slice the apples in half and place them in the pan, coating them in the mixture and cooking until they start to caramelize. Place them cut-side up on a baking tray, sprinkle with the cinnamon and roast in the oven for 10–15 minutes.

5 For the mash, peel and dice the potatoes and put them in a pan of salted cold water. Bring to the boil over a high heat, then reduce the heat and simmer for 15 minutes or until cooked. Drain and mash, blending with the milk and butter, then season with salt and black pepper. Set aside in a warm place.

6 Put the carrots, sugar and butter in a small saucepan and pour in enough water to come halfway up the carrots. Bring to a simmer over a medium heat and cook until the water evaporates, taking care not to scorch. Bring a separate pan of water to the boil over a medium heat and add the cabbage. Simmer for 5 minutes, then drain.

7 To serve, place a mound of mash on each of 4 warm plates, add the cabbage and lay the sliced pork on top. Add some carrots and a roast half-apple to each plate and spoon the cider sauce around.

Pheasant with wild rice and horseradish

Hearty and delicious, slow-cooking keeps this pheasant casserole deliciously juicy

Prep time 10–15 minutes
Cooking time 3 hours
Difficulty Medium

brace of pheasants
1 onion, quartered
1 celery stick, halved
1 bay leaf
1 carrot, roughly chopped
8 streaky bacon rashers
2 tbsp butter
8 shallots, finely chopped
60ml (2fl oz) brandy
150g (5½oz) wild rice
500ml (16fl oz) double cream
4 sprigs of fresh tarragon,
  chopped, plus extra,
  to garnish
sea salt and freshly ground
  black pepper

For the horseradish sauce
60g (2oz) fresh horseradish
  root
150ml (5fl oz) double cream
1 tsp sugar
½ tsp mustard powder
½ tsp salt
½ tsp ground white pepper
2 tsp white wine vinegar

For the vegetables
60g (2oz) butter
4 Little Gem lettuces, halved
2 bunches of spring onions,
  chopped
1 tsp sugar
400g (14oz) green peas
3 sprigs of fresh mint
120ml (4fl oz) fresh vegetable
  stock
salt and black pepper

For the game chips
2 or 3 large parsnips
vegetable oil for deep-frying

1 Skin and quarter the pheasants. Put the backs and necks in a large saucepan and pour in 1.2 litres (2 pints) water. Add the onion, celery, bay leaf and carrot. Bring to a simmer over a low heat, then cook gently for 1 hour or until reduced by half. Strain the stock into a large bowl and set aside.

2 Preheat the oven to 180°C (350°F/Gas 4). Wrap the pheasant pieces in the bacon and secure with cocktail sticks. Melt the butter in a flameproof casserole over a medium heat, then add the shallots and the pheasant, turning until browned.

3 Gently warm the brandy in a small high-sided pan or large ladle. Pour into the casserole and carefully ignite, standing well back. When the flames subside, add 600ml (1 pint) of the pheasant stock, season with salt and black pepper, cover and cook in the oven for up to 2 hours until tender. Remove the cocktail sticks.

4 To make the horseradish sauce, grate the horseradish into a small bowl. Add the remaining sauce ingredients and stir to combine. Leave to infuse for about 30 minutes.

5 Cook the wild rice in water for 35–40 minutes, then drain.

6 For the vegetables, melt the butter in a saucepan over a medium heat. Add the lettuces, onions and sugar and season with salt and black pepper. Cover and cook for 5 minutes. Add the peas and mint, then the stock. Cover and cook for 5 minutes more. Remove the lid and heat until all the juices have disappeared.

7 To make the game chips, peel the parsnips into long ribbons. Heat a large pan half-filled with vegetable oil (or a deep-fryer) until the temperatures reaches 170°C (340°C) on a cook's thermometer. Drop in the parsnip ribbons and deep-fry for 5 minutes, or until crisp and browned. Remove from the oil with a slotted spoon, drain well on kitchen paper and season generously.

8 Remove the casserole from the oven, add 100ml (3½fl oz) horseradish sauce (to taste), the cream, tarragon and wild rice.

9 Serve the pheasant on 4 warm plates with the vegetables and game chips (if using), garnished with the extra tarragon.

Creole salted cod with rice and peas

A vibrant tomato and pepper sauce enlivens this tasty dish with piquant flavours

Prep time 30 minutes, plus overnight soaking
Cooking time 1 hour
Difficulty Easy

1 Soak the cod in cold water for 24 hours, changing the water two or three times. Pour the milk into a large sauté pan, add the fish and place over a medium heat. Poach for 5 minutes, then allow to cool. Tear the cod into bite-sized pieces (do not use a knife) and season generously with black pepper. Sprinkle with the flour and set aside.

2 Preheat the oven to 180°C (350°F/Gas 4). Bake the whole sweet potato in the hot oven for 1 hour or until tender.

3 Meanwhile, pour the oil into a heavy pan over a medium heat. Add the onion and garlic and sauté until nicely brown. Now add the red and green peppers and chilli and sauté for a few more minutes until soft.

4 Add the tomatoes, the prepared cod and the thyme. Pour in just enough water to cover and simmer until it has reduced by half and the sauce has thickened. Taste and adjust the seasonings.

5 To make the rice and peas, pour the stock into a medium saucepan. Bring to the boil over a medium heat, add the rice and beans and bring back to the boil. Reduce the heat and simmer for 20 minutes or until all the stock has evaporated.

6 Meanwhile, make the braised cabbage. Place a small frying pan over a medium heat and add the oil and butter. Allow the butter to brown a little, then add the onion, garlic and green and red peppers. Cook, stirring, for 2 minutes, then add the cabbage, season with salt and black pepper and add a little water to prevent it sticking to the pan. Reduce the heat, cover and allow to sweat for 5 minutes, stirring once or twice.

7 Remove the sweet potato from the oven and cut into 8 slices.

8 Measure out the rice into a small cup and turn out in the middle of each of 4 warm plates. Surround with the fish, cabbage and a couple of slices of sweet potato and serve immediately.

For the salt cod
500g (1lb 2oz) salted cod fillet
200ml (7fl oz) milk
1 tbsp plain flour
2 tbsp olive oil
1 onion, chopped
2 garlic cloves, minced
1 red pepper, deseeded and chopped
1 green pepper, deseeded and chopped
1 small fresh red chilli deseeded and chopped
3 tomatoes, skinned, deseeded and chopped
sprig of fresh thyme
freshly ground black pepper

For the sweet potato
1 small white-fleshed sweet potato

For the rice and peas
500ml (16fl oz) chicken stock
175g (6oz) basmati rice
1 x 175g can black-eye beans, drained

For the cabbage
1 tbsp olive oil
15g (½oz) butter
1 small onion, finely sliced
1 garlic clove, crushed
½ green pepper, deseeded and finely sliced
½ red pepper, deseeded and finely sliced
½ small Savoy cabbage, trimmed and shredded
salt and black pepper

Prep time 10–15 minutes,
plus 24 hours' marinating
Cooking time 25–30 minutes
Difficulty Medium–hard

For the chicken
1–2 tsp lemon juice
¼ tsp freshly ground nutmeg
500g (1lb 2oz) skinless
  chicken breast fillet, diced
3 small white onions
4 garlic cloves
2.5cm (1in) fresh root ginger
6 fresh green chillies
handful of coriander leaves
handful of mint leaves
200g (7oz) Greek-style yogurt
1 tbsp single cream
115g (4oz) butter, melted
salt and black pepper
1 lime, quartered, to serve

For the raita
2 baby cucumbers
150g (5½oz) Greek-style
  yogurt

For the masala
1 tbsp vegetable oil
knob of unsalted butter
1 tsp cumin seeds
4 black peppercorns
2 whole cloves
1 bay leaf
2.5cm (1in) cinnamon stick
4 green cardamom pods
1 black cardamom pod
3 small onions
2.5cm (1in) fresh root ginger
2 garlic cloves
½ tsp ground turmeric
1 tsp ground coriander
1 tsp paprika

For the rice
250g (9oz) basmati rice
1 tsp vegetable oil
1 tsp cumin seeds
4 green cardamom pods

Chicken tandoori masala

A subtle marinade and superb blend of spices make this a classic curry favourite

1 Mix together the lemon juice, nutmeg, a pinch of black pepper and salt to taste. Rub this mixture into the chicken pieces and set aside for 15–30 minutes.

2 Combine all the other ingredients for the chicken, except the butter and lime, until evenly mixed, then scrape into the bowl of a food processor and whizz until well chopped. Transfer to a clean bowl. Add the chicken, mix until very well coated and leave to marinate in the refrigerator for 24 hours.

3 To make the raita, peel the baby cucumbers and chop into even dice. Put the yogurt in a bowl, add the cucumber and mix well. Set aside in the refrigerator until needed.

4 Prepare the masala, which is a blend of aromatic spices. Heat a large saucepan over a medium heat and add the vegetable oil and butter. When the butter has melted, add the whole spices and fry until they begin to make popping noises, stirring to avoid any scorching. Finely chop the onions, ginger and garlic, add them to the pan and fry until golden brown. Add all the ground spices and stir until blended. Remove from the heat and set aside.

5 Preheat the oven to 240°C (475°F/Gas 9), to replicate the fierce heat of an Indian tandoor oven, which is essentially a ceramic jar placed over white-hot charcoal. (If you are lucky enough to have access to a tandoor, grill the chicken over a medium-high heat.)

6 Thread the marinated chicken onto metal skewers and cook in the oven (or tandoor) for 12–15 minutes. While the chicken is cooking, melt the butter in a small saucepan over a low heat. Baste the chicken with the melted butter and cook for a further 2 minutes.

7 To make the rice, soak the grains in a bowl of water for 10 minutes, then drain. Put the oil in a large saucepan and add the cumin and cardamom. Add twice the volume of water as there is rice, bring it to the boil over a medium heat, then tip the rice into the pan. Bring back to the boil and cover first with a wet tea towel, then with the lid. Reduce the heat to low and cook for 10–15 minutes until the rice is tender.

8 Remove the cooked chicken from the skewers and – being careful not to burn your hands – transfer it to the pan of masala sauce. Simmer for 5 minutes, adding a little more water if you prefer a sauce with a thinner consistency.

9 Divide the rice between 4 warm plates. Spoon some hot chicken tandoori masala onto each plate and add a lime quarter, leaving your guests to squeeze it over to taste. Serve the chilled raita in a bowl on the side.

"**Absolutely gorgeous. The chicken is so tender and there are so many layers of gorgeous flavours there... really first-rate.**"
— Jilly Goolden

Duck breast, roast potatoes and gravy

Rich, flavourful duck combines beautifully with classic sage and onion stuffing

Prep time 30 minutes
Cooking time 1½ hours
Difficulty Medium

125g (4½oz) duck fat
800g (1¾lb) Desiree potatoes
45g (1½oz) plain flour
750ml (1¼ pints) good-
   quality chicken stock
4 Gressingham duck breasts
salt and freshly ground
   black pepper

For the stuffing
1 onion, finely chopped
1 tbsp dried sage
1 small bunch of fresh sage
1 small Bramley apple,
   finely chopped
100g (3½oz) fresh white
   breadcrumbs
45g (1½oz) butter, melted
1 small egg, beaten
pinch of freshly ground
   nutmeg
drizzle of truffle oil (optional)
salt and black pepper

For the vegetables
350g (12oz) early East
   Anglian carrots, peeled
2 tbsp caster sugar
2 large knobs of butter
1 pointed cabbage,
   finely sliced
salt and black pepper

1 Preheat the oven to 200°C (400°F/Gas 6). Put the duck fat in a baking tray and place the tray on the highest shelf of the oven. Peel the potatoes, cut into even chunks and put them in a saucepan of boiling water to cover. Add a pinch of salt and simmer for 10–15 minutes until the outer edges are fluffy. Drain, cover and, holding the lid firmly, shake the saucepan to rough up the edges.

2 Put the potatoes in the hot duck fat, baste and season with salt. Roast in the oven for 40–50 minutes. Check after 20 minutes, turn and, if necessary, baste again.

3 Meanwhile, to make the stuffing, put the onion in a small pan of boiling water, add the dried sage and 3 or 4 leaves of the fresh sage, chopped. Boil for 5 minutes or until the onion is soft. At the last minute, add the apple. Strain through a sieve and discard the liquid.

4 Combine the breadcrumbs with the onion mixture and add the butter and some of the egg to bind, taking care that the stuffing doesn't become too wet. Season with salt and pepper, then add the nutmeg and remaining chopped sage leaves and mix together well.

5 Line a non-stick tray with a sheet of greaseproof paper. Make 4 balls of the stuffing mixture, pressing them together firmly, then put them on the tray. Brush the tops with any remaining beaten egg and a very small drizzle of truffle oil (if using). Cook in the oven with the potatoes for 25–35 minutes until crispy.

6 To make the gravy, mix the flour in a small bowl with a little cold water, pouring it in gradually to form a thin paste, whisking all the while to ensure that there are no lumps. Add the stock, little by little, until the mixture has the consistency of pouring cream. Place over the heat, continuing to stir. The gravy should thicken. Continue to add the remaining stock, stirring all the time. Set aside.

7 Take the duck breasts and remove any sinew from the flesh side. Score the skin with a sharp knife, just penetrating the fat and not the flesh. Season with a little salt on the skin side.

8 Place a non-stick frying pan over a high heat and wait until it becomes very hot.

continued...

...continued from p.86

9 Place the duck breasts skin-side down in the hot pan. Season the flesh side with salt and black pepper. Cook for 5 minutes to render the excess fat, turning the breasts over when the skin is crisp and golden. If there is too much fat in the pan, carefully drain it off, standing well back and being careful that it does not splatter.

10 Meanwhile, put the carrots in a pan of boiling water with the caster sugar. Cook for 4–5 minutes. Drain off most of the water, add a knob of butter and reduce until the little remaining liquid forms a glaze for the carrots.

11 Cook the pointed cabbage in boiling water for 4–5 minutes, drain and season well with salt, black pepper and a knob of butter.

12 Once the duck breasts have been turned over, transfer to a baking tray in the oven to finish cooking. Cover loosely with foil and leave to roast for a further 4–5 minutes for pink duck, or 2–3 minutes longer if you prefer well-done meat. Remove from the oven and leave to rest for 5 minutes in a warm place.

13 Reheat the gravy and season to taste. Slice each duck breast thinly across the grain and place one breast portion on each of 4 warm plates. Serve with the stuffing, roast potatoes, carrots, and cabbage. Serve the hot gravy in a jug on the side.

"I think this is sensational British home cookery ... I think it's brilliant. The vegetables taste wonderful. The gravy's spot-on."

— Ed Baines

Venison pudding

Wonderfully succulent venison encased in suet pastry, served with sweet baby leeks

Prep time 35 minutes
Cooking time 40–50 minutes
Difficulty Medium

1 Lightly grease four 250ml (8fl oz) pudding basins with a little unsalted butter. Sift the flour and salt into a food processor, add the suet and whizz a couple of times. Transfer to a bowl and add iced water, little by little, stirring until it forms a dough. Divide into 4 and take a larger part of each one. Roll out each one on a floured work surface to make 4 circles to line the basins. Reserve the remaining pastry for the lid of each pudding.

2 To make the filling, put the flour on a broad plate and season well with salt and pepper. Pat the venison dry with kitchen paper and toss in the flour to coat. Heat the butter in a sauté pan over a medium heat. Brown the venison on all sides to seal; remove to a warm plate. Brown the bacon lardons in the same pan, then add the onion, garlic, carrot, mushrooms, thyme and bay leaf. Sweat for a few minutes until soft. Pour in the wine and stock and cook for 4–5 minutes. Return the venison to the pan and remove from the heat.

3 Spoon the venison into the lined pudding basins, making sure not to fill right to the top. Spoon over enough sauce to cover the meat and tap each basin to settle the mixture. Roll out the remaining pastry into circles for the lids. Dampen the edges of the pastry lids, drape over the puddings and press together the edges to seal. Place a double layer of pleated baking parchment and foil over the top of each basin and secure tightly with kitchen string.

4 Put the basins in a large steamer over a low heat and steam for 30–40 minutes. Pass the remains in the venison pan through a sieve, return to the rinsed-out pan and reduce. Keep warm.

5 Meanwhile, preheat the oven to 220°C (425°F/Gas 7). Heat the goose fat in a heavy roasting tin in the oven. Peel and cut the potatoes into roast potato-sized chunks. Bring the stock to the boil over a high heat, drop in the potatoes and par-boil for 8 minutes. Drain. Roast in the hot fat for 30 minutes until golden.

6 Cook the leeks in a saucepan of boiling water for 5 minutes. Drain, add the butter and keep warm over a low heat.

7 To serve, out a pudding onto each of 4 warm plates and serve with the potatoes, leeks and the jug of warm sauce.

For the pastry
225g (8oz) self-raising flour
pinch of sea salt
115g (4oz) shredded beef
  suet

For the filling
3 tbsp plain flour
800g (1¾lb) venison fillet,
  diced
25g (scant 1oz) butter
150g (5½oz) smoked
  bacon lardons
1 large onion, grated
2 garlic cloves, very finely
  grated
1 large carrot, very finely
  grated
100g (3½oz) field
  mushrooms, sliced
2 sprigs of fresh thyme
1 bay leaf
250ml (8fl oz) red wine
300ml (10fl oz) fresh
  beef stock
sea salt and freshly ground
  black pepper

For the roast potatoes
4 tbsp goose fat
4 large Maris Piper potatoes
2 litres (3½ pints) fresh
  chicken stock

For the leeks
8 baby leeks
100g (3½oz) unsalted butter

Whisky-flamed peppered beef fillet

A slightly decadent dish, with prime beef, Yorkshire puds and béarnaise sauce

Prep time 30 minutes, plus resting and chilling time
Cooking time 30 minutes
Difficulty Medium

For the beef
1kg (2¼lb) British beef fillet
3 tbsp olive oil
100g (3½oz) black pepper corns, cracked
1 glass of whisky such as Bell's or Famous Grouse

For the Yorkshire puddings
2 free-range eggs
150ml (5fl oz) milk
100g (3½oz) plain flour
2 tbsp fresh horseradish, finely grated
50g (1¾oz) beef dripping

For the vegetables
500g (1lb 2oz) new potatoes
3 sprigs of fresh mint
200g (7oz) fresh peas
1 tbsp sugar
500g (1lb 2oz) asparagus, trimmed

For the béarnaise sauce
2 shallots, finely chopped
2 sprigs of fresh tarragon
2 bay leaves
2 sprigs of fresh thyme
120 ml (4fl oz) tarragon vinegar, or to taste
4 tbsp dry white wine
350g (12oz) butter
3 free-range egg yolks
salt and freshly ground black pepper

1 Trim off any excess fat from the beef fillet. Smear a little olive oil over the meat. Spread the peppercorns on a plate and roll the meat through, making sure that the fillet is well covered. Set aside.

2 Put all the ingredients for the Yorkshire puddings, except the dripping, in a bowl and whisk, adding 2 tbsp water, then refrigerate for 20 minutes. Preheat the oven to 240°C (475°F/Gas 9).

3 Put the remaining oil in a large frying pan over a high heat. Once hot, sear the beef fillet on each side until nicely browned. Pour in the whisky and carefully ignite, standing well back. When the flames subside, transfer the meat to a rack in a roasting dish, pour over the excess sauce from the bottom of the pan and roast in the oven for 15–20 minutes.

4 Meanwhile, put the new potatoes in a pan of cold water with 2 sprigs of the mint. Put the peas in a separate pan of cold water with the remaining mint and the sugar. Put the asparagus in a separate steamer pan that can fit above the potatoes.

5 Remove the beef from the oven, wrap it tightly in foil and leave to rest for 20 minutes. Put a little beef dripping into each hole of a Yorkshire pudding tin and place in the oven to heat.

6 To make the béarnaise sauce, mix together the shallots, tarragon, bay leaves, thyme, tarragon vinegar and white wine in a small pan and bring to the boil, allowing the liquid to reduce by two-thirds; strain into a heatproof bowl. In a separate pan, melt 300g (10oz) of the butter. Meanwhile, place the potatoes over a medium heat. Remove the Yorkshire pudding tin from the oven and pour in the batter. Cook in the oven for 20 minutes.

7 Put the steamer of asparagus over the cooking potatoes and put the peas over a medium heat, then place the reduced vinegar mixture, in its bowl, over a pan of simmering water. Add the egg yolks and whisk. Remove from the heat and slowly whisk in first the melted butter, then the remaining 50g (2oz) butter, in small pieces – the sauce should thicken. Season.

8 Slice the beef onto 4 warm plates with the Yorkshire puddings and vegetables, serving the béarnaise sauce on the side.

Sri Lankan chicken curry

Infused with exotic flavours, with refreshing mango and cucumber salsa

Prep time 20 minutes
Cooking time 1 hour
Difficulty Easy

1 To make the curry, heat the oil and butter in a large saucepan over a medium heat, then add the garlic and ginger. Fry for 2 minutes, then add the sliced onion. Gently fry for about 5 minutes until soft and translucent.

2 Add 1 tsp of the chilli flakes and 1 tsp of the curry powder, and fry for 2 minutes, then add the chicken pieces and brown on all sides. Tip in the curry leaves, cumin and mustard seeds, and stir for 4 minutes, then add the pepper, salt and remaining chilli flakes and curry powder. Leave to cook for 10 minutes, turning the pieces, then add the chillies and tomatoes. Cook for 5 minutes.

3 Pour in 750ml (1¼ pints) water, cover the pan and reduce the heat slightly. Gently simmer for 35 minutes, stirring occasionally.

4 Meanwhile, make the salsa. Put the mango, cucumber, spring onions, chilli, herbs and lime juice in a bowl, and mix well. Season with salt and black pepper and dress with a splash of virgin olive oil and balsamic vinegar. Set aside.

5 Bring a saucepan of salted water to the boil over a medium heat, add the rice and reduce the heat to a simmer. Cook for 20 minutes or until tender.

6 Taste the curry and adjust the seasoning, then stir in the coriander and sugar. Serve hot on 4 warm plates, with the rice, mango and cucumber salsa and poppadoms.

For the curry

1 tbsp vegetable oil
knob of butter
4 garlic cloves, finely chopped
2.5cm (1in) piece of fresh root ginger, finely sliced
1 large onion, sliced
2 tsp red chilli flakes
3 tsp Sri Lankan curry powder such as Jaffna
1.4kg (3lb) chicken pieces
handful of curry leaves
1 tsp ground cumin
1 tsp mustard seeds
½ tsp freshly ground black pepper
½ tsp salt
2 fresh green chillies, finely chopped
3 large tomatoes, chopped
300g (10oz) basmati rice
3 tsp chopped coriander
pinch of sugar
4 poppadoms, to serve

For the mango and cucumber salsa

1 ripe mango, diced
½ cucumber, deseeded and diced
2 spring onions, finely chopped
1 fresh red chilli, deseeded and finely chopped
2 tbsp chopped coriander leaves
3 sprigs of fresh mint
juice of 1½ limes
splash of virgin olive oil
splash of balsamic vinegar
salt and black pepper

Best end of lamb with puréed swede

Served with a port reduction, this may be the tastiest Sunday lunch you'll ever eat

Prep time **45 minutes**
Cooking time **45 minutes**
Difficulty **Medium**

For the lamb
3 large garlic cloves, peeled
1 tsp sea salt
sprig of fresh rosemary
sprig of fresh thyme
500g (1lb 2oz) best end
   of new-season English
   lamb fillet
a little olive oil
freshly ground black pepper

For the potatoes
500g (1lb 2oz) goose fat
1kg (2¼lb) King Edward
   potatoes
sprig of fresh rosemary, finely
   chopped, or a little olive oil

For the port reduction
a little olive oil
a few lamb bones
1 carrot, chopped
1 celery stick, chopped
1 streaky bacon rasher,
   chopped
100ml (3½fl oz) port
150ml (5fl oz) good red wine
   such as Shiraz
500ml (16fl oz) good-quality
   fresh chicken stock

For the vegetables
and black pudding
1 organic swede, peeled
   and diced
30g (1oz) unsalted butter
4–6 organic shallots, peeled
a little olive oil
I carrot, peeled
1 bundle of fresh organic
   asparagus
200g (7oz) black pudding,
   skinned and sliced

1 Preheat the oven to 180°C (350°F/Gas 4). Crush together the garlic, salt, rosemary and thyme to make a paste. Put the lamb fillet in a bowl, add the herb paste and a little olive oil and rub all over the meat. Cover and leave to marinate for 30 minutes.

2 Put the goose fat in a roasting tin and place in the oven to heat. Bring a large saucepan of water to the boil over a high heat. Peel the potatoes, chop into chunks, add them to the water. Bring to a simmer and par-boil for 8 minutes, then drain. Remove the roasting tin from the oven and place over a medium heat. Add the potatoes, turn until coloured, then roast in the oven for 45 minutes.

3 To make the reduction, pour a little olive oil into a saucepan over a medium heat. Fry the bones, carrot, celery and bacon until caramelized. Stand well back, add the port and carefully ignite at the edge of the pan. When the flames subside, add the wine and reduce by at least half. Pour in the chicken stock and reduce again to a consistency you like. Check the seasoning, serve and keep warm.

4 Put the swede in a pan, cover with water, bring to the boil over a high heat and cook for 10–12 minutes. Drain. Mash or put through a potato ricer, then whip the swede with most of the butter. Keep warm. Meanwhile, in a small frying pan over a medium heat, slowly caramelize the shallots with a little olive oil for 20 minutes, stirring occasionally and adding the remaining butter at the end.

5 Twelve minutes before the potatoes are ready, add a little oil to a frying pan over a high heat and sear the lamb on all sides for 3–4 minutes. Transfer to a baking tray and roast for 6 minutes. Remove from the oven and leave to rest. Sprinkle the rosemary over the roast potatoes. Meanwhile, bring a small pan of water to the boil over a high heat. Using a vegetable peeler, slice the carrot into very thin ribbons. Plunge into the boiling water for 1 minute; drain. Steam the asparagus for 3–4 minutes until just cooked. Make 4 small asparagus bundles by wrapping them in a couple of carrot ribbons. Fry the black pudding over a high heat until crisp.

6 Put a little swede on each of 4 warm plates. Top with slices of the lamb. Add the black pudding and shallots and drizzle with the port reduction. Serve with the potatoes and an asparagus bundle each.

Slow-cooked pheasant casserole

Flavourful pheasant with wild mushrooms is cooked slowly for a tender, juicy result

Prep time **20 minutes**
Cooking time **4½ hours**
Difficulty **Easy**

brace of pheasants
3 tbsp sunflower oil
225g (8oz) smoked bacon
   scraps, diced
4 celery sticks, chopped
3 large onions, chopped
1 whole head of garlic,
   cloves separated, peeled
   and crushed
3 carrots, chopped
225g (8oz) swede, chopped
1 large red pepper, chopped
100g (3½oz) wild mushrooms,
   chopped
100g (3½oz) soft or semi-
   cured Spanish chorizo,
   skinned and chopped
1 tbsp plain flour
300ml (10fl oz) fresh
   chicken stock
300ml (10fl oz) red wine
1 tbsp elderberry or
   redcurrant jelly
1 tbsp Worcestershire sauce
1 tbsp chopped parsley
1 tbsp chopped thyme
   leaves
500g (1lb 2oz) new potatoes
200g (7oz) mangetout
salt and freshly ground
   black pepper
1 small bunch of flat-leaf
   parsley, finely chopped,
   to garnish

1 Preheat the oven to 140°C (275°F/Gas 1). Tie the legs of each bird together tightly with kitchen string. Pour the oil into a flameproof lidded casserole set over a medium heat and add the pheasants. Brown them all over, remove and set aside. In the same casserole, fry the bacon, then add all the chopped vegetables and the chorizo. Cook, stirring, until the onion is soft and translucent.

2 Stir in the flour. Continue stirring for a minute or so, then add the stock, wine, elderberry or redcurrant jelly and Worcestershire sauce and bring to the boil. Return the pheasants to the casserole and cover with the lid. Cook very slowly in the oven for 3–4 hours until the meat is tender.

3 Lift the birds out of the casserole onto a plate and leave until cool enough to handle. Pull all the meat off the bones, discard the bones and return the meat to the casserole. Season with salt and black pepper and add the chopped parsley and thyme.

4 Meanwhile, bring a large pan of water to the boil. Add the potatoes to the boiling water and cook for 15 minutes or until tender. Steam the mangetout over another pan of boiling water for 4–5 minutes until cooked.

5 Serve the pheasant casserole in 4 warm soup plates with the mangetout and new potatoes, with the finely chopped parsley liberally sprinkled over the top.

"It's delicious … a great depth of flavour. Yep, lovely casserole, that one."
— John Burton Race

Blade steak with tandoori tatties

This lively, unusual dish combines Scottish flavours with sub-continental seasonings

1 Preheat the oven to 220°C (425°F/Gas 7).

2 Peel and halve the potatoes and put in a large pan of water over a medium heat. Bring to a simmer and par-boil for 5 minutes.

3 Make the tandoori masala paste by blending together all the ingredients. Mix 2 tbsp of the paste with the crème fraîche, lemon juice and Tabasco, to taste.

4 Drain the potatoes and pat dry. Put them in a non-stick baking tray, cover with the masala paste and bake in the oven for 40 minutes.

5 Coat a heavy baking tray with olive oil and add the blade steaks. Rub the steaks with the Tabasco, balsamic vinegar and salt and black pepper to taste. Roast in the oven for 15 minutes, then remove and leave to rest in a warm place for 5 minutes.

6 To make the curried leeks, melt the butter over a low heat, add the leeks and gently sweat without colouring for 15 minutes. Once softened, add the curry powder and cream, stir through, and cook for a further 5 minutes.

7 To make the mushrooms, melt the butter in a pan over a low heat and add the mushrooms and whisky. Cook for 15 minutes until the mushrooms have softened.

8 Serve 2 slices of the blade steak on each of 4 warm plates, accompanied by the mushrooms, leeks and tandoori tatties.

Prep time 20 minutes
Cooking time 45 minutes
Difficulty Easy

For the potatoes
900g (2lb) Maris Piper
 potatoes
200ml (7fl oz) crème fraîche
1 tbsp freshly squeezed
 lemon juice
Tabasco sauce, to taste

For the masala paste
½ tbsp grated garlic
½ tbsp grated fresh root
 ginger
1 tbsp paprika
1 tsp ground cinnamon
1 tsp ground cumin
½ tsp ground coriander
¼ tsp chilli powder
pinch of ground cloves
200ml (7fl oz) plain yogurt

For the blade steak
extra virgin olive oil
8 slices of blade steak
splash of Tabasco sauce
1 tbsp balsamic vinegar
sea salt and freshly ground
 black pepper

For the curried leeks
30g (1oz) salted butter
3 large leeks, trimmed
 and chopped
1½ tbsp hot curry powder
3 tbsp double cream

For the mushrooms
15g (½oz) butter
8 button mushrooms
splash of single-malt
 Scotch whisky

Roast beef and Yorkshire pudding

Polishing perfection – a sumptuous rib of beef with all the classic accompaniments

Prep time 10–15 minutes
Cooking time 2 hours
Difficulty Medium

For the beef
olive oil
2.5kg (5½lb) 30-day-hung
 rib of salt-marsh beef
sea salt and black pepper

For the Yorkshire pudding
2 eggs, plus 1 egg yolk
125g (4½oz) plain flour
pinch of mustard powder
250ml (8fl oz) whole milk
sunflower oil

For the vegetables
900g (2lb) Maris Piper
 potatoes, cut into chunks
8 mini cauliflowers
olive oil
1.35kg (3lb) new potatoes
1 summer cabbage
900g (2lb) small carrots

For the cheese sauce
15g (½oz) butter
15g (½oz) plain flour
275ml (9fl oz) whole milk
85g (3oz) Mrs Kirkham's
 Lancashire cheese, grated
salt and black pepper

For the gravy
½ bottle full-bodied red wine
2 red onions, chopped
2 plum tomatoes, chopped
500ml (16fl oz) beef stock
2 tbsp plain flour (optional)

For the horseradish sauce
150ml (5fl oz) crème fraîche
pinch of mustard powder
60g (2oz) fresh horseradish
 root, finely grated

1 Preheat the oven to 200°C (400°F/Gas 6). Heat a little olive oil in a large roasting tin over a medium heat. Rub the beef with more olive oil and season with salt and pepper. Put in the hot roasting tin and seal for a couple of minutes on each side. Roast in the oven for 1 hour 10 minutes for rare meat, or until done to your liking.

2 Meanwhile, for the Yorkshire puddings, whisk together all the ingredients, except the oil, in a bowl, until smooth, then set aside. Bring 2 large saucepans of water to the boil. Add the Maris Pipers to one and par-boil for 10 minutes. Drain in a colander, then shake to rough up the edges. Put the cauliflowers in the second pan and par-boil for 4 minutes. Drain and set aside in an ovenproof dish.

3 Remove the beef from the oven. Leave to rest for 30 minutes, covered with foil. Increase the temperature to 220°C (425°F/Gas 7). Half-fill a Yorkshire pudding tin with sunflower oil, pour 5mm (½in) olive oil into a baking tray and put both in the oven for 15 minutes. Rub the par-boiled Maris Pipers with olive oil and place on the hot tray. Pour the batter into the pudding tin and cook for 30 minutes.

4 For the cheese sauce, melt the butter in a saucepan over a low heat. Sprinkle in the flour and mix to form a smooth paste. Gradually add the milk, stirring constantly to prevent lumps and season. Add the cheese and heat gently until it thickens. Pour over the cauliflowers and bake in the oven for 15–20 minutes. Bring 2 saucepans of water to the boil. Add the new potatoes to one, cooking for 15 minutes or until tender; shred the cabbage and add to the other pan for 5 minutes and steam the carrots until cooked.

5 Meanwhile, place the beef roasting tin over a medium heat. Pour in a little red wine, scraping the tin, then sieve into a saucepan and add the onions and tomatoes. Cook for 10 minutes, then add the remaining red wine and reduce for 5–10 minutes. Add the stock and reduce again. Whisk in some plain flour to thicken (if using).

6 For the horseradish sauce, put the crème fraîche in a bowl with the mustard powder, season, then mix with the horseradish.

7 Slice the meat and serve with the vegetables, Yorkshire puddings, gravy and horseradish sauce.

Spicy chicken with roasted tomatoes

A fresh-tasting, aromatic dish using the juiciest dark meat of the chicken

1 Using a mortar and pestle, or a food processor, blend the garlic, ginger and chillies with all the other ingredients for the chicken – apart from the chicken itself – to a smooth paste. Make one deep lengthways cut in each piece of chicken and place in the marinade. Leave to marinate in the refrigerator for 24 hours.

2 Preheat the oven to 190°C (375°F/Gas 5). Put the marinated chicken in a shallow roasting dish, cut-side up and roast in the oven for 50 minutes. Remove, set aside and keep warm.

3 Increase the oven temperature to 240°C (475°F/Gas 9). To make the roasted potatoes and tomatoes, drizzle olive oil into a roasting tin and add the shallots, tomatoes and garlic. Place in the oven to heat the oil. Bring a large saucepan of water to the boil over a high heat, add the potatoes, par-boil for 5 minutes, then drain.

4 When the oil is sizzling, add the potatoes and turn to coat well in the flavourings. Roast in the oven for 30 minutes or until golden, basting at 10-minute intervals.

5 Stir the chives into the soured cream and form it into 4 ovals, or quenelles, between two dessertspoons.

6 Arrange a chicken thigh and drumstick, crossed one over the other, on each of 4 warm plates. Add a small mound of roasted potatoes and cherry tomatoes to each plate, together with a few leaves of mixed salad and one of the quenelles of soured cream.

Prep time 35 minutes, plus 24 hours' marinating
Cooking time 1½ hours
Difficulty Medium–easy

For the spicy chicken
2 garlic cloves, chopped
2cm (¾in) piece of fresh root ginger, chopped
2 small fresh green chillies, chopped
handful of fresh coriander leaves, chopped
3 tbsp extra virgin olive oil
1 tbsp white wine vinegar
1 tbsp plain yogurt
2 tsp tandoori masala
1 tsp ground coriander
½ tsp chilli powder
¼ tsp ground turmeric
1 tsp salt
½ tsp sugar
4 organic chicken thighs, skinned
4 organic chicken drumsticks, skinned

For the roasted baby potatoes and tomatoes
extra virgin olive oil
250g (9oz) shallots, sliced
250g (9oz) cherry tomatoes, halved
5 large garlic cloves
1kg (2¼lb) baby potatoes, halved

To serve
small bunch of fresh chives, snipped
3 tbsp soured cream
handful of mixed leaf salad

MAINS • SPICY CHICKEN WITH ROASTED TOMATOES

Prep time 40 minutes, plus
6–12 hours' marinating time
Cooking time 1 hour
35 minutes
Difficulty Medium–hard

For the garam masala
32 green cardamom pods
35 whole cloves
3 x 2cm (¾in) cinnamon sticks
1 star anise
½ tsp daagad phool
    (optional)
1 blade of mace

For the lamb
4 tbsp sunflower oil
450g (1lb) onions, sliced
300g (10oz) Greek-style yogurt
juice of 2 lemons
1 tsp grated fresh root ginger
1 tsp grated garlic
3 fresh green chillies, slit
1½ tsp salt
2 tsp chilli powder
½ tsp ground turmeric
2 tbsp finely chopped mint
    leaves
2 tbsp finely chopped
    coriander leaves
1kg (2¼lb) lamb shoulder
    (trimmed weight), cubed

To garnish the rice
120ml (4fl oz) milk
½ tsp saffron threads
juice of 2 lemons
6 tbsp ghee, melted
handful of cashew nuts

For the fragrant rice
500g (1lb 2oz) basmati rice
8 green cardamom pods
8 whole cloves
1½ tsp jeera seeds
2 x 2cm (¾in) cinnamon sticks
3 bay leaves
2 tbsp sunflower oil
1½ tsp salt
1 black cardamom pod

Lamb biryani

Redolent with fragrant spices and Persian influences, this is a feast worthy of effort

1 Put all the ingredients for the garam masala in a spice grinder (or a coffee grinder set aside for the purpose). Grind until you have a fine powder. Alternatively, use a mortar and pestle, adding a few of the spices at a time and being careful not to overcrowd the mortar.

2 Prepare a marinade for the lamb by heating 1 tbsp of the oil in a frying pan over a medium-high heat. Add the onions and fry until golden brown, then remove from the pan. Put half the onions into a large bowl and set aside the other half for garnishing the rice. Add the garam masala to the bowl (reserving 1½ tsp), along with the yogurt, lemon juice, ginger, garlic, chillies, salt, ground spices and chopped herbs, and mix well. Add the lamb and toss until well coated in the marinade. Cover, and leave to marinate in the refrigerator for 6–12 hours.

3 In a small saucepan over a very low heat, gently heat the milk for the rice garnish until lukewarm, then crumble in the saffron, and leave to colour and infuse for 30 minutes.

4 Mix together all the ingredients for the rice in a large saucepan. Add 750ml (1¼ pints) water and place over a high heat. Bring to the boil, then reduce the heat, cover and simmer for 10 minutes or until the water is at the same level as the top of the rice. Remove the pan from the heat.

5 Put the marinated lamb into a large heavy pan into which you can also fit all the rice, then pour in the par-cooked rice. Carefully pour a line of saffron milk, running down the centre of the rice, over the top, adding the lemon juice on either side of the line, then cover all the rice with the melted ghee. The rice should be soaked in a lovely lemon-butter mixture, which sinks down into the biryani.

6 Sprinkle the top with the reserved fried onions and the cashew nuts, then cover with a tight-fitting lid. Place the biryani pan over a high heat and cook for 10–15 minutes, then reduce the heat to medium and cook for another 10–15 minutes. Finally, reduce the heat to low and cook for 5–10 minutes more. While the biryani is cooking, prepare the egg masala, raita, and lassi (overleaf).

continued...

For the egg masala

3–4 tbsp sunflower oil
4 green cardamom pods
4 whole cloves
1 cinnamon stick
2 bay leaves
1 tsp caraway seeds
2 small onions, grated
¾ tsp grated fresh root
 ginger
¾ tsp grated garlic
½ tsp ground turmeric
1 tsp chilli powder
2 tsp ground coriander
1½ tsp garam masala
1 x 400g can chopped
 tomatoes
5 or 6 large eggs
200ml (7fl oz) single cream
2–3 tbsp finely chopped
 coriander leaves

For the raita

1 onion, finely chopped
1 tbsp chopped mint leaves
1½ tbsp chopped coriander
 leaves
500ml (16fl oz) Greek-style
 yogurt
½ fresh green chilli, finely
 chopped

For the mango lassi

6 tsp caster sugar
¼ tsp ground cardamom
500ml (16fl oz) Greek-style
 yogurt
1 x 850g can mango pulp

...continued from p.98

7 To make the egg masala, heat the oil in a frying pan over a medium heat. Add the whole spices and fry for 30 seconds. Add the onions and fry for a further 4–5 minutes. Tip in the ginger and garlic and cook for 30 seconds, then add all the powdered spices and sauté for another 30 seconds to release the aromas. Lastly, add the tomatoes and simmer for 4–5 minutes.

8 Meanwhile, bring a saucepan of water to the boil over a high heat, add the eggs and boil for 8 minutes. Drain and, when cool enough to handle, peel.

9 Add the hard-boiled eggs, left whole, to the masala and cook for 5–6 minutes, then add the cream, 200ml (7fl oz) water and the chopped coriander. Reduce the heat to low and simmer gently for 4–5 minutes.

10 To make the raita, mix together the onion, mint, coriander, and yogurt in a bowl. Season, then top with the chillies. Set aside in the refrigerator until needed.

11 For the mango lassi, put all the ingredients into a blender with 250ml (8fl oz) water and blend thoroughly until smooth.

12 To serve, divide the biryani among 6–8 warm plates, sitting a small ramekin of egg masala on each one, with a bowl of the raita on the side. Serve with a glass of mango lassi.

Roast rack of pork with apricot stuffing

Succulent roast pork is perfectly accompanied by fruity stuffing

1 Make the stuffing by mixing all the stuffing ingredients with 1 tbsp cold water. Season well with pepper. Roll into a sausage shape long enough to extend almost the length of the pork joint. Wrap in cling film and put in the freezer for 30 minutes.

2 Preheat the oven to 240°C (475°F/Gas 9). Cut along the inside of the pork's rib bones as far down as the spinal column, to make a cavity for the stuffing. Remove the sausagemeat from the freezer and use to stuff the cavity, folding the top of the pork over. Tie each end of the joint with string to help prevent stuffing escaping. Loosely tie the joint together between each rib. Splash a little cold water over the pork rind, sprinkle with salt and rub in thoroughly.

3 Put the pork in a roasting tin and roast for 25 minutes. Reduce the oven temperature to 200°C (400°F/Gas 6) and roast for 1 hour 20 minutes. Meanwhile, put the potatoes in a saucepan. Cover with cold salted water, bring to the boil, reduce the heat and simmer for 10 minutes. Drain and shake vigorously. Add to the roasting tin with the pork. When the pork is cooked, remove it from the oven, transfer to a warm plate and leave to rest for 10–15 minutes.

4 Put the parsnips and carrots in a saucepan of boiling water and boil for 5 minutes. Drain. Measure the oil and honey into a small dish, then put the carrots and parsnips into a large plastic bag, and pour over the honey mixture, shaking well to coat the pieces. Transfer the vegetables to a roasting tin and roast in the oven for 20–30 minutes, turning once.

5 For the gravy, remove excess fat, if any, from the pork roasting tin. Put the flour in the tin and gradually add the stock, stirring continuously to avoid lumps. Season and add the sage. Place over a medium heat and bring to the boil, stirring continuously. Simmer for 20–30 minutes, then strain through a sieve. Meanwhile, to make the greens, melt half the butter in a large saucepan or wok over a high heat. Add the greens and stir-fry for 3–5 minutes until just wilted. Remove from the heat. Add the remaining butter, season with salt and black pepper and toss well.

6 To serve, carve the pork onto 4 warm plates and serve with the potatoes, honey-roasted vegetables, greens and sage gravy.

Prep time 25 minutes
Cooking time 2 hours
Difficulty Medium

For the stuffing
100g (3½oz) coarsely minced belly pork
20g (¾oz) smoky bacon, coarsely chopped
20g (¾oz) dried apricots
20g (¾oz) dried breadcrumbs
freshly ground black pepper

For the meat and potatoes
1.25–1.5kg (2¾lb–3lb 3oz) best end loin of pork, bone in, rind finely scored and French-trimmed
800g (1¾lb) King Edward potatoes, peeled and cut into chunks
salt

For the honey-roasted parsnips and carrots
2 large parsnips, cut into batons
2 large carrots, cut into batons
½ tbsp rapeseed oil
1 tbsp clear honey

For the sage gravy
1 tbsp plain flour
450ml (15fl oz) pork stock
1 tbsp finely chopped sage leaves

For the greens
30g (1oz) butter
500g (1lb 2oz) curly kale or spring greens, shredded
salt and black pepper

Prep time 30 minutes,
plus overnight marinating
Cooking time 2 hours
Difficulty Medium

For the curry
juice of ½ lemon
1kg (2¼lb) leg of goat, cubed
3–4 tbsp curry powder
5mm (¼in) piece of fresh root
    ginger, finely chopped
1 tbsp paprika
6 green cardamom pods,
    crushed
6–8 garlic cloves, crushed
2–3 fresh chillies, deseeded
    and finely chopped
3 tbsp vegetable oil
2–3 large onions, chopped
sprig of fresh thyme
2 good-quality lamb stock
    cubes, crumbled
1 tbsp soft dark brown sugar
handful of fresh coriander,
    chopped
salt and coarsely ground
    black pepper

For the dumplings
1½ tsp baking powder
450g (1lb) self-raising flour
1 tsp salt
knob of unsalted butter
a little iced water
vegetable oil for deep-frying

For the rice
550g (1¼lb) basmati rice
pinch of salt

Caribbean curried goat

Heavenly flavours come to the fore in this spicy curry with crisp-fried dumplings

1 Pour the lemon juice into a large bowl of water. Add the goat, swirl it around to rinse the meat, then drain and put in a clean bowl. Add the curry powder, ginger, paprika, cardamom, half the garlic and half the chilli and season with salt and coarse black pepper. Cover with cling film and leave to marinate in the refrigerator overnight.

2 Add the oil to a large saucepan and place over a medium heat. Add the onions and the rest of the garlic and chilli and gently sauté for a few minutes until soft. Add the meat, together with any marinade and increase the heat to high. Turn and mix the meat in all the other ingredients. Cover, reduce the heat to low and leave for 10 minutes or until the meat has produced some liquid. Add the thyme, stock cubes, brown sugar and coriander and stir well. Cover and cook for 1½–2 hours until tender, stirring occasionally and adding splashes of water if it threatens to dry out.

3 Meanwhile, make the crisp-fried dumplings. Mix together the baking powder, flour and salt in a large bowl and rub in the butter with your fingertips until the mixture resembles breadcrumbs. Add ice-cold water, little by little, combining first with a knife, then your hands, until the mixture comes together into a dough. Pour enough oil into a large saucepan to come halfway up the sides – or use a deep-fryer – and place over a high heat until the oil measures 170°C (340°F) on a cook's thermometer. Take small amounts of the dough and roll between your hands to make dumpling-sized balls. Fry the dumplings for 3 minutes on each side, turning with a slotted spoon. Remove with the slotted spoon and drain on kitchen paper.

4 To make the basmati rice, wash the rice until the water runs clear. Put into a non-stick saucepan, adding water to cover – about 2.5cm (1in) above the level of the rice – and a pinch of salt. Bring to the boil over a high heat, then reduce the heat to a simmer, cover and cook until the water has evaporated.

5 To serve, divide the rice and curry among 4–6 warm plates, adding dumplings to each portion.

Fish and chips with minty mushy peas

A perennial favourite with a modern twist, fresh from your own kitchen

Prep time 10 minutes, plus overnight soaking
Cooking time 1 hour 20 minutes
Difficulty Medium–hard

1 Soak the marrowfat peas overnight in plenty of cold water with a good pinch or two of bicarbonate of soda. Drain the peas and rinse well in cold water. Put in a saucepan, add fresh cold water to cover and bring to the boil. Simmer for about 1 hour, topping up with water if needed, until tender and mushy. Remove from the heat, stir in the butter and season with salt and black pepper. Set aside and keep warm. Pour the vinegar and sugar into a small saucepan and place over a low heat. Stir until dissolved and leave to cool for 30 minutes. Transfer to a small basin and add the mint.

2 To make the batter, pour 500ml (16fl oz) water into a large bowl. Add the flour, bicarbonate of soda and salt. Whisk with an electric hand whisk for 5 minutes or until there is plenty of air in the batter. It should be just pourable. Set aside.

3 For the tartare sauce, put the egg yolks in a bowl and whisk until pale. Pour the vinegar and sugar into a small pan over a low heat. Stir until dissolved. Gradually pour this into the egg yolks, whisking, then season and pour in the oils very slowly, continuing to whisk constantly. Add the gherkins, capers, parsley, shallot, mustard, and lemon juice and stir through. Chill until needed.

4 Peel the potatoes and cut into chunky-sized chips. Heat the oil in a deep-fat fryer until the temperature reaches 130°C (265°F). Add the chips and fry for 5–6 minutes until soft but not coloured. Remove from the pan and drain on kitchen paper. Increase the temperature of the oil to 190°C (375°F).

5 Wipe the fish clean with a damp cloth, then coat in the batter, making sure that it is evenly coated. Put the fish in the hot fat, skin facing upwards. Deep-fry, turning occasionally, for 5–6 minutes.

6 Remove the fish from the pan and drain on kitchen paper. Allow the oil to return to 190°C (375°F). Carefully put the chips into the hot oil once again and fry until they become a crispy golden colour. Remove from the pan and drain on kitchen paper.

7 Put a fish fillet on each of 4 warm plates. Add the chips and hot peas, drizzling the mint sauce over the peas. Serve with the tartare sauce, lemon wedges, buttered bread and pickled onions.

For the minty mushy peas
450g (1lb) marrowfat peas
good pinch or two of bicarbonate of soda
90g (3oz) unsalted butter
250ml (8fl oz) malt vinegar
3 tbsp sugar
1 small bunch of fresh mint, finely chopped
salt and black pepper

For the battered fish
350g (12oz) plain flour
1 tsp bicarbonate of soda
3 tsp salt
4 fresh haddock fillets, about 200g (7oz) each

For the tartare sauce
2 egg yolks
50ml (2fl oz) white wine vinegar
15g (½oz) caster sugar
125ml (4fl oz) sunflower oil
125ml (4fl oz) olive oil
3 gherkins, finely chopped
2 tsp capers, rinsed and finely chopped
2 tsp finely chopped parsley
1 shallot, finely chopped
½ tsp Dijon mustard
juice of ½ lemon

For the chips
1 large Maris Piper potato
handful of Accord potatoes
groundnut oil for deep-frying

To serve
2 lemons, halved and wrapped in muslin
4 slices bread, buttered
1 jar pickled onions

Jerk chicken with rice and peas

The invigorating flavours of Jamaica shine through in this absolutely gorgeous dish

Prep time 30 minutes, plus overnight marinating
Cooking time 3 hours 10 minutes
Difficulty Medium

For the jerk chicken
1 large free-range chicken
juice of ½ lemon
2 tbsp jerk seasoning (or use 2 tsp dried thyme, 2 tsp anatto and 2 tsp pimento)
50g (1¾oz) plain flour
3 tbsp oil, preferably infused with garlic and spices
1 large white onion, chopped
1 red onion, chopped
1 spring onion, chopped
1 fresh Scotch bonnet chilli, deseeded and chopped
1 fresh tomato, chopped
1 x 230g can chopped tomatoes
1cm (½in) piece of fresh root ginger, finely chopped
1 garlic clove, chopped
100g (3½oz) red, yellow and green peppers, chopped
½ tsp salt
½ tsp ground black pepper
1 tsp ground turmeric
1 good-quality vegetable stock cube, crumbled
sprig of fresh thyme
sprig of fresh rosemary

For the rice and peas
225g (8oz) dried kidney beans
½ x 400g can coconut milk
pinch of salt
1 spring onion
sprig of fresh thyme
250g (9oz) long-grain rice
1 fresh Scotch bonnet chilli

For the plantain chips
3 tbsp vegetable oil
1 large, firm underripe plantain

1 Joint and cut the chicken into 8 pieces. Put in a bowl, add the lemon juice and turn the meat over until well coated. Drain off the excess lemon juice, then add the jerk seasoning (if making your own, crumble together first) and flour. Cover tightly with cling film and leave to marinate in the refrigerator overnight.

2 At the same time, soak the kidney beans overnight in a large bowl of cold water, changing the water once or twice during the soaking time if possible.

3 On the day of cooking, drain and rinse the kidney beans, then tip them into a saucepan of fresh water and place over a high heat. Bring to the boil for 10 minutes, then reduce the heat and simmer for 2 hours or until tender. It is important to ensure that the beans are at a proper rolling boil for the first 10 minutes, to remove any residual toxins. Set aside.

4 Heat the oil for the chicken in a large, heavy frying pan over a medium heat. Add the chicken and turn it over in the oil until it is a lovely golden brown on all sides. Remove from the heat, and set aside on a large plate.

5 Put the onions, spring onion, chilli, fresh and tinned tomatoes, ginger, garlic, sweet peppers, salt, pepper and turmeric in a blender and pulse to a purée. Make sure you have removed all the seeds from the Scotch bonnet, as they are scorching hot.

6 Transfer the purée to the pan in which the chicken was browned. Add the stock cube and 120ml (4fl oz) water and bring to the boil over a high heat. Reduce the heat and simmer for 5 minutes.

7 Return the chicken to the pan and stir. Ensure that there is enough juice to cover; if not, add a little more water, but don't add too much or you will dilute the flavour. Add the thyme and rosemary and simmer over a very low heat for 15–20 minutes until very tender and completely cooked through.

8 Put the pan of kidney beans back over a low heat and add the coconut milk, pinch of salt, spring onion and thyme, mixing very well. The beans will soak up all the delicious aromatic flavourings like a sponge, so take it slow.

continued...

…continued from p.104

9 Bring the beans to the boil, add the rice and stir. Sit the whole Scotch bonnet pepper on top, making sure that it is intact and not broken or pierced in any place, to avoid the rice becoming too fiery, as Scotch bonnets are among the hottest chillies. Ensure that the liquid is just covering the rice (too much will make it soggy). Reduce the heat to very low and simmer for 30 minutes or until the rice is tender and the liquid has been absorbed. Remove the Scotch bonnet, spring onion and thyme and stir.

10 To make the fried plantain chips, pour the oil into a large frying pan, place over a high heat and peel and slice the plantain. Fry the plantain in the hot oil on both sides until golden brown, then drain on kitchen paper.

11 Serve the rice and peas on 4 warm plates, dividing the jerk chicken evenly among each and adding some crispy plantain chips.

"How good was that. I love food, but I could marry that dish – absolutely delicious. It's a very, very special dish"

— Ed Baines

Stargazy pie with Cornish Yarg

Warm spiced rhubarb chutney enlivens this version of a traditional Cornish dish

Prep time 45 minutes
Cooking time 1 hour
Difficulty Medium

1 Put the cod and haddock in a saucepan and cover with the milk. Add the parsley and season with white pepper. Bring to a simmer over a medium heat and poach for 2 minutes. Allow to cool for 5 minutes, then strain, reserving the poaching milk. Flake the fish and set aside.

2 Cook the potatoes in a large pan of salted water over a high heat for 15–20 minutes. Preheat the oven to 180°C (350°F/Gas 4).

3 In a small saucepan over a medium heat, melt 25g (scant 1oz) of the butter and stir in the onion. Cook for 1–2 minutes, then add 15g (½oz) of the flour and stir. Gradually pour in the cream, stirring to prevent lumps. Add a little of the poaching milk until you have a white sauce with a creamy consistency. Season and add the leek.

4 Mash the potatoes and lightly combine with the fish and sauce. Spread into a baking dish and level off. Push the sardines into the fish mixture so that the heads stick up in a rough pattern.

5 For the pastry, tip the remaining flour into a bowl with a pinch of salt. Rub in the suet and remaining butter with your fingertips until it resembles breadcrumbs. Gradually add a little iced water and mix until it forms a dough. Roll out on a floured work surface to about 3mm (¼in) thick and big enough to cover the pie dish.

6 Crumble the cheese over the filling, then put the pastry on top. Trim the edges. Using a sharp knife, cut slits in the pastry where the sardine heads are and pull through. Brush the top of the pie with beaten egg. Bake in the oven for 35 minutes or until lightly golden.

7 To make the chutney, pour the vinegar and 2–3 tbsp water into a saucepan and bring to a simmer. Add the spices and 2 tbsp of the sugar. Stir, then simmer for 10 minutes. Add the diced rhubarb and cook for 10 minutes. Melt the butter in a small frying pan and gently sauté the extra rhubarb chunks in the butter for 5 minutes. Sprinkle in the remaining sugar and allow to caramelize. Strain the vinegar mixture and return it to the rinsed-out pan with the rhubarb chunks and stem ginger.

8 Serve the pie cut into large wedges on 4 warm plates, accompanied by the warm chutney and some crusty bread.

For the stargazy pie

200g (7oz) cod loin
100g (3½oz) undyed smoked haddock
250ml (8fl oz) whole milk
sprig of fresh parsley
2 Maris Piper potatoes, peeled and cut into chunks
75g (2½oz) salted Cornish butter
1 onion, finely chopped
115g (4oz) plain flour
200ml (7fl oz) double cream
4 leek leaves, chopped
6 fresh sardines, gutted and boned
25g (scant 1oz) shredded beef suet
a little iced water
100g (3½oz) Cornish Yarg cheese
1 egg, beaten
salt and ground white pepper
fresh crusty bread, to serve

For the spiced rhubarb chutney

200ml (7fl oz) distilled white wine or cider vinegar
1 tsp ground cumin
1 tsp freshly ground nutmeg
1 tsp cayenne pepper
1 cinnamon stick
3–4 tbsp golden caster sugar
2 rhubarb stalks, diced, plus 1 extra, chopped into 2cm (3¾in) chunks
50g (1¾oz) Cornish butter
75g (2½oz) preserved stem ginger in syrup, chopped

Prep time 10–15 minutes, plus chilling time
Cooking time 1 hour 40 minutes
Difficulty Medium

For the cranberry sauce
300g (10oz) fresh cranberries
juice of ¼ lemon
250g (9oz) caster sugar
1 tsp lemon thyme leaves

For the chicken
1 chicken, about 1.35kg (3lb)
2 onions
2 unwaxed lemons
20g (¾oz) fresh lemon thyme
40g (1¼oz) butter
2 carrots, sliced
200g (7oz) swede, diced
200g (7oz) celeriac, diced
2 tsp cornflour
600ml (1 pint) chicken stock
50ml (2fl oz) dry white wine
salt and black pepper

For the potatoes
85g (3oz) duck or goose fat
1kg (2¼lb) potatoes, peeled
salt

For the vegetables
300g (10oz) Chantenay carrots, trimmed
1 tbsp olive oil
1 tsp soft brown sugar
100g (3½oz) streaky bacon
1 Savoy cabbage, shredded
salt and black pepper

For the bread sauce
4 garlic cloves
50g (1¾oz) butter
1 onion, finely chopped
500ml (16fl oz) whole milk
8 whole cloves
30g (1oz) porridge oats
1 tbsp double cream
50g (1¾oz) white breadcrumbs

Roast chicken with Scots bread sauce

With its home-made cranberry sauce, this is a delicious traditional family recipe

1 To make the cranberry sauce, tip the cranberries into a saucepan with the lemon juice and sugar. Place over a medium heat and bring to the boil, then reduce the heat and simmer for 20 minutes. Remove from the heat and sprinkle in the thyme. Allow to cool, then refrigerate for at least 1½ hours.

2 Preheat the oven to 200°C (400°F/Gas 6). Stuff the chicken cavity with 1 onion, 1 lemon, quartered and the lemon thyme. Rub the chicken all over with the butter and sprinkle very generously with salt and freshly ground black pepper.

3 Arrange the remaining vegetables for the chicken in a roasting dish and place the chicken breast side-down on top. Pour in 200ml (7fl oz) water and roast for 30 minutes, then stir the vegetables. Roast for another 15 minutes, then turn the chicken over and baste. Cut the remaining lemon into wedges and push these between the wings or legs. Roast for a further 30–45 minutes.

4 To make the roast potatoes, put the fat in a baking tray and sit in the oven for 15 minutes or until very hot. Meanwhile, chop the potatoes to "roast-tattie"-sized chunks and boil for 8 minutes. Drain, then add to the hot fat in the tray. Season with salt, spoon over the fat and roast in the oven for 30 minutes or until golden.

5 For the vegetables, put the carrots in a baking tray. Drizzle with the oil, sprinkle with the sugar and season with salt and black pepper. Roast in the oven for 40 minutes.

6 To make the bread sauce, put the whole garlic cloves in foil in a frying pan and soften over a medium heat for 10 minutes. Melt the butter in a saucepan over a medium heat, add the onion and fry until soft. Season, then add the milk, cloves, garlic, oats and cream. Cook over a low heat for 15 minutes. Remove the cloves, then blend the remaining ingredients in the pan using a hand-held blender. Add the breadcrumbs and cook for a further 10 minutes.

7 When the chicken is ready, remove it and the vegetables from the dish. Mix the cornflour with 200ml (7fl oz) water, add it to the dish and place over a medium heat. Cook, stirring from time to time, until the gravy thickens slightly. Keep warm.

8 To finish the vegetables, chop the bacon, place in a large frying pan over a fairly low heat and fry gently in its own fat for 5 minutes. Add the cabbage and cook for a further 5–10 minutes until tender but not overcooked.

9 Pour the gravy into a jug or fat separator and remove and discard the fat. Pour the gravy into a saucepan, add the stock, wine and a little water. Reduce until it measures about 300ml (10fl oz). Taste and season with salt and black pepper.

10 Serve the chicken on a pool of bread sauce on each of 4 warm plates, with the roast potatoes, cabbage and carrots, gravy and home-made cranberry sauce.

"Again, perfectly cooked chicken. Lovely flavour of the lemon and the thyme... I defy anyone to get a better roast chicken than this."
— John Burton Race

Dexter beef and mushroom pie

Succulent and utterly irresistible, top-quality beef makes this dish sing

Prep time **1 hour**
Cooking time **2 hours**
Difficulty **Medium–hard**

For the filling
400g (14oz) mushrooms, sliced
150ml (5fl oz) vegetable oil
1 onion, chopped
900g (2lb) grass-fed Dexter beef, cut into large dice
2 tbsp Worcestershire sauce
2 tbsp thyme leaves
1 tbsp English mustard
120ml (4fl oz) Hobsons Old Henry or Town Crier ale
salt and freshly ground black pepper

For the pastry
225g (8oz) plain flour
pinch of salt
75g (2½oz) butter, diced
75g (2½oz) lard, diced
juice of 1 lemon
iced water
1 egg, beaten

For the vegetables
1 Spanish onion, sliced
2 tbsp olive oil
3 courgettes, sliced
6 large potatoes, peeled and cut into chunks
6 carrots, sliced
115g (4oz) butter
freshly ground black pepper

1 Heat a large frying pan over a medium heat and fry the mushrooms in half the oil until crispy. Remove with a slotted spoon and drain on kitchen paper. Add the onion to the same pan and sweat gently until soft but not coloured. Add the beef to the pan and cook, stirring, until nicely browned. Return the mushrooms to the pan and add the Worcestershire sauce, thyme, mustard and ale. Reduce the heat to low and simmer for 1½ hours. Taste and season, remove from the heat and allow to rest for 5 minutes.

2 While the filling is cooking, make the pastry. Sift the flour and salt into a bowl. Add the butter and lard and "cut" the fat into the flour with a knife, then add enough of the lemon juice and some iced water, little by little, to form a dough.

3 Roll out the dough into a square on a floured work surface. Fold the bottom third up and the top third down. Give the pastry half a turn so that the folds are at the sides. Seal the edges with a rolling pin. Roll out again into a square and repeat the process 4 times. Wrap in greaseproof paper and chill for 30 minutes. Preheat the oven to 220°C (425°F/Gas 7).

4 Remove the pastry from the refrigerator. Roll out 225g (8oz) of it on a floured work surface until 5mm (¼in) thick. Pour the warm filling into a pie dish. Brush the beaten egg around the rim. Top with the pastry and crimp the edges. Cut a slit in the middle of the lid and decorate with the excess pastry, cut into leaf shapes, then brush with beaten egg. Bake in the oven for 15–20 minutes until golden brown, then allow to cool for a few minutes.

5 While the pie cooks, prepare the vegetables. In a frying pan over a medium heat, fry the onion in the oil until soft, then add the courgettes, reduce the heat to low and cook slowly for 20 minutes. Bring 2 saucepans of water to the boil over a high heat. Add the potatoes to one and carrots to the other. Reduce the heat under both pans and simmer for 20 minutes or until tender. Drain. Mash the potato with most of the butter and add black pepper. Add the remaining butter to the carrots.

6 Serve a portion of pie on each of 4 warm plates with the carrots, braised onions and courgettes and mashed potato.

Corned beef pie with duchess potatoes

This is the real deal – juicy, spicy and worlds away from the tinned stuff

Prep time 1 hour, plus
5 days to corn the beef
Cooking time 4½ hours
Difficulty Hard

For the corned beef
2 tbsp mustard seeds
2 tbsp coriander seeds
1 cinnamon stick, crushed
2 tbsp whole cloves
1 tbsp grated fresh root
    ginger
150g (5½oz) salt
43g (1½oz) pink salt
150g (5½oz) sugar
10 bay leaves
2 tsp allspice
2.5kg (5½lb) beef brisket,
    in 1 piece
1 tbsp Worcestershire sauce
200ml (7fl oz) red wine
200ml (7fl oz) light beer

For the pie filling
2 large onions, finely sliced
1 whole carrot, halved
600ml (1 pint) beef stock
1kg (2¼lb) home-made
    corned beef (see above)
225ml (7½fl oz) red wine
3 tbsp chopped parsley
50g (1¾oz) butter

For the pastry
225g (8oz) plain flour
pinch of salt
60g (2oz) butter
60g (2oz) lard
1 egg, beaten

1 Mix together all of the dry spices and seasonings for the marinade. Reserve half in a dry, airtight container. Marinate the beef in the other half of the spice mixture. Put a weight on a saucer and place on top of the meat to keep it under the surface of the liquid that will come out. Marinate in the refrigerator for 4–5 days.

2 The meat will be tender and still red. Wash it thoroughly to remove the overly salty taste.

3 Put the brisket in a large pot with the reserved spice mixture and cover with water. Add the Worcestershire sauce, red wine and beer. Bring to the boil over a low heat and simmer for 3–3½ hours until really tender. Remove from the stock and allow the meat to rest and cool before slicing.

4 Put the onion, carrot and stock in a pan and cook for about 5 minutes until the onions start to soften.

5 Slice the corned beef into chunks. Discard the carrot. Drain the onions, reserving the stock. Put the onions back into the pan and gently fold in the corned beef. Remove from the pan and set aside.

6 Now put the stock in the rinsed-out pan, add the red wine and simmer together over a medium heat until the wine has reduced.

7 To make the pastry, sift together the flour and salt into a mixing bowl and rub in the butter and lard with your fingertips until the mixture resembles fine breadcrumbs. Add half the beaten egg and 1 tbsp water and mix to a firm dough. Wrap the dough in cling film and leave to rest in the refrigerator for 30 minutes.

8 Preheat the oven to 200°C (400°F/Gas 7).

9 Roll out half the dough thinly and use it to line a 20cm (8in) pie dish. Add the corned beef and onion filling. Sprinkle most of the chopped parsley over the top of the filling.

10 Roll out the remaining dough into a large round and use it to cover the pie. Seal the edges and crimp with a fork. Pierce air holes with the fork through the pastry and decorate with pastry leaves. Brush with the remaining egg.

11 Bake the pie in the oven for 15 minutes, then reduce the oven temperature to 190°C (375°F/Gas 5). Bake for a further 45 minutes or until golden. Meanwhile, return to the reserved stock. Heat once again in a pan over a low heat and gently whisk in the butter until thickened, to make a red wine jus. Keep warm.

12 To make the duchess potatoes, sieve and mash them, then add the remaining ingredients, except for 1 egg and beat well. Line a baking tray with non-stick paper.

13 Using a forcing bag with a star nozzle, pipe the potato onto the tray: form a 5cm (2in) base and pipe the potato on top until you have a pyramid. Repeat with the remaining potato until it has all been used and place in the refrigerator to firm up for 15 minutes. Beat the remaining egg and use it to glaze the pyramids. Cook in the oven for 20 minutes or until browned.

14 Make the cabbage. Put a large saucepan of salted water over a high heat and bring to the boil. Plunge in the cabbage, return to the boil and cook for 4–5 minutes. Drain, then gently mix in the cream cheese and single cream. Season well.

15 Place a piece of pie on each of 4 warm plates with the duchess potatoes and cabbage and pour over the warm red wine jus and sprinkle with the remaining parsley. Serve immediately.

For the duchess potatoes
1.3kg (3lb) boiled potatoes
50g (1¾oz) butter
2 large eggs
1 tsp salt
pinch of grated nutmeg
freshly ground black pepper

For the cabbage
1.3kg (3lb) cabbage, shredded
2 tbsp cream cheese
175ml (6fl oz) single cream
salt and pepper

Aromatic chicken curry

An exotic African-inspired dish with potato-filled roti and cucumber raita

Prep time 1 hour 15 minutes
Cooking time 50 minutes
Difficulty Medium–hard

For the curry and rice

1 large boiling chicken
2 tbsp white wine vinegar
a little salt
75g (2½oz) mild curry powder
2 tsp ground cumin
2 tsp dried thyme
6–8 spring onions, chopped,
    plus extra to garnish
1 tsp garlic powder
1 head of garlic, chopped
3 bay leaves
½ tsp ground turmeric
pinch of chicken seasoning
juice of 1 lemon
3 tbsp vegetable oil
1 tsp cumin seeds
300ml (10fl oz) chicken stock
3 potatoes, diced
dash of coconut cream
2 African seasoning stock
    cubes, crumbled
250g (9oz) basmati rice
shredded Iceberg lettuce,
    to garnish

For the potato roti

500g (1lb 2oz) strong white
    flour
250g (9oz) self raising flour
1 tsp salt
1 tbsp baking powder
2 potatoes, peeled and diced
2 spring onions, chopped
1 tsp curry powder
1 tsp ground cumin
salt and black pepper
vegetable oil for frying

For the raita

½ cucumber, diced
½ onion, sliced
150ml (5fl oz) plain yogurt
salt and black pepper

1 With a cleaver, cut and joint the chicken, taking the meat off the bones and discarding the skin. Put in a bowl and sprinkle with the vinegar and salt. Set aside for 10 minutes.

2 In a small bowl, mix together 2 tsp of the curry powder, the cumin, thyme, spring onions, garlic powder, half the fresh garlic, the bay leaves, turmeric, chicken seasoning and lemon juice. Pour this over the chicken pieces and turn them until coated in the mixture. Set aside for another 10–15 minutes.

3 To make the roti, in another bowl, mix together the flours, salt and baking powder. Add warm water, little by little, until it comes together as a dough. Cover with a damp, clean tea towel and leave to rise in a warm place for 10–15 minutes.

4 Mix the remaining curry powder with a little water to make a paste. Heat the oil in a large pan over a medium heat, then add the cumin seeds, the remaining fresh garlic and the curry paste. Cover and cook for 2–3 minutes, then add the chicken and stir well. Add 400ml (14fl oz) water, replace the lid and reduce the heat to low. Cook for 20 minutes, checking and adding a splash of water if it threatens to dry out. Stir in the stock, potato, coconut cream and crumbled stock cubes. Cover and cook for a further 20 minutes.

5 For the raita, mix together the cucumber, onion and yogurt in a small bowl and season with salt and black pepper. Set aside in the refrigerator until needed.

6 To make the roti filling, bring a saucepan of water to the boil over a high heat. Add the potatoes and cook for 5–10 minutes until tender, then drain very well. Mash the boiled potatoes in a bowl using a fork, then add the spring onions and mix well. Season with salt and black pepper and add the curry powder and cumin.

7 Divide the roti dough into 8 equal pieces and roll each piece out into a circle on a floured work surface. Spoon a quarter of the potato mixture onto the centre of each one, then fold the dough around it, pressing with the rolling pin to seal the ball completely. Carefully roll each out again into a circle, being very gentle so that the filling does not break through the surface.

8 In a saucepan of boiling water over a medium heat, cook the rice for 10 minutes, then drain. Meanwhile, put a little oil on a roti pan, or a large frying pan, place it over a high heat and let it get very hot. Add a roti circle, cook for just 1 minute, then turn over and cook on the other side. Transfer to greaseproof paper and keep warm. Repeat with the remaining roti.

9 To serve, place a mound of rice on each of 4 warm plates. Spoon on the curry. Fold the roti into triangles and place one on the side of each plate, then garnish with lettuce and spring onions. Serve the raita in a bowl on the table.

"This is a feast … and it is so cleansing. Really delightful."

— John Burton Race

Pan-fried sea bass with sauté potatoes

Roasted fennel and crispy pancetta help to make this sophisticated and delicious dish

Prep time 15 minutes
Cooking time 50 minutes
Difficulty Medium

1 Preheat the oven to 180°C (350°F/Gas 4). Bring a large pan of salted water to the boil over a high heat, add the potatoes and par-boil for 10–15 minutes. Drain, leave to cool, then slice.

2 Place the fennel on a baking tray, toss with 60ml (2fl oz) of the olive oil and bake for 25 minutes.

3 Heat a wok or large frying pan over a medium heat and add 30g (1oz) butter, then add the onion, garlic and sliced potatoes. Cook, stirring, for 10 minutes or until turning crisp at the edges. Add the curly parsley.

4 Meanwhile, put the flour on a large plate and season with salt and white pepper. Roll the sea bass fillets in the flour and pat off any excess. Melt 50g (1¾oz) of the butter and the remaining 1 tbsp oil in a large frying pan over a medium heat, add the fish skin-side down and fry for 5 minutes.

5 Melt the remaining butter in a saucepan with the capers and lemon juice, taste and season. Put the pancetta on a baking sheet and bake in the oven for 3 minutes or until crisp.

6 To serve, put some potatoes on each of 4 warm plates, place the sea bass on top and add the fennel and pancetta. Whisk the sauce until amalgamated, then spoon it over, scatter with the flat-leaf parsley and serve each with a halved lemon.

500g (1lb 2oz) Jersey Royal potatoes
1 large bulb of fennel, chopped
75ml (2½fl oz) olive oil
175g (6oz) unsalted butter
1 Spanish onion, finely chopped
1 garlic clove, finely chopped
1 small bunch of fresh curly parsley, finely chopped
plain flour, for coating
4 sea bass fillets
2 tbsp baby capers, rinsed
juice of 1 lemon, plus 2 lemons, halved, to serve
75g (2½oz) thinly sliced pancetta
salt and ground white pepper
1 small bunch of fresh flat-leaf parsley, finely chopped, to garnish

Trafalgar steak and shallot pudding

A rich, unctuous, old-fashioned pudding, with a warming port wine sauce

Prep time 55 minutes
Cooking time 1 hour
45 minutes
Difficulty Medium–hard

For the port sauce
2 tbsp olive oil
4 celery sticks, chopped
2 red onions, chopped
600ml (1 pint) fresh
  vegetable stock
600ml (1 pint) fresh beef
  stock
350ml (12fl oz) red wine
250ml (8fl oz) port
2 tbsp Worcestershire sauce
4 banana shallots, peeled
  but left whole
12 small shallots, peeled
  but left whole
salt and freshly ground
  black pepper

For the pastry
200g (7oz) plain flour
pinch of salt
40g (1¼oz) lard
30g (1oz) butter
2 tbsp whole milk, to glaze

For the filling
500g (1lb 2oz) rump steak
4 tsp English mustard
4 tbsp plain flour, seasoned
  with salt and freshly ground
  black pepper
olive oil

For the mash
4 baking potatoes
30g (1oz) butter
4 tbsp single cream
salt

1 Preheat the oven to 160°C (325°F/Gas 3). Peel all the vegetables, except the potatoes for the mash and the parsnips, and trim the meat for the filling. Set the vegetables and meat aside. Make the port wine sauce by heating the olive oil in a pan over a medium heat and adding all the vegetable and meat trimmings, along with the chopped celery and red onion. Sauté for 2–3 minutes until soft and browned. Set aside in the pan.

2 Pour the stocks, red wine, port and Worcestershire sauce into a separate, large pan. Set over a medium heat and bring to a simmer for about 30 minutes until reduced to about half its original volume. During this process, add all the whole shallots and poach for 5 minutes. Remove with a slotted spoon and set aside.

3 Use a little of the reduced liquid to deglaze the pan of sautéed vegetables, then tip the contents of the pan into the simmering reduced liquid. Continue to reduce the port sauce for 20 minutes or until about 600ml (1 pint) remains. Strain the sauce through a fine sieve, season and set aside. Discard the vegetable trimmings.

4 To make the pastry, sift the flour and salt into a bowl. Melt the lard and butter in a small pan over a low heat. Add 2 tbsp water, then mix into the flour until it comes together as a soft dough.

5 Roll the dough into a ball, then separate off one-third; set aside. Roll out the larger dough ball and use to line a buttered and floured large pudding basin. Press into the bowl. Roll out the smaller ball of dough to make a lid for the pudding. Leave both lots of pastry to rest in the refrigerator for 10 minutes.

6 To make the pudding filling, cut the steak into 5cm (2in) squares, sandwich each between cling film and pound until evenly flattened and about twice the surface area. Spread a little mustard on each meat square, add a piece of poached banana shallot and fold the meat over it into a parcel. Spread the seasoned flour onto a plate and pat the meat parcels in it. In a frying pan over a medium heat, gently fry the meat in a little olive oil until golden all over, turning occasionally. Add the parcels to the pastry-lined pudding bowl with 3–4 tablespoons of the reduced sauce (don't overfill the basin).

7 Wet the edges of the pastry with water, then place the smaller pastry circle on top; seal the edges well. Pinch the lid lightly to form a peak, then brush with a little milk. Double up a piece of foil and butter one side. Wrap it around the top of the pudding bowl and seal tightly by twisting the foil. Sit the bowl in a tray of hot water and cook in the oven for 40–45 minutes, topping up the water as needed. Take the foil lid off the pudding, increase the oven temperature to 195°C (380°F/Gas 5½) and cook the pudding for further 10 minutes or until golden.

8 While the pudding is cooking, prepare the vegetables. For the mash, bring a large saucepan of salted water to the boil, add the unpeeled potatoes and simmer for 10–15 minutes until cooked. Drain, peel and put through a ricer. Add the butter and cream, stir very well and set aside, keeping warm.

9 Scoop out balls from the swede and potato with a melon baller. Bring a large pan of salted water to the boil. Gently boil the swede and potato for 10 minutes until tender. Drain. Heat a little olive oil in an ovenproof frying pan over a medium heat. Tip in the potato and swede balls and the reserved small shallots, sauté until golden, then transfer the pan to the oven and roast for 10 minutes.

10 Bring a pan of salted water to the boil over a medium heat. Add the carrots and brown sugar, reduce the heat and simmer for 10 minutes. Drain and add a knob of butter and the parsley.

11 Peel the parsnips and use a vegetable peeler to create broad, thin "crisps". Slice into straws using a julienne cutter or a small sharp knife. Heat the oil in a sauté pan over a high heat, drop in the parsnip straws and fry for a couple of minutes. Blot on kitchen paper. Repeat the process, frying the thin crisps until golden.

12 To make the horseradish sauce, briefly soak the breadcrumbs in the milk. Add the cream, vinegar and horseradish and season with salt and black pepper. Mix well and check the seasoning.

13 To serve, turn out the pudding and serve with the vegetables on each of 4 warm plates. Decorate each with parsnip crisps, sprinkle all over with parsley and serve the two sauces alongside.

For the vegetables
1 swede
2 baking potatoes
a little olive oil
12 baby carrots, with green tops
pinch of brown sugar
knob of butter
1 small bunch of fresh parsley, finely chopped

For the parsnip crisps
2 parsnips
4 tbsp vegetable oil

For the horseradish sauce
2 tbsp white breadcrumbs
2 tbsp whole milk
2 tbsp double cream
2 tbsp vinegar
40g (1½oz) horseradish, grated
salt and black pepper

MAINS • TRAFALGAR STEAK AND SHALLOT PUDDING

Luxurious Cornish paella

With lobster, mussels, prawns and squid, this is decadent and divinely moreish

Prep time 45 minutes
Cooking time 1 hour
30 minutes
Difficulty Medium

For the paella
1 free-range whole chicken, about 1kg (2¼lb), with giblets
2 pork, garlic and black pepper sausages
3 tbsp olive oil
1 onion, diced
4 garlic cloves, finely chopped
225g (8oz) paella or long-grain rice
pinch of saffron
1 yellow pepper, sliced
450g (1lb) local mussels, cleaned and de-bearded
1 squid, cleaned and sliced
2 tomatoes
225g (8oz) cooked prawns in their shells
1 cooked lobster, meat extracted and chopped
225g (8oz) frozen peas, defrosted
nam pla (Thai fish sauce), to taste
2 lemons, one juiced, the other cut into wedges
salt and freshly ground black pepper
4 granary buns or chunks of crusty white bread, to serve

For the stock
carcass and giblets from the chicken (see above)
1 bouquet garni
3 celery sticks with leaves, chopped
1 onion, chopped
2 carrots, chopped
2 garlic cloves
salt

120

1 To make the stock, joint the chicken and set the meat aside. Put the carcass and giblets in a large pan, add the bouquet garni, celery, onion, carrots and garlic. Season, cover with water and bring to a simmer over a low heat. Cook for 1 hour, then strain into a large bowl and set aside.

2 Preheat the grill to its highest setting, then grill the sausages, turning to brown all sides, for 10 minutes or until cooked. Slice, and set aside.

3 In a paella pan or your widest frying pan, heat the olive oil over a medium heat. Add the chicken joints and brown on all sides, then transfer them to a plate. Add the onion and garlic to the pan and fry until soft. Add the rice and turn to coat it in oil. Stir in the saffron and return the chicken to the pan with the yellow pepper. Add enough stock to cover the rice, reduce the heat and simmer for 10 minutes. Keep topping up with stock from time to time.

4 Put a separate pan with a lid over a high heat, tip in the mussels and add a dash of the stock. Replace the lid and steam for 3–5 minutes, until the mussels open, shaking the pan once. Pour into a colander and discard any that have not opened. Add the mussels to the paella, keeping a few aside to garnish. Add the squid. Cook for a further 10 minutes.

5 Meanwhile, put the tomatoes in a bowl, cover with boiling water and leave for a couple of minutes. Plunge them into iced water, slip off and discard the skins, then chop and add to the pan. Add the prawns, lobster, sausage and peas to the pan and heat through. Season and add the fish sauce and lemon juice to taste.

6 Serve the paella in 4 large warm bowls garnished with lemon wedges and the reserved mussels, with the bread alongside.

Chicken marinated in lemon and thyme

A light and refreshing summer dish with sparkling, lively flavours

Prep time 20 minutes, plus overnight marinating
Cooking time 45 minutes
Difficulty Medium

For the chicken
6 tbsp olive oil
2 tsp dried thyme
4 or 5 garlic cloves, crushed
grated zest and juice of
   4 small lemons
4 organic chicken thighs
4 organic chicken breasts,
   on the bone
250g (9oz) basmati rice
600ml (1 pint) chicken stock
Maldon sea salt and freshly
   ground black pepper

For the dressing
juice of 1 small lemon
2 tbsp white wine vinegar
8 tbsp sunflower oil
2 garlic cloves, crushed
2 bay leaves
2 heaped tsp Dijon mustard

For the vegetables
200g (7oz) cherry tomatoes
   on the vine
4 endives

For the salad
12–16 cherry tomatoes
2 handfuls of rocket
2 handfuls of watercress
2 shallots, finely sliced
2 avocados, sliced

1 The day before, marinate the chicken. Pour the olive oil into a large bowl and add the thyme, garlic and lemon zest. Season, add the chicken and turn to coat. Cover and leave to marinate in the refrigerator. At the same time, make the dressing. Shake all the ingredients in a screw-top jar and keep refrigerated until needed.

2 Wash the rice thoroughly and soak in plenty of cold water for 1–2 hours. Add the lemon juice to the marinating chicken, and mix thoroughly. Return to the refrigerator for 30 minutes.

3 Preheat the oven to 190°C (375°F/Gas 5). Remove the chicken thighs from the marinade and place skin-side down in a baking tray. Add half the stock and cover with foil. Repeat for the chicken breasts, using a separate baking tray.

4 Cook the thighs for 20 minutes in the top of the oven, then remove the foil, turn the thighs over and add a little stock. Return to the oven for a further 25 minutes or until the skins are golden brown. Cook the breasts in the same way, but for only 15 minutes before removing the foil and 15 minutes afterwards.

5 Meanwhile, put the rice in a pan with twice its volume of water and plenty of salt. Bring to a boil, simmer for 5 minutes, then remove from the heat. Keep covered, allowing the rice to absorb the water completely.

6 Add the cherry tomatoes on the vine to the chicken–breast baking tray and roast for 10 minutes. Remove the chicken from the oven and allow to rest. Gently reheat the juices from both baking trays in a small saucepan.

7 Meanwhile, bring a saucepan of water to the boil over a high heat. Slice the endives lengthways, plunge them into the pan for 2 minutes, then drain. Place a ridged cast-iron grill pan over a high heat and char the endives for a couple of minutes on each side. Dress and season the salad and arrange in a side dish.

8 Serve the chicken on each of 4 warm plates, with the chicken juices, charred endives, roast cherry tomatoes, rice and salad.

Pork Wellington with a cider sauce

A new twist on an old favourite, with flaky pastry hiding juicy apples and mushrooms

1 To make the pastry, mix the flour with the salt. Cut the butter into cubes and fold through the flour with a knife, without breaking up the butter too much. Gradually add up to 150ml (5fl oz) of iced water until it comes together as a dough, wrap in cling film and place in the refrigerator for 30 minutes. Roll out the pastry on a floured surface into a rectangle, fold one of the short sides one-third of the way over, then bring in the other side to cover. Roll again, trying not to break up the butter pieces. Repeat, wrap in cling film and refrigerate for 20 minutes.

2 Peel and slice the apples, put into a saucepan over a moderately low heat and bring to a gentle boil, adding 80ml (2½fl oz) water and the sugar. Simmer for 20 minutes, stirring.

3 Preheat the oven to 220°C (425°F/Gas 7). Pour the oil into a frying pan over a medium heat. Tip in the bacon and onion and fry for 5 minutes, then add the mushrooms and cook for 5 minutes more. Remove from the heat, season and add the breadcrumbs.

4 Melt the butter in a frying pan over a medium heat, add the pork and turn to seal. Remove the pastry from the refrigerator, and roll it out so that it is big enough to wrap around the pork. Place the mushroom stuffing in the middle of the pastry and top with the pork. Spread with the apple and wrap the pastry right around, sealing the edges very well with the egg. Turn over so that the fold is on the bottom and brush with the remaining egg. Cook in the oven for 45 minutes.

5 To make the cider sauce, pour the double cream into a saucepan over a medium heat, season and reduce for 5 minutes. Add the cider and reduce for another 20 minutes until thick. Keep warm.

6 Bring the potatoes to the boil in salted water for 25 minutes or until tender. Mash and beat in the butter. Keep warm. Plunge the beans into boiling water for 5 minutes, drain and keep warm.

7 Put some mash on each of 4 warm plates and top with a slice of the Wellington. Add a serving of beans to each plate and serve the sauce on the side.

Prep time **30 minutes, plus 50 minutes' resting time**
Cooking time **1¼ hours**
Difficulty **Medium–hard**

For the puff pastry
250g (9oz) plain flour
pinch of salt
250g (9oz) butter

For the Wellington
2 Bramley apples
25g (scant 1oz) sugar
1 tbsp olive oil
3 smoked bacon rashers, diced
1 onion, diced
4 field mushrooms, diced
50g (1¾oz) breadcrumbs
knob of butter
800g (1¾lb) pork tenderloin
1 egg yolk, beaten
sea salt and cracked black pepper

For the cider sauce
300ml (10fl oz) double cream
100ml (3½fl oz) local Somerset cider
salt and pepper

For the vegetables
750g (1lb 10oz) Maris Piper potatoes
25g (scant 1oz) butter
250g (9oz) green beans
salt

Prep time 10 minutes,
plus 24 hours' marinating
Cooking time 45 minutes
Difficulty Medium

For the tikka masala
2 tsp ground coriander
1 tsp smoked paprika
1 tsp ground cumin
pinch of salt
1 tsp garlic powder
1 tsp fenugreek
½ tsp ground cinnamon
1 tsp ground ginger
2 tsp mild chilli powder
1 tsp hot chilli powder
1 tsp black pepper
1 tsp ground cardamom
1 tsp ground cloves
1½ tsp ground turmeric

For the lamb
1 tsp smoked paprika
1 tsp mild chilli powder
6 garlic cloves, roughly
   chopped
1 tsp soy sauce
2 tbsp olive oil
500g (1lb 2oz) good-quality
   lamb steaks
2 tbsp vegetable oil
2 onions, finely sliced
1 red pepper, finely chopped
2–3 tomatoes, finely
   chopped
1 x 400ml can coconut milk
handful of finely chopped
   fresh coriander
salt and black pepper

For the raita
1 mango, finely chopped
284ml tub soured cream
1 cucumber, chopped
250ml (8fl oz) plain yogurt
4 spring onions, finely
   chopped
small bunch of fresh chives,
   chopped

Lamb tikka masala

An intriguing contemporary interpretation with a fruity raita and potato pancakes

1 Mix together all the spices for the tikka masala.

2 To make the lamb, in a large bowl, mix together 2 tsp of tikka masala, a pinch of salt and black pepper, the smoked paprika, chilli powder, 5 of the garlic cloves, the soy sauce and olive oil. Coat the lamb in the spices, cover and leave in the refrigerator for 24 hours.

3 When ready to cook, bring a large pan of water to the boil and add the rice, turmeric, salt and cumin. Simmer for 10 minutes or until cooked, then drain and set aside.

4 Prepare the potatoes for the pancakes: quarter the potatoes and add them to a large pan of salted water. Bring to the boil over a high heat, then reduce the heat and simmer for 10 minutes or until tender. Drain and allow to dry, then mash.

5 For the raita, put the mango, soured cream, cucumber, yogurt, spring onions and chives in a bowl and mix well. Set aside.

6 Remove the lamb from the refrigerator and bring it to room temperature. Heat the vegetable oil in a heavy frying pan until smoking hot. Add the lamb and quickly sear it on both sides for a minute or two. Remove to a warm plate, leaving the oil in the pan.

7 Add to the pan 2 large tsp tikka masala, the onions, remaining garlic clove, red pepper and tomatoes and fry for 2–3 minutes. Pour in the coconut milk. Add the lamb to the pan with the sauce and fry for about 5 minutes on each side. Remove the meat and allow to rest. Bring the sauce to a simmer until it thickens.

8 Meanwhile, make the pancakes. Mix the potatoes, plain flour, egg yolk, turmeric, chilli powder and a pinch of salt, add the black peppercorns, garlic powder and smoked paprika and mix until it comes together as a dough, adding a little more flour if the mixture seems too sticky. Divide the dough into small pieces, then roll each one out on a floured surface to form round pancakes. Set aside, interleaved with greaseproof paper.

9 Fry the rice. In a large non-stick frying pan, heat the oil and butter. Add the rice, stirring constantly, for 8–10 minutes until really well heated through with each grain distinct and shiny with oil.

10 At the same time, cook the potato pancakes. Place another large non-stick frying pan over a high heat and add the vegetable oil. When hot, add a potato pancake, cook for 2 minutes, then turn and cook for 2 minutes more. Remove and keep warm while you cook the remaining pancakes, adding more oil if needed.

11 Sprinkle the masala sauce with the fresh coriander.

12 Using a lightly oiled glass, pack in a quarter of the rice, then tip it out onto each of 4 warm plates, leaving a neat pile. Arrange slices of the lamb on each plate, spoon over some masala sauce and serve with the pancakes and raita on the side.

For the rice
250g (9oz) basmati rice
2 tsp ground turmeric
2 tsp salt
2 tsp cumin seeds
1 tbsp olive oil
knob of salted butter

For the pancakes
200g (7oz) Maris Piper
  potatoes
handful of plain flour
1 egg yolk
pinch of turmeric
pinch of chilli powder
pinch of salt
pinch of black peppercorns
1 tsp garlic powder
½ tsp smoked paprika
vegetable oil, for frying

"This raita is really lovely. Really fresh flavours. Complements the lamb beautifully. I think the spice mix is excellent. I like this dish very much."
— Jilly Goolden

Pigeon wrapped in bacon

Stuffed with pepper-walnut pesto, this is a wonderful dish for autumn

Prep time 10–15 minutes
Cooking time 1 hour
40 minutes
Difficulty Medium

For the pesto
2 red peppers, deseeded
1 tbsp olive oil
2 fat garlic cloves
75g (2½oz) walnuts
45g (1½oz) flat-leaf parsley
juice of 1 lemon
4 sun-dried tomatoes in oil

For the pigeon
8 pigeon breasts
8 local dry-cured streaky
  bacon rashers
olive oil
1 glass of red wine

For the red cabbage
2 red onions, chopped
1 tbsp vegetable oil
200ml (7fl oz) red wine
2–3 tbsp smoked pepper
  jelly or redcurrant jelly
2 whole cloves
2 juniper berries
1 red cabbage, shredded
6 Agen prunes, chopped
red wine vinegar, to taste
large knob of butter
salt and black pepper

For the rosti
10g (¼oz) dried porcini
700g (1lb 9oz) potatoes,
  scrubbed, skins left on
leaves from 2 sprigs of fresh
  lemon thyme
3 tbsp rapeseed oil
large knob of butter

For the carrots
bunch of baby carrots
2.5cm (1in) piece of fresh
  root ginger, sliced
1 tbsp clear honey

1 Preheat the oven to 200°C (400°C/Gas 6). To make the pesto, put the red peppers on a baking tray, drizzle with the oil, pop a garlic clove in each and roast for 15 minutes, then remove, put in a small plastic bag and seal. Spread the walnuts in a small ovenproof dish and cook for 5 minutes or until golden, watching closely so they don't burn. Slip the skins from the peppers and discard, then add the flesh with its garlic and juices to a blender. Add the nuts, parsley, lemon juice and tomatoes and blend to a purée, adding enough of the tomato oil to make a stiffish paste.

2 For the pigeon, make an incision into each breast and place a spoonful of the pesto inside. Carefully wrap each with bacon, and set aside in the refrigerator to firm up.

3 To make the red cabbage, place a saucepan over a moderate heat, then cook the onions in the oil until soft. Add the red wine, jelly, cloves, juniper, cabbage and prunes, mixing well and reduce the heat to low. Cover the saucepan with foil, then with its lid and cook for 1–1½ hours, stirring every 20 minutes.

4 Meanwhile, prepare the rosti. Put the porcini in a small bowl, and cover with boiling water. Leave for 10 minutes, then drain and chop. Boil the potatoes for 5 minutes, then grate coarsely, adding the mushrooms and lemon thyme. Mix gently and season. Heat the oil and butter in a large frying pan over a medium heat, add a large spoonful of rosti mixture and fry for 5–6 minutes on each side until golden brown. Set aside and keep warm.

5 To make the carrots, bring a pan of water to the boil, add the carrots, ginger and honey and simmer for 8–9 minutes.

6 Heat a little olive oil in a frying pan over a high heat and add the pigeon. Fry for 3 minutes on each side, then rest in a warm place. Pour the wine into the pan and reduce until syrupy, then season.

7 Add a little vinegar to the cabbage and taste; you want a good balance of sweet and sour flavours. Add the butter and stir.

8 Serve 2 pigeon breasts on each of 4 warm plates with the rosti, red cabbage, carrots and sauce.

Squirrel pie with vegetables

The subtle, nutty taste of squirrel is a delight – ask your butcher for the meat

Prep time 45 minutes
Cooking time 1 hour
20 minutes
Difficulty Medium

For the filling
3 tbsp olive oil
1 small onion, finely chopped
1 garlic clove, finely chopped
2 or 3 bacon rashers, sliced
3 squirrels, jointed, deboned
  and cubed
a little plain flour
100ml (3½fl oz) red wine
500ml (16fl oz) beef stock
1 tsp tomato purée
6 button mushrooms, sliced
1 bay leaf
sprig of fresh thyme
6 juniper berries
salt and pepper

For the pastry
115g (4oz) plain flour
30g (1oz) hard margarine
30g (1oz) white vegetable fat
30g (1oz) unsalted butter
1 egg, beaten

For the potato cakes
4 large new potatoes
knob of butter
bunch of spring onions,
  chopped
bunch of fresh chives, finely
  chopped
1 egg, beaten
60g (2oz) white breadcrumbs
knob of butter
60ml (2fl oz) olive oil

For the vegetables
olive oil
2 parsnips, sliced
4 small turnips
2 handfuls of carrots, sliced
2 knobs of butter
2 tsp clear honey

1 Pour the oil into a saucepan and place over a medium heat. Add the onion, garlic and bacon and cook, stirring, until lightly coloured. Remove from the pan with a slotted spoon, leaving the fat behind. Toss the cubes of squirrel in plain flour and pepper, then shake off any excess. Add the meat to the pan and brown on all sides. Pour in the red wine and reduce by half, then add the beef stock. Return the onion, garlic and bacon to the pan and add the tomato purée, mushrooms, herbs and juniper berries. Reduce the heat and simmer for 45 minutes. Taste, season and set aside.

2 Meanwhile, make the pastry. Put the flour in a large bowl, and dice in all the fats. Rub together with your fingertips until it resembles fine breadcrumbs, then gradually add iced water until it comes together as a dough. Wrap in cling film and refrigerate for 30 minutes. Preheat the oven to 180°C (350°F/Gas 4).

3 Pour the filling into a pie dish. Roll out the pastry on a floured work surface until slightly larger than the dish, then cover the pie. Brush with the egg, then cook for 30–35 minutes until golden.

4 Bring a large pan of water to the boil over a high heat and add the potatoes. Boil for 15 minutes or until tender, then drain and crush with a fork. Melt the butter in a saucepan over a medium heat and add the spring onions. Cook gently, stirring, until soft, then add to the potatoes with the chives. Season. Shape the mixture into 4 cakes. Put the egg and breadcrumbs on 2 separate plates. Dip each cake first in the egg, then in breadcrumbs.

5 For the vegetables, heat the oil in a small roasting tin in the oven for 15 minutes. Add the parsnips and roast for 30 minutes or until golden brown. Put the butter and oil for the potato cakes in a large frying pan and fry the potato cakes for 5 minutes on each side or until golden and cooked through. Keep warm.

6 Bring 2 small saucepans of water to the boil and put the turnips in one and the carrots in another. Simmer for 10 minutes or until just tender, then drain and add a knob of butter to each.

7 Serve the pie hot on 4 warm plates, adding a potato cake and vegetables to each.

Lamb in hay

Cooking in hay was once common,
and it gives a deliciously aromatic result

Prep time **10 minutes**
Cooking time **3 hours**
Difficulty **Medium**

1 Preheat the oven to 240°C (475°F/Gas 9). Rub the lamb all over with salt, then cover with butter. Evenly sprinkle over the chopped herbs. Lay half the hay on a trivet in a large roasting tin. Sit the meat on top, then pack more hay around to cover the lamb completely. Sprinkle with water.

2 Cover with foil, making sure that the roasting tin is completely sealed and put in the hot oven for 30 minutes. Reduce the oven temperature to 200°C (400°F/Gas 6) and cook for 2 hours.

3 Remove the lamb from the oven, take off the foil and hay, and transfer the meat to a carving board. Keep warm and allow to rest for 15 minutes. Strain the juices from the bottom of the tin into a bowl, then remove the fat. Put this gravy in a saucepan over a medium heat. Mix the cornflour in a small bowl with enough water to make a smooth paste, then add to the juices. Heat, stirring occasionally, until thickened.

4 Heat the oil in a wok or large saucepan over a medium high heat. Add the mustard seeds and, when they finish popping, the red chilli. Stir once, then add the carrot, cabbage and green chilli. Stir-fry for 30 seconds, then add the coriander, salt and sugar. Stir-fry for a further 5 minutes, then add the lemon juice.

5 Carve the lamb onto 4 warm plates and serve with the spiced cabbage and carrots.

For the lamb
1 leg of Welsh spring lamb,
  about 2.7kg (6lb)
sea salt
125g (4½oz) butter
2 tbsp mixed chopped herbs
  (rosemary, mint or thyme)
bag of hay
1 tbsp cornflour

For the spiced cabbage with carrots
4 tbsp vegetable oil
1 tsp black mustard seeds
¼ fresh red chilli, finely sliced
350g (12oz) carrots, grated
350g (12oz) Savoy cabbage,
  trimmed and shredded
½ fresh green chilli, finely
  sliced
2 tbsp chopped coriander
1 tsp salt
pinch of organic white sugar
dash of freshly squeezed
  lemon juice

"I love this whole concept and I love that rather curious hay-ey flavour that goes into the meat and comes into the gravy."
— Jilly Goolden

Prep time 15–20 minutes,
plus 24 hours' soaking
Cooking time 3 hours
35 minutes
Difficulty Medium–hard

For the sausages
salted hog casings
300g (10oz) pork shoulder
125g (4½oz) belly pork
20g (¾oz) runny honey
185g (3oz) fresh white
  breadcrumbs
sprig of fresh sage, chopped
45g (1½oz) black pudding
1 tbsp vegetable oil
salt and freshly ground
  black pepper

For the stock
2 chicken carcasses
2 onions, chopped
2 carrots, chopped
2 celery sticks, chopped

For the onion gravy
20g (¾oz) salted butter
4 onions, sliced
20g (¾oz) plain flour

For the mash
6 Maris Piper potatoes, diced
50g (1¾oz) salted butter
200ml (7fl oz) milk
salt and black pepper

For the mushy peas
300g (10oz) frozen peas
30g (1oz) salted butter
salt and black pepper

Bangers and mash

Traditional, hearty and warming, with superb home-made sausages

1 Soak the hog casings in a large bowl of water for at least 24 hours, changing the water a few times, then rinse and dry very well.

2 To make the stock, put the chicken carcasses in a large pan with the onions, carrots and celery and pour in 2 litres (3½ pints) water. Bring to the boil over a moderately low heat then simmer for 2–3 hours. Cool, chill overnight, then skim off and discard the fat. Put back in a large pan over a high heat and reduce until it measures half its original volume. Set aside.

3 Make the sausages. Dice, then mince the pork shoulder and belly. Add the honey and 110ml (3¾fl oz) cold water, the breadcrumbs and sage. Season and mix together. Finely dice the black pudding and gently stir into the mixture, trying to keep the dice intact. Fill the hog casings with the mixture, and tie off at intervals into sausages.

4 Put a wide, shallow pan over a low heat, half-fill with water, and bring to a simmer. Drop in the sausages and poach for 5 minutes, then drain and set aside.

5 To make the onion gravy, melt the butter in a frying pan over a low heat, add the onions and fry very gently for 1 hour or until caramelized. Add 500ml (16fl oz) of the reduced chicken stock, and bring to a simmer. Cook until the stock has reduced again by half its volume, to intensify the flavour.

6 Remove a little of the onion liquor from the pan and put in a small bowl. Add the flour and mix into a smooth paste.

7 Whisk the paste back into the onion pan until the gravy has thickened and cook for another 3 minutes, whisking. Set aside.

8 To make the mash, bring a large saucepan of salted water to the boil over a high heat and add the potatoes. Simmer for 15 minutes or until soft. Drain and pass through a potato ricer back into the rinsed-out pan, or mash with a potato masher. Add the butter and milk, season and stir to combine.

9 Meanwhile, make the mushy peas. Bring a saucepan of salted water to the boil, add the peas and simmer for 5 minutes. Drain.

10 Remove a fifth of the peas and set aside in a bowl. Pour the remaining peas into a blender and whizz, or process with a stick blender, until they make a purée. Transfer the pea purée and reserved whole peas to a saucepan over a gentle heat and add the butter. Stir everything together and season to taste.

11 Put the vegetable oil for the sausages in a large frying pan and place over a medium-high heat. Add the sausages and fry for 15–20 minutes, turning, or until well coloured and thoroughly cooked. Meanwhile, gently reheat the onion gravy.

12 Serve the sausages on warm plates with the mash, mushy peas and onion gravy.

"I love the sauce, I love the onions ... It's a very good bangers and mash."
— John Burton Race

Lamb with chicken mousseline

A horseradish and chicken mousse elevates this lovely spring-time dish

Prep time 25 minutes
Cooking time 3 hours
Difficulty Medium

For the mousse
100g (3½oz) chicken breast
1 small egg white
pinch of coarse sea salt
100ml (3½fl oz) double cream
10g (¼oz) horseradish, grated
15g (½oz) capers, rinsed
salt and black pepper

For the lamb
350g (12oz) 5-bone rack
  of new-season lamb
a little olive oil
1 sheet of caul fat
salt and black pepper

For the jus
1 or 2 lamb bones
200g (7oz) lamb trimmings
1 carrot, finely diced
1 onion, finely diced
1 celery stick, finely diced
1 tsp tomato purée
1.2 litres (2 pints) lamb stock
1 bay leaf
sprig of fresh thyme
5 peppercorns

For the vegetables
300g (10oz) new potatoes
a few fresh mint leaves
olive oil
2 shallots, finely sliced
45g (1½oz) asparagus
45g (1½oz) peas
45g (1½oz) broad beans
salt

For the dressing
100ml (3½fl oz) olive oil
1 tbsp tarragon vinegar
1 tsp sugar
handful of fresh mint leaves
handful of fresh basil leaves

1 Put the chicken breast, egg white and salt in a blender or food processor and mix to a purée, then pass the mixture through a sieve to remove any sinew.

2 Slowly add the cream, stirring, until it reaches the consistency of a light mousse, then season. Add the horseradish and capers and mix carefully. Set aside in the refrigerator until needed.

3 Cut off two cutlets from the lamb to make a canon and trim off the fat and sinew. Take the rest of the meat from the bones and trim off the sinew. Reserve all the trimmings.

4 Season the trimmed canon and cutlets. Put a large frying pan over a high heat, add a little oil and lightly sear the meat on all sides. Set aside.

5 To make the jus, place a saucepan over a medium-high heat and add the lamb bones, trimmings, carrot, onion and celery until well browned.

6 Add the tomato purée and stock, herbs and peppercorns. Bring gently to the boil, then reduce the heat and simmer for 2–3 hours.

7 Strain the jus and pour into a small saucepan set over a medium heat. Reduce until syrupy, remove from the heat and set aside until needed.

8 Preheat the oven to 210°C (410°F/Gas 6½).

9 When the meat has cooled, spread a layer of mousse evenly on the top of the canon and over the lamb chop. Gently wrap both with the caul fat.

10 Place a large frying pan over a high heat, add a little oil and sear the meat once more, then roast in the oven for 4 minutes for the chop and 7 minutes for the canon. This will give medium-rare meat. If you prefer your lamb more well done, leave each piece in the oven for 1–2 minutes more. Allow to rest for 10 minutes.

11 Meanwhile, bring a large pan of salted water to the boil, then add the potatoes and mint. Simmer for 20 minutes or until cooked. Drain and slice the potatoes.

continued...

...continued from p.132

12 Heat a little olive oil in a frying pan over a medium-high heat and add the shallots and potatoes. Sauté for 5 minutes.

13 Bring another pan of salted water to the boil. Add the asparagus, cook for 1 minute, then add the peas and beans, and cook for 1 minute more. Drain.

14 Mix together the oil, vinegar and sugar for the dressing, and warm gently in a pan.

15 Drizzle the vegetables with the dressing and season. Add the mint and basil, finely chopped.

16 Gently reheat the pan of lamb jus.

17 Slice the canon and divide it and the cutlets among 4 warm plates, adding a stack of potatoes and pouring on the jus. Arrange the vegetables around the edge of the plate.

"Absolutely delightful ...
the sweetness – the lamb
was perfectly cooked.
Fantastic effort."
— John Burton Race

Torbock's pie with pheasant and ham

A winning combination of game, ham and vegetables served as a hearty pie

1 Soak the ham shank in plenty of cold water overnight. The next day, put the pheasant and ham shank in a large pan. Add the carrots, leeks, onion, celery and bouquet garni. Pour in enough cold water to cover. Bring to the boil over a low heat and gently simmer for 2 hours. Cover and leave in a cool place overnight.

2 To make the pastry, sift the flour and salt into a bowl. Rub in the vegetable fat and the unsalted butter with your fingertips until the mixture resembles breadcrumbs. Gradually add enough iced water, little by little, until the mixture just comes together into a dough. Wrap in cling film and leave to chill for 30 minutes.

3 Preheat the oven to 180°C (350°F/Gas 4). Remove the pheasant and ham from the cooking liquor and take the meat off the bones. Cut it into bite-sized pieces. Strain the liquor, reserve 600ml (1 pint) and add the tarragon. (Freeze the rest to use in soups.)

4 Melt the butter for the filling in a saucepan over a medium heat. Add the flour and cook for 2–3 minutes, stirring. Gradually add the cooking liquor, stirring constantly to prevent lumps. Bring to the boil, reduce the heat and simmer until slightly thickened. Season and stir in the cream. Put the filling in four 10cm (4in) diameter pie dishes, cover with the sauce and arrange the mushrooms on top.

5 Roll out the rested pastry to around the thickness of a pound coin. Cover each pie with pastry and brush with the egg. Decorate with a thistle cut from the trimmings. Bake for 15–20 minutes until the pastry is golden, then brush the tops with a little melted butter.

6 Meanwhile, in 3 separate pans of boiling water, blanch the cabbage, green beans and carrots for a few minutes. Drain and refresh in cold water. Sweat the onion and garlic in a little butter until soft. Add the wine, cumin and cream. Season, then stir in the cabbage. Cook until the sauce has reduced. Whisk together the mustard, oils, a splash of water, a pinch of sugar, the lemon juice, thyme and shallot. Gently reheat the beans, pour in the dressing and toss to coat. Dissolve 1 tsp sugar in a warm pan over a medium heat. Add the vinegar, a knob of butter and tarragon. Once the butter has melted, add the stock and carrots and season. Serve one pie on each of 4 warm plates with the warm vegetables.

Prep time 20 minutes
Cooking time 2 hours day before, 1 hour on the day
Difficulty Medium

For the filling
1 ham shank
1 pheasant
2 carrots, roughly chopped
2 leeks, roughly chopped
1 onion, roughly chopped
1 celery stick, chopped
1 bouquet garni
2 sprigs of fresh tarragon
50g (1¾oz) salted butter
50g (1¾oz) plain flour
250ml (8fl oz) double cream
115g (4oz) button mushrooms
salt and freshly ground black

For the pastry
225g (8oz) plain flour
pinch of salt
115g (4oz) vegetable fat,
60g (2oz) unsalted butter,
1 egg, beaten, for egg wash

For the vegetables
1 Savoy cabbage, shredded
large handful of green beans
16 Chantenay carrots
1 onion, finely chopped
2 or 3 garlic cloves
50g (1¾oz) butter
splash of dry white wine
pinch of ground cumin
splash of double cream
½ tbsp Dijon mustard
1 tbsp olive oil
1 tbsp groundnut oil
pinch of sugar
dash of lemon juice
sprig of fresh thyme
1 small shallot
1 tsp sugar
1 tbsp white wine vinegar
sprig of fresh tarragon
2–3 tbsp chicken stock
salt and black pepper

Boozy beef with roasted vegetables

Gorgeous, rich, alcohol-laced beef with roast vegetables and fluffy mash

Prep time 15 minutes
Cooking time 1½ hours
Difficulty Medium

For the beef
knob of unsalted butter
600g (1lb 5oz) fillet of beef
1 onion, diced
100g (3½oz) unsmoked
   streaky bacon, chopped
3 garlic cloves, sliced
100g (3½oz) button
   mushrooms
4 tbsp Cognac
1 x 75cl bottle red wine
2 or 3 carrots, peeled
   and sliced
2 bouquet garni
1 tbsp tomato purée
600ml (1 pint) beef stock
rock salt and black pepper

For the roasted vegetables
3 small organic courgettes
1 red pepper
1 orange pepper
1 onion, chopped
1 red onion, chopped
1 garlic bulb, cloves
   separated and peeled
1 sweet potato, chopped
   into 1cm (½in) cubes
1 banana shallot, sliced
6 small Chanterelle carrots
good-quality olive oil

For the mash
4 large organic potatoes
2 knobs of butter
milk
cream
salt and pepper

To serve
350g (12oz) green beans,
   trimmed
chopped parsley, to garnish

1 For the beef, melt the butter in a large pan over a medium-high heat. Season the beef with a little rock salt and black pepper, put in the pan, brown all over. Remove to a warm plate.

2 Add the onion to the same pan and sauté until soft. Add the bacon, garlic and mushrooms and fry until the bacon is cooked.

3 Put the Cognac in a small pan and heat gently, then tilt the pan to one side, light the brandy and allow the alcohol to burn off. Once the flames have subsided, add to the main pan ingredients.

4 Return the beef to the pan with the bacon, onions, garlic and mushrooms. Increase the heat and add enough wine to cover half the beef. Let it bubble for a few minutes, then add the carrots and bouquet garni. Mix the tomato purée with the stock and add it to the pan, reduce the heat, cover loosely with a lid and leave to simmer gently for 1½ hours or until the beef is very tender. Keep turning the beef in the wine and basting the top with the liquid.

5 Remove the beef from the pan and leave to rest for 5 minutes. Slice the beef and put in a serving dish. Pour over the juices and spoon the contents of the pan into the serving dish. Season with salt and black pepper. Leave to rest for 30 minutes.

6 While the beef is simmering, to make the roasted vegetables, preheat the oven to 200°C (400°F/Gas 6). Cut the vegetables into chunks and put them in an ovenproof dish. Drizzle with olive oil and place on the top shelf of the oven for 40–45 minutes, stirring occasionally to stop them sticking, until the vegetables are soft.

7 To make the mash, peel the potatoes and boil in a pan until soft. Remove from the pan and drain. Add 2 knobs of butter and a little milk and mash until fluffy. Add a little cream and continue to mash. Taste and add more cream and season to suit. For the green beans, cook in a saucepan of boiling water until tender.

8 To serve, put the roasted vegetables on the plate at one end and the slices of beef on top of the vegetables. Put the mash on the opposite side of the plate, then put a portion of green beans in the centre of the dish between the beef and potatoes. Spoon the sauce over the beef and sprinkle with a little chopped parsley.

Rack of roe venison with barley risotto

A stunning centrepiece dish with a rich red wine sauce and earthy, sweet barley

1 Preheat the oven to 200°C (400°F/Gas 6).

2 Rinse the barley well. Put in a pan and cover with water. Bring to the boil over a medium heat, then drain and rinse again. Return the barley to the rinsed-out pan, cover again with water and bring to the boil. Half-cover, reduce the heat and simmer for 45 minutes or until tender. Season with the salt, then drain and set aside.

3 Trim the racks of venison and set aside the trimmings. To make the sauce, melt the butter in a frying pan over a moderate heat and tip in the shallot, carrot, celery, garlic and herbs and cook, stirring, until coloured. Remove the vegetables to a dish.

4 Add the oil to the pan and colour the meat trimmings on all sides. Return the vegetables to the pan and stir. Add the wine, increase the heat and boil until almost dry. Add the chicken stock and simmer gently for 15 minutes. Remove the bay leaf and thyme and pour the sauce into a blender. Blend the sauce, then pass the mixture through a sieve. Season and set aside.

5 Return to the risotto. Toast the sunflower seeds in a dry frying pan over a medium heat, stirring, for 1–2 minutes. Set aside. Heat the oil in a deep frying pan over a medium heat. Cook the onion slowly until golden yellow. Add the celery and cook for 5 minutes, then add the carrots and cook for a further 2–3 minutes. Add the barley, then add the chicken stock, a little at a time, until you have the consistency of a risotto. Set aside.

6 Cover each rack of venison with a little oil, then season with black pepper. Place a frying pan over a high heat and sear the venison until browned all over. Lightly salt, then transfer to a baking tray. Roast in the hot oven for 10 minutes. Remove from the oven and allow to rest in a warm place for about 10 minutes. Meanwhile, reheat the barley, stirring in the butter and parsley. Reheat the sauce, stir in the redcurrant jelly and whisk in the knob of butter.

7 Place a ring of risotto on each of 4 warm plates and scatter with roasted sunflower seeds and celery leaves. Cut each rack into individual chops and place these against each barley mound. Pour the sauce around the plate.

Prep time 30 minutes
Cooking time 1 hour
Difficulty Medium–easy

For the barley
100g (3½oz) pearl barley
1 tbsp sunflower seeds
1 tbsp extra virgin olive oil
1 onion, chopped
100g (3½oz) celery, finely sliced, with leaves, to garnish
175g (6oz) carrots, coarsely grated
100ml (3½fl oz) chicken stock
2 tsp unsalted butter
2 tbsp chopped parsley
sea salt and freshly ground black pepper

For the venison
2 x 500g (1lb 2oz) racks of roe venison, each with 6–8 bones
1 tbsp olive oil

For the wine sauce
2 tsp unsalted butter, plus a knob to finish
1 shallot, finely sliced
1 small carrot, finely sliced
½ celery stick, finely sliced
½ garlic clove, crushed
1 bay leaf
sprig of fresh thyme
dash of olive oil
200ml (7fl oz) red wine
300ml (10fl oz) chicken stock
1 tbsp redcurrant jelly

Beef Wellington with red wine gravy

A deserved classic, served with rosemary-roasted new potatoes and asparagus

Prep time 1 hour, plus
overnight chilling
Cooking time 40 minutes
Difficulty Medium–hard

MAINS • BEEF WELLINGTON WITH RED WINE GRAVY

For the puff pastry
450g (1lb) strong plain flour
pinch of salt
225g (8oz) hard margarine,
  diced
225g (8oz) lard, diced
squeeze of lemon juice
275ml (9fl oz) iced water

For the Wellington
375g (13oz) organic beef fillet
olive oil
3 large shallots, chopped
10 chestnut mushrooms,
  chopped
60g (2oz) soft brown
  breadcrumbs
2½ glasses of red wine
600ml (1 pint) beef stock
1 tsp cornflour
1 tsp wholegrain mustard
1 egg, beaten
salt and freshly ground
  black pepper

For the vegetables
20 new potatoes
olive oil
1 small bunch of fresh
  rosemary, chopped
6 fresh asparagus spears,
  trimmed

1 To make the pastry, sift the flour and salt into a bowl. Add the margarine and lard and pour in the lemon juice. Gradually add up to 275ml (9fl oz) iced water little by little, making cuts across the mixture with a palette knife and turning the bowl all the time, until it forms a dough. Put in the refrigerator to chill for 30 minutes.

2 Remove the pastry and roll into a rectangle on a floured work surface. Fold one of the short sides a third of the way over the rectangle, then fold in the other short side to cover. Press together the edges with the rolling pin. Chill again.

3 Repeat this rolling, folding and chilling four times, then replace the pastry in the refrigerator and leave overnight.

4 Season the beef fillet. Heat a little oil in a large frying pan over a high heat, then seal the meat on all sides. Remove from the pan and set aside, reserving the fat.

5 Tip the shallots and mushrooms into the same pan and fry until soft. Add the breadcrumbs and fry for another 30 seconds, then pour in 1 glass of the wine. Transfer to a bowl. Preheat the oven to 200°C (400°F/Gas 6).

6 To make the gravy, pour the stock into a pan set over a high heat, bring to the boil, add the remaining red wine and reduce by half. In a bowl, mix the cornflour with just enough water to make a smooth paste, then add this to the gravy, stirring, until it has thickened enough to coat the back of a spoon. Set aside.

7 On a floured work surface, roll out a third of the pastry to the size of the beef and spread it with the mustard.

8 Place the beef on top of the mustard-coated pastry and cover the beef all over with the shallot and mushroom mixture.

9 Roll out another piece of pastry big enough to cover the fillet. Place it over the fillet to make a parcel, sealing the edges carefully and brush the pastry with the egg.

10 Place the Wellington on a baking tray and cook in the oven for 15–20 minutes until the pastry is golden and cooked through.

continued...

...continued from p.138

11 Meanwhile, bring a saucepan of water to the boil, add the potatoes and cook for 10 minutes.

12 At the same time, heat a little oil in an ovenproof dish. Add the cooked potatoes to the dish and return the dish to the oven for 6 minutes.

13 Sprinkle the rosemary over the potatoes and roast for a further 10 minutes.

14 Bring a saucepan of water to the boil and plunge in the asparagus for 3 minutes, then drain.

15 Gently reheat the gravy and serve slices of the Wellington on the 4 warm plates with the potatoes, asparagus and red wine gravy.

"Beef is perfect. Absolutely excellent. Mushrooms gorgeous... Pastry brilliant on top. Overall, it's a pretty fab-o dish."

— Jilly Goolden

Chipole pudding with oxtail gravy

This rich suet pudding takes its name from an old country term for spring onions

1 Preheat the oven to 190°C (375°F/Gas 5). Season the oxtail, put in a baking tray with the onions and roast for 1 hour or until nicely browned and it has given up its juices. Take the meat off the bones. Let the juices in the bottom of the pan cool, then skim off and discard the fat. Simmer the bones with the juices and enough cold water to cover in a saucepan over a low heat for 1 hour, then strain, add the ale and simmer until the liquid has reduced to a tasty gravy. Set aside.

2 To make the pastry, mix the chipole (spring) onions in a bowl with the flour and suet. Add the egg and thyme and gradually mix in enough iced water to make a firm dough. Divide into four and roll out each piece on a floured work surface until about 1cm (½in) thick.

3 Make the filling by mixing the beef and chipole onions. Season with salt and black pepper and form the mixture into 4 balls.

4 Lay 4 pudding cloths on a clean surface and line each cloth with greaseproof paper. Place each piece of pastry on the paper and heap a ball of the meat mixture into the middle. Gather the pastry and cloth up to cover the meat and, before closing, use a funnel to pour some of the gravy into the pudding. Close the hole and tie the cloth as tightly as possible with kitchen string.

5 Put the puddings in a large pan of boiling water over a medium heat, making sure that the water comes no further than three quarters of the way up the sides of the puddings and maintain a rolling boil for 1 hour. Watch the water level and top up with boiling water if needed.

6 Meanwhile, boil the potatoes with a sprig of mint for 15 minutes. Drain and keep warm. Sprinkle a little rosemary over the baby carrots and steam them for about 15 minutes or until tender. Drain and mix with the butter and orange zest. Plunge the broccoli into boiling water for 3–5 minutes.

7 To serve, place a pudding on each of 4 warm plates with the vegetables and lashings of roast oxtail gravy.

Prep time 1 hour
Cooking time 3¾ hours
Difficulty Medium

For the gravy
1 oxtail
3 or 4 onions, chopped
150ml (5fl oz) real ale, preferably Teignworthy High Tide
salt and freshly ground black pepper

For the suet pastry
125g (4½oz) chipole (spring) onions, chopped
500g (1lb 2oz) self-raising flour
250g (9oz) shredded vegetable suet
1 egg yolk
1 tsp chopped fresh thyme

For the filling
500g (1lb 2oz) of Holberton beef mince
250g (9oz) chipole onions, chopped
600ml (1 pint) roast oxtail gravy (see above)
salt and black pepper

For the vegetables
340g (12oz) new potatoes
sprig of fresh mint
sprig of fresh rosemary
12–16 baby carrots
knob of butter
grated zest of 1 orange
2 heads of broccoli, broken into florets

Wild Norfolk venison Nelson

A luxurious dish with chicken liver pâté and home-made Cumberland sauce

Prep time 40 minutes, plus overnight marinating
Cooking time 50 minutes
Difficulty Medium–hard

For the venison
250ml (8fl oz) tawny port
1 tsp juniper berries, crushed
1 tsp peppercorns, crushed
1 bay leaf
pinch of salt
2 sprigs of fresh rosemary
4 sprigs of fresh thyme
4 sprigs of fresh parsley
500g (1lb 2oz) loin of venison
vegetable oil

For the puff pastry
200g (7oz) unsalted butter
225g (8oz) plain flour
pinch of salt
juice of ½ lemon
1 egg, beaten

For the pâté
125g (4½oz) butter
1 onion, finely chopped
1 garlic clove, crushed
300g (10oz) free-range chicken livers, chopped
1 small glass of port
60g (2oz) mushrooms, sliced
salt and black pepper

For the vegetables
450g (1lb) new potatoes
1 head of broccoli, in florets

For the Cumberland sauce
50g (1¾oz) unsalted butter
1 shallot, finely chopped
zest and juice of 2 oranges
zest and juice of 1 lemon
2 tbsp redcurrant jelly
½ tsp mustard powder
2.5cm (1in) piece of fresh ginger root, finely chopped
pinch of cayenne pepper

1 Put all the ingredients for the venison, except the meat, in a large bowl. Stir, add the meat, cover and leave to marinate in the refrigerator for up to 24 hours.

2 Make the pastry the night before. Put the butter in the freezer for an hour. Sift the flour and a pinch of salt into a large bowl, then coarsely grate in the firm butter. Add the lemon juice and just enough iced water, little by little, to make a dryish dough. Wrap in cling film and chill overnight.

3 Roll out the pastry until it is 5mm (¼in) thick and big enough to wrap the venison. Return to the refrigerator to rest until needed.

4 To make the pâté, melt half the butter in a saucepan over a low heat, tip in the onion and garlic and gently sweat, stirring, for 10 minutes, then add the livers. Season and add the port and wild mushrooms. Simmer for 4 minutes, then remove from the heat, and leave to cool. Pour into a blender, add the remaining butter and blend to a purée. Set aside in the refrigerator until needed.

5 Remove the venison from the marinade (reserve the marinade) and dab dry with kitchen paper. Place a frying pan over a high heat and add a little vegetable oil. When very hot, flash-fry the venison for a few seconds, turning, then reduce the heat to medium and continue to cook for 5 minutes. Set aside to cool.

6 Make the Cumberland sauce. Melt the butter in a saucepan over a medium heat, add the shallots and sweat for 5 minutes until soft but not coloured. Add the lemon and orange zests and juices, the redcurrant jelly, mustard, ginger and cayenne. Reduce the sauce for 5 minutes, then add the reserved marinade and simmer until reduced to the consistency you prefer.

7 Preheat the oven to 220°C (425°F/Gas 7).

8 Remove the pastry from the refrigerator and spread the middle generously with half the chicken liver pâté. Place the venison on top, then spread the remaining pâté over the meat.

9 Brush the edges of the pastry with beaten egg, then draw the sides of the pastry over the venison, sealing well to make a parcel.

10 Decorate the Nelson with leftover pastry trimmings.

11 Cook the Nelson in the oven for 20 minutes until the pastry is cooked through, then remove and leave to rest for 10 minutes.

12 While the Nelson is resting, steam the vegetables over a saucepan of boiling water until tender.

13 To serve, put 2 slices of the venison onto each of 4 warm plates. Add the vegetables and drizzle with Cumberland sauce.

Craster smoked fish pie

A fabulous dish that harnesses the gorgeous flavours of smoked fish

Prep time 10 minutes
Cooking time 1 hour
20 minutes
Difficulty Medium

For the filling
300g (10oz) salmon fillet
300g (10oz) natural smoked
　Craster haddock
360ml (12fl oz) milk
3 large free-range eggs
350g (12oz) peeled and
　de-veined cooked prawns
300g (10oz) smoked salmon
　fillet, cut into chunks

For the topping
600g (1lb 5oz) Desiree
　potatoes, peeled
　and quartered
50g (1¾oz) butter
50ml (1¾fl oz) milk
50g (1¾oz) breadcrumbs
salt and white pepper

For the cheese sauce
50g (1¾oz) butter
½ leek, chopped
1 celery stick, chopped
50g (1¾oz) plain flour
200ml (7fl oz) white wine
150ml (5fl oz) double cream
sprig of fresh tarragon, plus
　extra 1 tbsp, chopped
sprig of fresh flat-leaf parsley,
　plus extra 2 tbsp, chopped
1 tsp Dijon mustard
150g (5½oz) Cuddy's Cave
　cheese, grated

For the salad
75ml (2½fl oz) avocado oil
2 tbsp white balsamic
　vinegar
freshly squeezed lemon
　juice, to taste
1 x 110g bag of spinach,
　watercress and rocket

1 Put the fresh salmon and smoked haddock in a wide sauté pan, add the milk and poach over a gentle heat for 10 minutes. Leave to cool, then sieve. Set the poaching milk aside in the refrigerator.

2 Flake the fish into large pieces with your hands, being careful not to break it up too much. Put in the refrigerator until needed.

3 Bring a saucepan of water to the boil over a high heat, add the eggs and boil for 8 minutes. Drain, shell the eggs, cut into quarters and set aside. Do not boil the eggs for any longer than this, or they will dry out in the pie. It is best if the yolks remain slightly moist and soft.

4 For the topping, bring a large saucepan of water to the boil over a high heat, add the potatoes and cook for 15 minutes or until tender.

5 Drain the potatoes, mash them with the butter and milk, then season with salt and white pepper.

6 To make the cheese sauce, melt the butter in a saucepan over a medium heat and tip in the leek and celery. Cook, stirring, for 5 minutes, or until soft but not coloured.

7 Add the flour and cook, stirring, for 3 minutes, then slowly add the fish poaching milk, stirring constantly to prevent lumps, until you have a sauce with a creamy consistency.

8 Stir in a little of both the wine and cream, the whole and chopped tarragon, whole and chopped parsley and the mustard. Heat very gently, adding more wine and cream to taste, until you achieve a silky-textured sauce that is thick enough to coat the back of a spoon.

9 Remove from the heat, add 100g (3½oz) of the cheese and stir until melted. Discard the herb stalks and set aside until needed.

10 Preheat the oven to 180°C (350°F/Gas 4). Put the cooked fish and prawns in an ovenproof dish. Carefully arrange the smoked salmon and eggs in a layer over the top, being careful not to break up the eggs, as they are best kept in quarters.

continued...

...continued from p.144

11 Pour over the cheese sauce and carefully lay the mashed potatoes on top. Sprinkle with the remaining cheese and the breadcrumbs, making sure that they are evenly spread over the top of the pie.

12 Bake in the oven for 20–25 minutes until golden and bubbling, then remove from the oven and leave to rest for 5–10 minutes.

13 Meanwhile, pour the avocado oil into a small bowl and whisk in the balsamic vinegar and a little lemon juice. Season with salt and black pepper, adding more lemon to taste, and toss with the salad leaves.

14 Serve the fish pie on 4 warm plates, with the salad alongside.

"The thing I like about this pie is that it has lots of fish in there, bound with a little bit of sauce. That's lovely."
— Ed Baines

Toad in the hole

A fantastic take on a classic, served with mustard mash

1 To make the batter, mix together the flour, eggs and milk until they form a smooth batter. Add a little water if needed, season with salt and black pepper, then allow to stand at room temperature for 30 minutes.

2 Preheat the oven to 220°C (425°F/Gas 7).

3 Skin the sausages and wrap each in smoked streaky bacon.

4 Pour 1 tbsp rapeseed oil into each of 4 individual ovenproof serving dishes and heat in the oven for 10 minutes. Remove the dishes from the oven and pour in the batter. Place 2 sausages in each, return to the oven and cook for 30 minutes.

5 To make the gravy, melt the butter in a frying pan over a low heat, add the onions, cover and sweat until soft. Add the flour and cook, stirring, for 2–3 minutes, then add the stock, Worcestershire sauce and ale and stir. Set aside.

6 Boil the potatoes in a large pan of salted water for 10 minutes or until tender; drain. Mash with the milk, butter and mustard.

7 Set up a steamer over a high heat, add the asparagus and cabbage and steam for 5 minutes.

8 Serve a dish of toad in the hole on each of 4 warm plates with the mash and vegetables and offer a jug of gravy on the side.

Prep time **10 minutes**
Cooking time **1 hour 40 minutes**
Difficulty **Medium**

For the batter
150g (5oz) plain flour
2 large free-range eggs
150ml (5fl oz) milk
salt and freshly ground
  black pepper

**For the toad
in the hole**
8 pork sausages
8 thin-cut oak-smoked
  streaky bacon rashers
4 tbsp rapeseed oil

For the gravy
160g (5¾oz) salted butter
4 red onions, chopped
2 tbsp plain flour
360ml (12fl oz) good quality
  beef stock
splash of Worcestershire
  sauce
splash of Hobsons Postman's
  Knock real ale

For the vegetables
4 medium potatoes, peeled
  and cut into chunks
splash of milk
large knob of butter
2 tbsp wholegrain mustard
  with malt whisky
2 bunches of fresh
  asparagus, trimmed
½ red cabbage, shredded

Sussex partridge with berry stuffing

Arguably the best game bird of the lot, here served with sticky roast vegetables

Prep time 45 minutesr
Cooking time 1 hour, plus
20 minutes' resting
Difficulty Medium

For the stuffing
4 slices white bread
1 apple
3 Medjool dates, stoned
    and roughly chopped
1 tbsp olive oil
1 red onion, finely sliced
grated zest of 1 lemon
100g (3½oz) mixed dried
    berries
large handful of chopped
    sage, thyme and parsley
½ tsp cayenne pepper
pinch of ground cinnamon
splash of apple juice

For the bread sauce
450ml (15fl oz) milk
1 small onion
4 whole cloves
85–110g (3–4oz) fresh
    white breadcrumbs
freshly grated nutmeg,
    to taste
pinch of cayenne pepper
2 tbsp double cream
salt

For the potatoes
2kg (4½lb) potatoes, peeled
    and cut into chunks
350g jar goose fat
large handful of chopped
    rosemary
salt and black pepper

For the partridge
4 oven-ready Sussex
    partridges
4 garlic cloves, slightly
    crushed with a knife
large handful of fresh thyme
8 streaky bacon rashers
olive oil

1 Preheat the oven to 200°C (400°F/Gas 6). Make the stuffing. Toast the bread, then whizz it in a food processor to a fine crumb. Put in a bowl. Core and grate the apple (leave the skin on) into the bowl and add the dates.

2 Pour the oil into a small frying pan over a medium heat, tip in the onion and fry until just brown on the edges. Add to the bowl with all the other stuffing ingredients and mix. Form into 4 flattened balls each the size of a tangerine. Put in a non-stick baking tray and bake in the oven for 20–25 minutes until lightly browned.

3 To make the bread sauce, pour the milk into a heavy pan. Stud the onion with the cloves and place in the milk. Over a low heat, bring very slowly to the boil, then remove the onion and stir in enough breadcrumbs to make a thick sauce. Season with nutmeg, a pinch of cayenne and salt to taste. Stir in the cream and set aside.

4 For the potatoes, bring a large saucepan of salted water to the boil, add the potatoes and par-boil for 8–10 minutes. Drain and leave in the colander to steam dry. Put the goose fat in a baking tray and warm in the oven until melted. Carefully put the potatoes in the goose fat and toss liberally. Season with salt and black pepper and sprinkle over the rosemary. Roast in the oven for 30–40 minutes until golden, turning occasionally.

5 Turn to the partridge. Stuff each bird with 1 garlic clove and some thyme and place in a large roasting dish, breast-side up. Cover each bird neatly with 2 bacon rashers. Season and drizzle with olive oil. Roast in the oven for 18–20 minutes, then remove and reserve the juices and bacon. Rest the birds on a warm plate, breast-side down and wrapped in foil, for about 25 minutes.

6 Meanwhile, make the gravy. Melt the butter in a large saucepan, add the shallots and fry gently until softened. Add the reserved bacon and fry for a minute, then add the partridge juices, the stock and thyme. Bring to the boil, reduce the heat and cook for 10 minutes, stirring. Strain through a fine sieve, return to the saucepan and reduce the heat. Mix the cornflour with enough water to make a paste, then add this to the gravy. Cook until thick enough to coat the back of a spoon. Set aside and keep warm.

7 Put the parsnips in a large non-stick roasting tin. Pour over the olive oil and use your hands to toss the batons until liberally coated in the oil. Sprinkle over the turmeric and use a spoon to mix until well coated. Drizzle over the honey and roast in the oven for 20–30 minutes until slightly blackened and very sticky, stirring halfway through cooking.

8 Drop the carrots in a saucepan of water and bring to the boil. Simmer for 10 minutes, then refresh in cold water. Melt the butter in a saucepan, add the carrots, sugar, orange zest and juice, ground cinnamon and cinnamon stick. Stir over a high heat until the carrots are coated in a sticky glaze and caramelized.

9 Boil the beans for about 3 minutes, refresh in cold water to halt the cooking process and drain. Melt the butter in a pan until foaming. Add the mustard seeds and fry until they start to pop, then stir through the beans and chilli flakes and heat through.

10 Place a stuffing ball on each of 4 warm plates and perch a partridge on top. Arrange the vegetables on each plate, and serve the gravy in a jug on the side.

For the gravy
knob of unsalted butter
3 shallots, finely chopped
500ml (16fl oz) fresh chicken
  stock
1 tbsp chopped thyme
  leaves
2 tsp cornflour

For the parsnips
4 parsnips, cut in batons
2–3 tbsp olive oil
2 tsp ground turmeric
2–3 tbsp clear honey

For the carrots
500g (1lb 2oz) Chantenay
  carrots
knob of unsalted butter
2–3 tbsp soft light brown
  sugar
grated zest and juice
  of 1 large orange
1 tsp ground cinnamon
1 cinnamon stick

For the beans
handful of fine French beans
knob of butter
pinch of black mustard seeds
pinch of red chilli flakes

149

MAINS • SUSSEX PARTRIDGE WITH BERRY STUFFING

Prep time 15–20 minutes
Cooking time 1 hour
40 minutes
Difficulty Medium

For the bread sauce
600ml (1 pint) whole milk
1 large onion, peeled
4 bay leaves
10 whole cloves
pinch of black peppercorns
115g (4oz) fresh white
   breadcrumbs
50g (1¾oz) butter
4 tbsp double cream

For the cranberry sauce
150g (5oz) cranberries
2 clementines
100g (3½oz) caster sugar
2 tbsp port

For the roast potatoes
4 large potatoes
2 tbsp goose fat

For the gravy
olive oil
a few turkey bones
1 rasher streaky bacon, sliced
2 shallots, chopped
2 large garlic cloves, sliced
1 celery stick, sliced
5 baby carrots, chopped
500ml (16fl oz) good red wine
3 tbsp port
1 litre (1¾ pints) best-quality
   fresh chicken stock
knob of butter
salt and black pepper

For the roast turkey
1 turkey leg
1 turkey breast
olive oil
knob of butter
4 good-quality streaky
   bacon rashers

Contemporary Christmas lunch

A new take on the ultimate festive meal, complete with all the trimmings

1 Preheat the oven to 180°C (350°F/Gas 4).

2 To make the bread sauce, pour the milk into a saucepan and place over a low heat. Cut the onion in half and fix bay leaves to it, using the cloves. Add it to the milk, along with the peppercorns. Bring the milk to the boil and simmer for a few minutes. Remove from the heat, cover with a lid and leave to infuse for 30 minutes, then strain into a bowl and set the contents of the sieve aside. Place the saucepan back over a low heat and add the breadcrumbs, stirring, until they have absorbed all the milk. Add half the butter, mix well and cook very gently for 15 minutes, stirring occasionally. Remove from the heat, return the onions and spices from the sieve to the sauce, cover and set aside.

3 For the cranberry sauce, put the berries in a saucepan. Add the juice, pulp and a little zest from the clementines with half the sugar. Stir well and taste, adding more sugar if needed. Bring to a simmer over a low heat. Cover and simmer for 10–15 minutes until the cranberries are soft and splitting, stirring now and then. Remove from the heat, add the port, cover and set aside.

4 To make the roast potatoes, bring a large saucepan of salted water to the boil over a medium heat. Peel the potatoes and cut into large chunks. Add them to the water and boil for 6–8 minutes. Meanwhile, put the goose fat in a heavy oven tray and place it in the oven. Drain the potatoes very well and shake in the pan to rough up the edges. Remove the tray of fat from the oven, place over a medium heat and add the potatoes. Colour the potatoes on each side, then roast in the oven for 25 minutes, turning once.

5 To make the gravy, add a little olive oil to a frying pan over a medium-high heat. When hot, add the turkey bones and begin to brown. Add the bacon and fry gently for 1–2 minutes. Add the shallots, garlic, celery and carrots and season with salt and black pepper. Once the ingredients are all browned, pour in the red wine and port and reduce by half. Add the chicken stock and reduce by half again. Pass this sauce through a fine sieve and into a saucepan. Cover and set aside.

6 Season the turkey pieces well. Place a large ovenproof frying pan over a medium heat and, when hot, add a little oil and the turkey, skin-side down. Colour on all sides, adding the butter, then roast in the oven for 25–30 minutes. Remove, cover and leave to rest. Lay the bacon on a baking sheet. Cover with another sheet to prevent curling and cook in the oven for 5–10 minutes until crisp.

7 To make the parsnip crisps, using a vegetable peeler, peel thin slices from the parsnip. Brush lightly with olive oil, butter and honey and curl each slice around a cocktail stick. Roast in the oven for 10 minutes or until crisp. Carefully remove the cocktail sticks.

8 To make the stuffing, put all the ingredients, except the oil and butter, in a large bowl and mix well. Form into a ball, then flatten into two discs 10–12cm (4–5in) in diameter and 1cm (½in) thick. Put the oil and butter in a frying pan over a medium heat, add the discs to colour, then cook in the oven in a baking tray for 10 minutes.

9 To make the glazed carrots, bring a saucepan of water to the boil, add the carrots and simmer for 5 minutes. Plunge immediately into iced water, to prevent further cooking and retain the colour. Put in a small frying pan with a drop of water, the honey and a knob of butter and place over a very low heat, stirring, to glaze.

10 To make the cabbage, bring a saucepan of salted water to the boil, add the cabbage and simmer for 5–6 minutes until just cooked. Strain, return to the pan and add a knob of butter.

11 Remove the onions and spices once more from the bread sauce, add the remaining butter and the cream and warm through. Gently warm the cranberry sauce. Add the juices from the cooked turkey to the gravy, reheat gently and whisk in a knob of butter.

12 To serve, arrange the roast potatoes and carrots on opposite sides of 2 warm plates. Put a circle of Savoy cabbage in the middle. Carve the turkey leg and place slices on top of the cabbage, sit the stuffing disc on these, then arrange slices of turkey breast on top. Scatter parsnip crisps over the carrots. Put the crispy bacon on top of the turkey stack and pour over the gravy. Happy Christmas!

For the parsnip crisps
1 large parsnip
olive oil
knob of butter
1 tsp honey

For the stuffing
20g (¾oz) good-quality
  sausagemeat
1 shallot, finely chopped
handful of fresh thyme leaves
handful of fresh parsley,
  chopped
grated zest of 1 lemon, plus
  a squeeze of lemon juice
60g (2oz) fresh white
  breadcrumbs
1 egg, beaten
pinch of paprika
olive oil
knob of butter

For the carrots
3 or 4 Chantenay carrots
1 tsp clear honey
knob of butter

For the cabbage
1 Savoy cabbage, shredded
knob of butter

Desserts

Sweet perfection

When it comes to impressing guests and delighting the family, nothing beats a good pudding. The desserts featured in this chapter run the gamut from hearty traditional puds, such as Cloutie Dumpling, to sophisticated classics like Frangipane and Tarte Tatin, to more contemporary creations with fusion elements, such as a Chocolate Chilli Cheesecake.

Other recipes promise to dazzle diners with their demonstration of expert culinary techniques, such as a Cranachan Panna Cotta filled with raspberry sauce and served with oatmeal tuiles, or the Trio of Lavender Desserts that features cake, crème brulée and ice cream. And some are deliciously unusual, such as the Christmas Tree and Lime Granita, or the Trio of Scottish Profiteroles, which combines French pastry with the best of Scottish ingredients.

However, all this does not mean that old favourites are neglected. Plenty of the puddings in this chapter remain firmly rooted in

traditional home cooking. Canary Pudding with Home-Made Custard hails from the classic, homely British tradition of steamed puddings. And there is the meticulously made Traditional Apple Pie – the "Rolls-Royce of apple pies", according to John Burton Race. Its unusual pastry, made with lard, margarine and soured milk, is a triumph of flavour and texture. Indeed, some of the most successful recipes are surprisingly simple – Apple Crump could not be easier to make, but it is mouth-wateringly moreish. All three are tastebud-perfect renditions that bring new life to tried-and-tested classics.

And as always, Great British ingredients play a strong part – no chapter on British puddings would be complete without summer fruit recipes, such as Strawberry and Lime Hazelnut Stack, or the exquisite Summer Pudding. And naturally there is also plenty of chocolate, for those who feel a pudding is not a pudding without it.

Strawberry and lime hazelnut stack

Hazelnuts, strawberries and lime meld in a moreish blend of textures and flavours

Prep time 15 minutes
Cooking time 30 minutes
Difficulty Easy

For the stacks
175g (6oz) hazelnuts, plus
  30g (1oz) extra, to garnish
175g (6oz) strong white flour
175g (6oz) caster sugar
175g (6oz) butter
250ml (8fl oz) extra thick
  double cream
250ml (8fl oz) crème fraîche
500g (1lb 2oz) strawberries,
  hulled and sliced

For the lime glaze
300g (10oz) caster sugar
grated zest and juice of
  3 limes

1 Preheat the oven to 180°C (350°F/Gas 4).

2 Grind the 175g (6oz) hazelnuts in a blender or food processor until fine. Transfer to a bowl with the flour, sugar and butter and mix together.

3 Line a baking sheet with baking parchment and arrange four 10cm (4in) metal food rings on top. Press the hazelnut mixture evenly into the bottom of each ring to make the biscuits for your stack. (If you want to use 2 biscuits in your stack, make 8 biscuits about 1cm (½in) thick; if you are using 1 biscuit only at the bottom of the stack, you can make them slightly thicker.) Bake in the oven for 15–20 minutes until light golden brown.

4 Meanwhile, to make the lime glaze, gently heat together the sugar and lime zest and juice in a pan for 10 minutes until the sugar has dissolved. Leave to cool.

5 Spread the extra hazelnuts over a baking sheet and toast under a hot grill until golden brown, turning them frequently. Put the hazelnuts in a clean tea towel and rub off the skins. Roughly chop.

6 In a bowl, whisk together the double cream and crème fraîche until thick. Spread a little of the cream mixture over the hazelnut bases, then top with a layer of strawberries, followed by a layer of lime glaze. (If you are using 2 hazelnuts biscuits in your stack, align a biscuit on top of the cream at this point.) Finish with a layer of cream, a layer of strawberries and a layer of lime glaze. Sprinkle the chopped hazelnuts over the top and serve.

Prep time 20 minutes, plus
2 days' to set and churning
time for the ice cream
Cooking time 25 minutes
Difficulty Easy

For the summer pudding
200g (7oz) blackcurrants
200g (7oz) redcurrants
200g (7oz) fresh raspberries
200g (7oz) strawberries
200g (7oz) blueberries
200g (7oz) fresh gooseberries
about 2 tbsp caster sugar,
   to taste depending on
   the acidity of the fruit
about 300ml (10fl oz) crème
   de cassis
1 loaf slightly stale white
   bread

For the vanilla and Cognac ice cream
1.2 litres (2 pints) double
   cream
2 vanilla pods, split
   lengthways
splash of Cognac
4 large egg yolks
150g (5½oz) muscovado or
   other soft light brown sugar
100g (3½oz) sugar

Summer pudding with crème de cassis

Quintessentially summer, this classic oozes soft fruits laced with blackcurrant liqueur

1 Put all the fruit in a large pan with a little sugar to taste and a hearty glug of crème de cassis. Cook gently over a low heat for 2 minutes until the currants have burst and released their juice. Allow to cool and add more cassis to taste.

2 Slice the bread thinly and remove the crusts. Line a large pudding basin or glass or ceramic bowl with the bread slices.

3 Strain the fruit slightly and reserve the extra syrupy juice in a jug.

4 Spoon the fruit into the bread-lined basin or bowl and cover with more bread. Cover with a plate and place a heavy weight on top to compact the fruit; leave in the refrigerator for 2 days to set and soak up all the liquid. Top up with more cassis or juice syrup as needed and leave to be absorbed. Turn out the pudding onto a serving plate and drizzle extra sauce over any white patches.

5 To make the custard base for the ice cream, scald the cream with the vanilla pods in a pan, then allow to cool.

6 Using a teaspoon, scrape out the vanilla seeds into the hot cream mixture and discard the pods. Add a splash of Cognac, and stir through. Using an electric mixer, beat the egg yolks until smooth and mousse-like.

7 In a clean pan, mix together the sugars and 150ml (5fl oz) water. Bring to the boil and, once the sugar has dissolved completely, simmer for 2–3 minutes until thickened slightly, then remove from the heat. Allow to cool for 1 minute.

8 Slowly pour the sugar syrup into the egg yolk mixture, beating all the time. Now add the cream mixture and beat until the mixture is smooth and custard-like.

9 Transfer to an ice-cream machine and churn according to the manufacturer's instructions for 20 minutes or until frozen.

10 To serve, turn out the summer pudding onto a serving plate. Cut into slices and serve with a scoop of the vanilla and Cognac ice cream on the side.

Canary pudding and home-made custard

A very traditional and wonderfully light steamed pudding that is nigh irresistible

1 Grease a pudding basin.

2 In a bowl, cream together the butter and sugar until very light and fluffy. Add the eggs, one at a time, beating well after each addition until thoroughly combined.

3 Sift in the flour and baking powder and fold through gently, adding sufficient milk to give the mixture a dropping consistency.

4 Pour the mixture into the prepared pudding basin and cover with greaseproof paper with a pleat across the middle. Tie down the paper with string and steam for 1 hour.

5 To make the custard, whisk together the egg, sugar and cornflour. Heat the milk in a saucepan to just below boiling point.

6 Pour the milk into the egg mixture, whisking all the time, then return the mixture to the pan and cook gently for about a minute until thickened, stirring continuously.

7 Turn out the pudding into a deep dish or plate. Pour a generous helping of golden syrup over the top and serve warm with a jug of custard on the side for pouring over.

Prep time **15 minutes**
Cooking time **1 hour**
Difficulty **Easy**

For the canary pudding
50g (1¾oz) butter
75g (2½oz) caster sugar
2 eggs
100g (3½oz) plain flour
1 tsp baking powder
2 tbsp whole milk

For the home-made custard
1 egg
1 tbsp caster sugar
1 tsp cornflour
300ml (10fl oz) whole milk

1 small tin golden syrup, to serve

"It's delightful. It's delicious. It really is one of those great British puds."

— John Burton Race

Bramley apple crump

A cross between a crumble and a pudding, its simplicity belies the sublime results

Prep time **15 minutes**
Cooking time **1 hour**
Difficulty **Easy**

For the crump
4 heaped tbsp organic
   plain flour
100g (3½oz) white
   granulated sugar
100g (3½oz) butter
   (at room temperature)
450g (1lb) Bramley apples

**For the vanilla
custard**
300ml (10fl oz) whole milk
2 tbsp single cream
1 vanilla pod, split
   lengthways
1 tbsp soft light brown sugar
1 tsp cornflour
2 egg yolks, at room
   temperature

1 Preheat the oven to 160°C (325°F/Gas 3).

2 To make the crump topping, put the flour in an ovenproof bowl and add the sugar and butter. Transfer the bowl to the oven for 10–15 minutes until the butter has melted.

3 Meanwhile, for the filling, peel, core and slice the apples. Place in another ovenproof dish and put in the oven for 5 minutes.

4 Remove the crump mixture from the oven and stir together the ingredients. Spread over the part-cooked apples and bake in the oven for 40 minutes until golden.

5 To make the custard, put the milk, cream and vanilla pod in a small pan and bring to the boil. Remove from the heat, discard the vanilla pod and add the sugar. Stir for 30 seconds.

6 Add the cornflour to the egg yolks. Whisking the egg yolk mixture continuously, slowly add the milk and cream mixture.

7 Pour the custard into a heatproof bowl, place over a pan of simmering water and stir with a wooden spoon until the custard has thickened and coats the back of the spoon. Remove from the heat and pour into a serving jug.

8 Serve spoonfuls of the apple crump in bowls, with the custard poured over the top.

"It is like a butter biscuit –
a very, very rich, rustic butter
biscuit – with beautiful apple.
And the custard's fantastic."
— Ed Baines

Lincolnshire carrot pudding

Lighter than Christmas pud, this steamed pudding is no less flavoursome

1 Put the currants and raisins in a small bowl and pour over the cider. Add the grated ginger and leave to soak overnight.

2 The next day, sift together the flour, bicarbonate of soda, and mixed spice. Stir through to make sure that they are well combined. Add all the other ingredients except the egg and mix everything together thoroughly. Lastly, mix in the egg.

3 Divide the mixture among 4 well-greased small pudding basins, leaving space at the top to allow the mixture to expand during cooking. Cover each basin with a double layer of greaseproof paper with a pleat running across the middle and tie in place with kitchen string. Steam for 1½ hours.

4 To make the custard, heat the cream, vanilla pod and scraped-out seeds in a saucepan over a medium heat for 5–10 minutes. Remove from the heat, discard the vanilla pod and leave to stand for 20 minutes.

5 In a separate bowl, whisk together the egg yolks and caster sugar until pale and fluffy. Return the cream mixture to a low–medium heat and slowly whisk in the egg yolk mixture. Continue whisking over a medium-low heat for 10 minutes until the custard has thickened. Serve hot with slices of the steamed carrot pudding.

Prep time 10 minutes, plus overnight soaking
Cooking time 1½ hours
Difficulty Easy–medium

For the pudding
70g (2½oz) currants
70g (2½oz) raisins
150ml (5fl oz) cider
½cm (¼in) piece of fresh root ginger, grated
100g (3½oz) plain flour
½ tsp bicarbonate of soda
1 tsp mixed spice
100g (3½oz) suet, shredded
100g (3½oz) potato, grated
100g (3½oz) carrots, grated
100g (3½oz) demerara sugar
100g (3½oz) fine breadcrumbs
25g (scant 1oz) chopped glacé cherries
60g (2oz) apple, grated
1 large egg

For the custard
500ml (16fl oz) single cream
1 vanilla pod, split lengthways
5 egg yolks
1 tbsp caster sugar

Christmas tree and lime granita

This unusual granita, served with mulled wine trifle shooters, makes a festive treat

Prep time 30 minutes, plus several hour's freezing time
Cooking time 15 minutes
Difficulty Easy–medium

For the Christmas tree and lime granita
2 "twigs" from a pine tree, needles picked and rinsed
pared zest and juice of 2 limes
75g (2½oz) caster sugar

For the mulled wine trifle jelly shooters
50g (1¾oz) golden caster sugar
pared zest of 2 lemons
2 plums
1 cinnamon stick
3 star anise
1 heaped tbsp mixed dried fruit
5 whole cloves
375ml (13fl oz) red wine
4 fine leaves gelatine, soaked in cold water for about 10 minutes

For the vanilla custard
142ml (5fl oz) single cream
1 vanilla pod, split lengthways
3 egg yolks
40g (1½oz) caster sugar

For the Space Dust floss
100g (3½oz) white granulated sugar
2 packets Fizz Wiz Space Dust

1 To make the granita, grind the pine needles using a mortar and pestle. In a food processor, blend the lime juice, 250ml (9fl oz) water, sugar, pine needles and some of the lime zest.

2 Strain the liquid through muslin into a bowl, then transfer to a shallow freezerproof container and freeze. After 1 hour's freezing time, scrape the granita with a fork to create the ice crystals. Return to the freezer and repeat until you have the correct grainy texture.

3 To make the jelly shooters, in a small saucepan, heat the sugar, half the pared lemon zest and 150ml (5fl oz) water until the sugar has dissolved. Simmer for 2–3 minutes until thickened slightly.

4 Roughly chop 1 of the plums. Put in a separate saucepan with the cinnamon stick, star anise, mixed dried fruit, cloves, red wine, sugar syrup and the remaining lemon zest. Bring to the boil, then pour into a bowl and allow to cool slightly.

5 Remove the spices from the plum mixture and purée the fruit using a stick blender before passing through a muslin-lined sieve into a bowl. Squeeze out the gelatine and whisk into the puréed plum mixture. Allow to cool.

6 Skin, stone and finely dice the remaining plum. Put a little of the diced plum into the bottom of each of 8 shot glasses, reserving the rest for decorating. Pour over the plum jelly mixture, leaving a space at the top and chill until set (this will take up to 4 hours).

7 To make the custard, heat the cream, vanilla pod and scraped-out vanilla seeds in a saucepan, making sure that it does not boil.

8 In a heatproof bowl, whisk together the egg yolks and sugar, then gradually whisk in the heated cream. Place the bowl over a pan of simmering water and heat gently, stirring constantly until thickened. Remove from the heat and allow to cool.

9 Make the floss using a candy-floss maker according to the instructions. Wrap around a stick with a filling of Space Dust.

10 To serve, pour some of the custard over the jelly shot and top with a little more diced plum. Serve with the granita in 8 separate shot glasses, each with a stick of Space Dust-filled candy floss.

Orange liqueur tart with chocolate sauce

A mouth-watering melding of chilli-spiked pastry, rich chocolate and creamy filling

1 Preheat the oven to 200°C (400°F/Gas 6). Lightly grease a 25cm (10in) deep flan tin and line the bottom with greaseproof paper.

2 To make the pastry, cream together the butter and icing sugar until pale. Using a mortar and pestle, grind the chilli to a paste with a drop of water. Add to the butter and icing sugar mixture. Add the egg and continue mixing until the mixture is pale and light.

3 In a separate bowl, sift together the flour and cocoa powder. Combine with the butter and icing sugar mixture until it only just comes together into a soft, sticky dough. Wrap in cling film and rest in the freezer for 15 minutes, to allow the chilli to infuse.

4 Roll out the pastry onto a lightly floured work surface and gently fit into the prepared tin. Return to the freezer for 15 minutes.

5 Remove the pastry case from the freezer, line with greaseproof paper and baking beans and blind-bake on a tray in the oven for 15 minutes. Remove the beans and paper and glaze the bottom of the pastry case with the beaten egg yolk. Return to the oven for a further 10 minutes until the pastry is cooked and the bottom is dry. Reduce the oven temperature to 180°C (350°F/Gas 4).

6 In the meantime, make the filling. Whisk together the sugar and eggs in a bowl. Slowly stir in the cream, orange liqueur, orange zest and juice and orange essence until thoroughly mixed.

7 Very carefully pour the filling into the pastry case while it is still in the oven, to reduce spillage and bake for about 25 minutes until the filling is set, but still with a slight wobble in the middle. Remove from the oven and allow to cool in the tin.

8 To make the chocolate sauce, put the chocolate in a heatproof bowl. Set the bowl over a pan of simmering water over a low heat. Heat gently, stirring occasionally, until the chocolate has melted. Add the butter and honey, stirring from time to time, until the butter begins to melt. Gradually whisk in the milk to form a smooth sauce and warm through.

9 To serve, remove the tart from the tin, dust the top with icing sugar and serve with the chocolate sauce and fresh raspberries.

Prep time 10 minutes, plus 30 minutes' freezing time
Cooking time 50–55 minutes
Difficulty Medium

For the chilli chocolate pastry
75g (2½oz) unsalted butter
60g (2¼oz) icing sugar
2 fresh red bird's-eye chilies, halved and deseeded
1 egg
100g (3½oz) plain flour
25g (1oz) cocoa powder
1 egg yolk, beaten, for egg wash

For the orange liqueur filling
200g (7oz) caster sugar
4 large free-range eggs
175ml (6fl oz) double cream
50ml (1¾fl oz) orange liqueur such as Cointreau
grated zest of 2 large oranges
125ml (4fl oz) freshly squeezed orange juice
1 tsp natural orange essence

For the chocolate sauce
100g (3½oz) good-quality dark chocolate (at least 70% cocoa solids), broken into small chunks
15g (½oz) unsalted butter, cubed
1 tbsp clear honey
60ml (2fl oz) whole milk

icing sugar, to dust
fresh raspberries, to serve

Creamed rice with red fruit compote

Nursery food grows up in this delectable dessert with fruit compote and crisp tuiles

Prep Time **15 minutes**
Cooking Time **45 minutes**
Difficulty **Easy–medium**

1 To make the tuiles, preheat the oven to 180°C (350°F/Gas 4). Cut out round or triangular tuile shapes from acetate sheets to make stencils. Arrange the tuile templates on a non-stick baking sheet.

2 Cream together the butter and sugar, whisk in the egg white, then fold in the flour. Spread the mixture over each template to make the tuile shapes, then carefully remove to leave the tuiles on the tray. Bake in the oven for 3–5 minutes. Once cooked, remove from the oven and shape while still warm, curving the tuiles over a rolling pin until cooled. Increase the oven temperature to 200°C (400°F/Gas 6).

3 To make the creamed rice, in a large saucepan, heat the double cream, milk, vanilla pods and cinnamon for a couple of minutes. Add the caster sugar, then the rice and butter. Bring to the boil, reduce the heat and simmer gently, uncovered, for 25–30 minutes, stirring frequently, until the rice is creamy and tender, but the grains are still holding their shape. Remove from the heat and discard the vanilla pods. Allow the rice to cool slightly.

4 For the compote, gently mix the rhubarb, orange juice and zest and 500ml (16fl oz) water in an ovenproof dish and roast in the oven for 15 minutes. Turn off the oven and allow the compote to cool slightly.

5 Meanwhile, in a pan, gently heat the raspberries and light brown sugar. Add the roasted rhubarb and stir through.

6 To serve, briefly warm the tuiles in the oven. Pour a layer of rhubarb and raspberry compote into 6–8 glass tumblers and top up with the creamed rice. Serve with the crisp tuiles.

For the tuiles
100g (3½oz) unsalted butter
130g (4½oz) icing sugar
3 egg whites
100g (3½oz) plain flour

For the creamed rice
500ml (16fl oz) double cream
1 litre (1¾ pints) semi-skimmed milk
2 Madagascan vanilla pods, split lengthways
pinch of ground cinnamon
150g (5oz) caster sugar
500g (1lb 2oz) Arborio rice
100g (3½oz) unsalted butter

For the red fruit compote
500g (1lb 2oz) fresh rhubarb, peeled and cut into 2cm (¾in chunks
grated zest and juice of 2 oranges
500g (1lb 2oz) fresh raspberries
250g (9oz) soft light brown sugar

Prep Time 10 minutes
Cooking Time 1 hour
45 minutes
Difficulty Medium

For the ginger parkin
170g (6oz) self-raising flour
4 tsp ground ginger
½ tsp mixed spice
pinch of ground nutmeg
115g (4oz) medium oatmeal
6 heaped tbsp golden syrup
2 tbsp black treacle (the
   combined quantity of syrup
   and black treacle should
   measure 285ml/9fl oz)
170g (6oz) soft dark brown
   sugar
170g (6 oz) unsalted butter
2 medium free-range eggs,
   beaten
1 tbsp whole milk
1 tbsp ginger wine
2 large pieces preserved
   stem ginger, finely chopped

**For the vanilla
custard ice cream**
340ml (11fl oz) whole milk
1 x 284ml (9fl oz) carton
   whipping cream
1 vanilla pod, split
   lengthways
8 large free-range egg yolks
150g (5½ oz) golden caster
   sugar

For the baked rhubarb
3 sticks rhubarb, cut into 5cm
   (2in) pieces
golden caster sugar, to taste

For the ginger syrup
2 tbsp golden syrup
1 tbsp ginger syrup from
   a jar of preserved stem
   ginger
1 tbsp ginger wine

Yorkshire ginger parkin

Moist, treacley, spicy ginger cake served with that other Yorkshire classic: rhubarb

Ginger parkin

1 Preheat the oven to 140°C (275°F/Gas 1). Grease a deep baking tin, about 20cm x 30cm (8in x 12in) and line with baking paper.

2 Sift together the flour and dried spices into a bowl and stir in the oatmeal.

3 Gently heat the golden syrup, black treacle, brown sugar and butter in a small heavy saucepan until the sugar has dissolved. Add to the dry ingredients in the bowl and beat until combined.

4 In a separate bowl, whisk together the eggs and milk and add to the flour and syrup mixture, then add the ginger wine. Stir well. Pour into the prepared cake tin and sprinkle with the chopped stem ginger. Bake in the oven for 1–1¼ hours until firm to the touch in the centre. Remove from the oven and leave to cool in the tin for 15–20 minutes before serving.

5 To serve, cut into squares and serve warm with the vanilla custard ice cream, baked rhubarb and ginger syrup.

Vanilla custard ice cream

1 Put the milk and cream in a saucepan with the vanilla pod, and bring slowly to the boil. Remove from the heat just before it reaches boiling point and set aside to infuse for 15 minutes.

2 Beat together the egg yolks and sugar until thick and creamy.

3 Using a teaspoon, scrape out the seeds from the vanilla pod into the cream and milk mixture. Discard the pod. Pour the milk and cream mixture into the egg yolk mixture, stirring all the time, then return to the pan. Heat gently, stirring constantly with a wooden spoon. Do not allow to boil.

4 When the custard has thickened and coats the back of a spoon, remove the saucepan from the heat and plunge into a bowl of cold water for a few minutes. Set aside for about 30 minutes to cool completely.

5 Pour the cooled custard into an ice-cream machine and churn according to the manufacturer's instructions for 20–25 minutes until frozen. Alternatively, pour into a plastic freezerproof container and place in the freezer. Take out after 2 hours and stir with a whisk. Repeat this freezing–whisking process two more times, then leave until thoroughly frozen.

6 Transfer the ice cream to the refrigerator 20 minutes before serving to allow it to soften.

Baked rhubarb

1 When the ginger parkin is cooked, set aside until ready to serve and increase the oven temperature to 180°C (350°F/Gas 4).

2 Put the rhubarb in a small frying pan with sugar to cover and add a sprinkling of water.

3 Cook until the rhubarb starts to soften, then transfer to an ovenproof dish. Bake in the oven for 10–15 minutes until the rhubarb is soft and tender, but still holding its shape.

4 Serve hot with the warm ginger parkin.

Ginger syrup

1 Combine all ingredients and heat gently in a small saucepan until warm.

2 Serve drizzled over the warm ginger parkin.

"The flavours here are phenomenal. The ginger's absolutely knockout ... It is a very cleverly thought-out pudding and very, very delicious."

— Ed Baines

Frangipane and raspberry tart

Almonds and soft raspberries complement each other divinely in this summery tart

Prep time 20 minutes
Cooking time 50 minutes
Difficulty Medium

For the Amaretto cream
splash of Amaretto liqueur
1 tbsp caster sugar
250g (9oz) mascarpone
  cheese
150ml (5fl oz) soured cream

For the pastry
225g (8oz) plain flour
3 tbsp caster sugar
pinch of Maldon sea salt
170g (6oz) salted butter,
  cut into cubes
1 medium egg

For the filling
2 medium eggs
50g (1¾oz) icing sugar
50g (1¾oz) caster sugar, plus
  a little extra for sprinkling
100g (3½oz) salted butter,
  roughly chopped
100g (3½oz) ground almonds
225g (8oz) ripe English
  raspberries
25g (scant 1oz) flaked
  almonds

1 To make the Amaretto cream, in a bowl, mix together the Amaretto, sugar, mascarpone and soured cream until well combined. Leave to chill in the refrigerator.

2 To make the tart, preheat the oven to 180°C (350°F/Gas 4). Grease a 23cm (9in) tart tin.

3 Sift the flour into a bowl, add 2 tbsp of the caster sugar and the salt and stir through. Using your fingertips, rub in the butter until the mixture resembles breadcrumbs. Add the egg to bind the mixture and form into a ball.

4 On a floured work surface, roll out the pastry and use to line the prepared tart tin. Line the pastry case with greaseproof paper and fill with baking beans. Blind-bake in the oven for 10 minutes, then remove the beans and paper. Return the pastry case to the oven for about 10 minutes until cooked. Do not turn off the oven.

5 To make the filling, using a hand-held blender, mix together the eggs, icing sugar, caster sugar and butter until light and fluffy. Add the ground almonds and stir thoroughly.

6 Pour the filling into the tart case and push in the whole raspberries. Top with the flaked almonds and a sprinkling of caster sugar. Bake in the oven for 30 minutes, than remove and allow to cool in the tin.

7 Serve the tart in wedges with dollops of the Amaretto cream.

Spotted dick with fruit and custard

An old standard receives star treatment
with a fruity filling and liqueur custard

1 To make the fruit filling, peel, core and slice the apples.
Put in a saucepan with the butter, sultanas or currants, raspberries,
marmalade and sugar. Add a splash each of cider and cider vinegar
and cook over a medium heat until caramelized.

2 To make the spotted dick, sift together the flour and baking
powder into a large bowl. Add the shredded suet, sugar, currants
and lemon zest. Add the milk to the dry ingredients and combine
to make the pastry.

3 Grease 4 dariole moulds well with the butter. Press the pastry
into the greased moulds, reserving some for the lids.

4 Fill the moulds with the caramelized fruit filling and top each one
with a pastry lid. Cover the moulds in greaseproof paper, then wrap
in foil and tie with string to secure. Steam the puddings for 50
minutes.

5 To make the custard, gently heat the milk and cream in a pan
until just below boiling point.

6 In a heatproof bowl set over a pan of simmering water, mix
together the egg yolks, sugar and vanilla. Cook, stirring, for
5 minutes, then add the Grand Marnier or other orange liqueur.
Gradually pour the hot cream and milk mixture into the egg
mixture and continue stirring for about 10 minutes until thickened.

7 To serve, turn out each spotted dick onto an individual serving
plate and cut open to allow some of the filling to spill out. Serve
with the custard poured around the sides of each pudding.

Prep time 25 minutes
Cooking time 1 hour
Difficulty Medium

For the fruit filling
2 Pink Lady apples
1 Bramley apple
50g (1¾oz) butter
50g (1¾oz) sultanas or
  dried currants
50g (1¾oz) fresh raspberries
1 x 454g jar good-quality
  orange marmalade
50g (1¾oz) sugar
splash of dry cider
splash of cider vinegar

For the spotted dick
300g (10oz) organic plain
  flour
10g (¼oz) baking powder
150g (5½oz) shredded suet
75g (2½oz) caster sugar
100g (3½oz) dried currants
finely grated zest of 1–2
  lemons
225ml (7½fl oz) whole milk
50g (1¾oz) butter, for
  greasing

For the custard
300ml (10fl oz) whole milk
300ml (10fl oz) double cream
8 egg yolks
150g (5½oz) caster sugar
2 vanilla pods, split
  lengthways
1 glass of Grand Marnier
  or other orange liqueur

**"This is an old British
classic, brought up to date.
Fantastic."**

— John Burton Race

Best of British cupcakes

Sensational cupcakes with seriously delicious toppings

Prep time 30 minutes
Cooking time 1 hour
Difficulty Easy–medium

For the basic vanilla cupcakes

170ml (6fl oz) organic
  soya milk
½ tsp apple cider vinegar
80ml (2½fl oz) rapeseed oil
170ml (6fl oz) agave syrup
2 tsp Nielsen-Massey organic
  vanilla extract
185g (6½oz) self-raising flour
½ tsp bicarbonate of soda
1 tsp baking powder
¼ tsp vanilla sea salt such
  as Halen Môn

For the basic chocolate cupcakes

175ml (6fl oz) organic
  soya milk
1 tsp apple cider vinegar
80ml (2½fl oz) rapeseed oil
180–200g (6–7oz) caster
  sugar
1½ tsp Nielsen-Massey
  organic vanilla extract
1 tsp chocolate essence
  or extract
185g (6½oz) self-raising flour
30g (1oz) cocoa powder
1 tsp bicarbonate of soda
1 tsp baking powder
¼ tsp vanilla sea salt such
  as Halen Môn

For the vegan buttercream icing

50g (1¾oz) pure dairy-free
  soya spread
50g (1¾oz) white vegetable
  fat such as Trex
300g (10oz) icing sugar
splash of soya milk
2 tsp vanilla extract

Basic cupcakes

1 Preheat the oven to 180°C (350°F/Gas 4) and line 1 or 2 cupcake tins with paper cases.

2 Whisk together the soya milk and cider vinegar and leave to stand for 5 minutes. Add the oil, agave syrup and vanilla extract and beat until smooth.

3 In a separate bowl, sift together the flour, bicarbonate of soda, baking powder and vanilla sea salt. Slowly incorporate the dry mixture into the wet, mixing until only a few little lumps appear. Divide the mixture evenly among the cupcake cases.

4 Bake in the oven for 20–22 minutes – if a toothpick inserted into the centre come out clean, they are ready. Cool slightly in the pan, then leave to cool completely on a wire rack. Decorate as desired.

Note Make the chocolate cupcakes as above, adding the caster sugar instead of agave syrup. Bake in the oven for 18–20 minutes.

Vegan buttercream icing

1 Beat the fats together until light. Add the icing sugar (and cocoa, if using) and continue beating for about 3 minutes.

2 Add the soya milk, vanilla extract and any other flavourings. Beat for a further 4–5 minutes until the icing looks like the fluffiest clouds you've ever seen! Use to ice the cupcakes.

Note For a chocolate version of the buttercream icing, use 250g (9oz) icing sugar and 50g (1¾oz) cocoa powder.

Variations

1 For the vanilla cupcakes, make 1 quantity vanilla cake batter, and divide the mixture into 4 equal portions. Make 1 quantity vanilla buttercream icing and divide the icing into 4 equal portions. Each portion makes about 12 petit four-sized cupcakes.

2 For the chocolate cupcakes, make 1 quantity of chocolate cake batter and divide the mixture into 3 equal parts. Make 1 quantity of chocolate buttercream icing and divide into 3 equal parts. Each portion makes about 16 petit four-sized cupcakes.

continued...

Lovely Lyle
4–6 tbsp golden syrup

School fête
pink or blue gel food
    colouring
sugar flowers
hundreds and thousands
coloured sugar, to sprinkle

Cherry Bakewell
10g (½oz) sliced almonds,
    toasted
about 1 tsp almond extract
a little raspberry jam
marzipan, to decorate
12 undyed glacé cherries

Lemon drop
1½ tsp grated lemon zest
1 tsp lemon extract
yellow gel food colouring
vegan lemon curd or lemon
    marmalade
strips of lemon zest, to
    decorate

Birmingham bliss
good-quality dark chocolate,
    broken into chunks

Kendal mint
5 peppermint teabags
1 tsp peppermint extract
green gel food colouring
silver and green dragees
chocolate shavings

Death by Jaffa
1 tbsp grated orange zest
1 tsp orange extract
orange marmalade, to taste
fresh orange zest or candied
    orange peel, to decorate

...continued from p.170

...continued from p.170

3 For Lovely Lyle cupcakes, spoon vanilla batter into 12 petits fours cases. Add a small blob of golden syrup on top of each cake, bake and cool. Cover in buttercream icing and drizzle with golden syrup.

4 To make School Fête cupcakes, spoon the vanilla batter into 12 petits fours cases, bake and cool. Ice the cupcakes with the vanilla icing mixed with a little pink or blue gel food colouring. Top with sugar flowers, hundreds and thousands and coloured sugar.

5 To make Cherry Bakewell cupcakes, chop half the almonds and mix into the vanilla batter with ¼–½ tsp almond extract. Spoon into 12 petits fours cases, bake and cool. Mix ½ tsp almond extract into the vanilla icing. Put a dollop of raspberry jam on top of each cake, cover in almond icing and decorate with toasted almonds, marzipan flourishes and a glacé cherry.

6 To make Lemon Drop cupcakes, mix the grated lemon zest and ¼–½ tsp lemon extract into the vanilla batter. Spoon into 12 petits fours cases, bake and cool. Mix ¼ tsp lemon extract and a little yellow gel food colouring into the vanilla icing. Put a dollop of lemon curd or marmalade on top of each cake, cover in lemon icing and decorate with lemon zest.

7 To make Birmingham Bliss cupcakes, spoon chocolate batter into 16 petits fours cases. Add 1 or 2 chocolate chunks to each one, bake and cool. Top with chocolate icing and chocolate chunks.

8 To make Kendal mint cupcakes, barely cover 5 peppermint teabags with boiling water. Add ½ tsp peppermint extract. Reduce the liquid to about 1½ tsp. Mix with the chocolate batter. Spoon into 16 petits fours cases, bake and cool. Cover the cupcakes with chocolate icing mixed with ½ tsp peppermint extract. Add a small amount of vanilla icing coloured with a couple of drops of green gel food colouring. Decorate with dragees and chocolate shavings.

9 To make Death by Jaffa cupcakes, mix the grated orange zest and ½–1 tsp orange extract into the chocolate batter. Spoon into 16 petit fours cases, bake and cool. Put a dollop of orange marmalade on the top of each cake. Ice with chocolate icing mixed with about ½ tsp orange extract and top with zest or peel.

Strawberry soufflés with panna cotta

Light-as-air soufflé, vanilla panna cotta and strawberry coulis – who could resist?

Prep time 25 minutes, plus
2 hours' chilling time
Cook time 20 minutes
Difficulty Medium–hard

1 To make the panna cotta, heat the cream with the vanilla pod in a heavy saucepan over a medium heat until small bubbles appear around the edge of the pan. Remove from the heat and set aside to infuse.

2 Grease 4 dariole moulds with vegetable oil. Pour the milk into a small saucepan. Squeeze the excess liquid out of the gelatine and add to the milk in the pan. Heat the milk and gelatine over a low heat until the gelatine has dissolved; do not allow to boil. Add the sugar and whisk briefly.

3 Remove the vanilla pod from the cream mixture. Scrape out the vanilla seeds into the pan; discard the pod. Gradually add the milk mixture to the warm cream, gently whisking all the time. Carefully pour the mixture into the prepared moulds. Tap the moulds on the work surface to level and chill for about 2 hours.

4 To make the soufflés, preheat the oven to 220°C (425°F/Gas 7). Grease 4 ramekins well with butter. Pour a little extra caster sugar into each one and roll around to coat; tip out any excess.

5 Blend the strawberries and lemon juice in a food processor until smooth. Press 500g (1lb 2oz) of the purée through a sieve into a heavy saucepan, and stir in 115g (4oz) of the caster sugar. Heat until the sugar has melted, then increase the heat and cook for about 5 minutes, stirring, until the mixture has reduced.

6 In a clean bowl, whisk the egg whites with the remaining 50g (2oz) of sugar until they form stiff glossy peaks. Then, carefully fold the egg mixture into the strawberry purée until well mixed.

7 Divide the soufflé mixture between the ramekins and use your thumb to make a rim around the top of each soufflé, to help them rise. Bake for 7–8 minutes, or until well risen and golden on top.

8 To make the coulis, push the remaining liquidized strawberries through a fine sieve until smooth. Add the liqueur.

9 To serve, invert the panna cottas onto serving plates. Once the soufflés have risen, take out of the oven, sit on the plates with the panna cotta and serve immediately. Serve the coulis in a small jug.

For the vanilla panna cotta
300ml (10fl oz) double cream
1 vanilla pod, split
   lengthways
300ml (10fl oz) whole milk
4 leaves gelatine, soaked in
   a little cold water for about
   10 minutes
100g (3½oz) caster sugar

For the strawberry soufflé
750g (1lb 10oz) strawberries
juice of 1 lemon
175g (6oz) caster sugar, plus
   a little extra, to coat the
   ramekins
4 large egg whites

For the strawberry coulis
about 2 tbsp strawberry
   liqueur

Orange Bakewell tart

Classic Bakewell tart with a twist – using home-made orange curd

Prep time 10 minutes, plus
50 minutes' chilling time
Cooking time 1 hour
20 minutes
Difficulty Medium

For the orange curd
grated zest of 2 oranges
    and juice of 1
60g (2oz) unsalted butter
125g (4½oz) caster sugar
2 eggs, lightly beaten

For the pastry
225g (8oz) plain flour
150g (5½oz) unsalted butter,
    diced
2 egg yolks

For the frangipane
125g (4½oz) unsalted butter
125g (4½oz) caster sugar
2 eggs, lightly beaten
125g (4½oz) ground almonds
2 tbsp plain flour
60g (2oz) flaked almonds

For the zesty orange cream
125g (4½oz) mascarpone
    cheese
150ml (5fl oz) double cream
2 tbsp icing sugar
grated zest of 1 orange
    and juice of ½
a few drops of orange
    flower water

1 To make the orange curd, combine the orange zest and juice, butter and sugar in a heatproof bowl set over a pan of simmering water. When the butter has melted, add the eggs. Stir until the mixture is thick enough to coat the back of a spoon (this can take up to 30 minutes). Pour into hot sterilized jars with tight-fitting lids, cool for 5 minutes, then seal. Cool on a wire rack, then refrigerate. It will keep for up to 1 month; use within a week once opened.

2 To make the pastry, put the flour and butter in a food processor and pulse until the mixture resembles breadcrumbs. Add the egg yolks and pulse again. The mixture should come together into bigger clumps; if not, add a few drops of ice-cold water, but be sparing. Pulse again. Tip out the mixture onto the work surface and draw together into a ball, kneading lightly until smooth. Be careful not to overwork, as this will make the pastry tough. Flatten into a disc, wrap in cling film and chill for 30 minutes.

3 To make the frangipane, cream together the butter and sugar in a medium bowl. Little by little, add the eggs, then fold in the ground almonds and flour. Set aside.

4 Lightly flour the work surface and rolling pin and roll out the pastry to fit a 25cm (10in) round loose bottomed tart tin. Line with greaseproof paper and fill with baking beans. Chill again for a further 20 minutes.

5 Preheat the oven to 190°C (375°F/Gas 5). Blind-bake the pastry case for 10 minutes. Remove the paper and beans and return the pastry case to the oven for a further 10 minutes. Cool slightly. Do not turn off the oven.

6 Spread half a jar of the orange curd over the bottom of the tart and top with the frangipane, spreading it carefully to cover the curd. Sprinkle with the flaked almonds and bake for a further 30 minutes until golden brown. Remove from the oven and allow to cool slightly.

7 To make the zesty orange cream, using a hand-held mixer, beat together all the ingredients in a bowl until soft peaks form.

8 Serve slices of the warm tart with the zesty orange cream.

Toffee Bakewell tarts

Indulgent toffee Bakewell tarts, served with clotted cream and a lemon martini

1 To make the pastry, divide the butter into four portions. Leave three-quarters in the refrigerator; rub the remaining quarter into the flour. With a knife, add the salt, lemon juice and cold water, little by little, until it just comes together into a dough. Knead on a floured work surface for 5 minutes, then chill for at least 15 minutes.

2 For the toffee filling, melt the butter and sugars in a non-stick pan over a low heat. Add the condensed milk and bring to the boil, stirring constantly. Remove from the heat and leave to cool.

3 On a floured work surface, roll out the pastry into a rectangle. Dot the top two-thirds with one portion of the chilled butter. Fold up in thirds and seal the edges with a rolling pin. Turn the dough around and roll into a rectangle again. Dot the third portion with a portion of the butter as before; roll into thirds. Seal the edges with a rolling pin. Wrap in cling film and chill for at least 20 minutes.

4 To make the lemon syrup, put the lemon zest and juice and the sugar in a small saucepan over a low heat. Once the sugar has dissolved, bring to the boil for 4–6 minutes until slightly thickened. Remove from the heat and allow to cool.

5 To make the frangipane filling, cream the butter and sugar together in a food processor. On a low speed, add the eggs and the almond essence and stir in the ground almonds.

6 Take out the pastry and repeat as per the last rolling, using the last of the butter. Repeat a final time without adding butter; roll again if still streaky. Wrap in cling film and chill for 15 minutes.

7 Preheat the oven to 180°C (350°C/Gas 4). Lightly grease a muffin tray. Roll out the pastry thinly, cut into rounds with a pastry cutter and gently place in the muffin tray holes. Put 1 tsp of the toffee filling on the bottom of each one and top with 1 tbsp of the frangipane. Bake in the oven for about 20 minutes until risen and golden. Leave in the tin for 5 minutes before gently removing.

9 To serve, make lemon martinis by adding crushed ice to each glass with equal parts of vodka and limoncello. Top up with Champagne. Serve the tarts with clotted cream, a drizzle of the lemon syrup on the cream and, of course, the lemon martinis!

Prep time 10 minutes
Cook time 45–50 minutes
Difficulty Medium

For the flaky pastry
175g (6oz) chilled unsalted
 butter, cut into cubes
225g (8oz) plain flour
pinch of salt
2 tsp freshly squeezed lemon
 juice
90–120ml (3–4fl oz) cold
 water

For the toffee filling
175g (6¼oz) unsalted butter
85g (3oz) caster sugar
85g (3oz) soft dark brown
 sugar
1 x 400g can condensed milk

For the lemon syrup
grated zest and juice of
 3 unwaxed lemons
85g (3oz) caster sugar

For the almond frangipane
125g (4½oz) unsalted butter
125g (4½oz) caster sugar
2 eggs
a few drops of almond
 essence
2 tbsp ground almonds

For the champagne lemon martini
crushed ice, to serve
equal parts of vodka and
 limoncello
Champagne, to top

clotted cream, to serve

Pear tarte Tatin
with pear schnapps

In a twist on the French classic, luscious
pears combine with irresistible caramel

Prep time **25 minutes**
Cooking time **40 minutes**
Difficulty **Easy–medium**

For the pastry
225g (8oz) plain white flour
75g (2½oz) caster sugar
pinch of ground cinnamon
110g (4oz) butter, cut into
  rough cubes

DESSERTS • PEAR TARTE TATIN WITH PEAR SCHNAPPS

For the pears
150g (5½oz) butter
200g (/oz) caster sugar
8 ripe pears
pinch of ground cinnamon
dash of pear schnapps
200ml (7fl oz) double cream,
  whipped until firm, to serve

1 Using your hands, mix together the sifted flour, sugar, cinnamon
and butter; do not overwork. Add 1–2 tbsp water, a very little at a
time, until the pastry just comes together into a dough and form
into a ball. Flatten slightly into a disc, wrap in cling film and leave
to chill for 30 minutes.

2 Preheat the oven to 180°C (350°C/Gas 4).

3 To make the caramel, smear the butter over the bottom of a
tarte tatin pan or ovenproof cast-iron frying pan. Sprinkle over the
caster sugar and dissolve over a medium heat until the sugar starts
to caramelize. Keep turning the pan now and again, so that the
sugar does not catch. Stir until the butter just starts to separate
and the sugar has started to turn a light golden toffee colour.

4 Meanwhile, peel, core and cut the pears into quarters. Remove
the pan from the heat and carefully add the pears to the butter
and sugar mixture in the pan, arranging them in a layer over the
bottom of the pan and packing them in tightly. Return to the heat
and cook for 10–15 minutes until really golden. Sprinkle with the
cinnamon and add a few drops of pear schnapps. Leave to cool
for 10 minutes.

5 On a floured work surface, roll out the pastry into a round large
enough to cover the pan. Carefully lay the pastry on top of the
pears, tucking the edges down in between the fruit and the edge
of the pan. Bake in the oven for about 30 minutes until the pastry
is crisp and golden. Leave the tart to cool in the pan for 10 minutes,
then carefully invert onto a serving plate.

6 To serve, cut into slices while still warm and serve with a generous
dollop of whipped cream.

"Formidable!"
— John Burton Race

Prep time 25 minutes, plus
1 hour 10 minutes' chilling
and churning time
Cooking time 40 minutes
Difficulty Medium

For the ice cream
500ml (16fl oz) double cream
500ml (16fl oz) semi-skimmed
  milk
1 vanilla pod, split
  lengthways
150g (5½oz) golden caster
  sugar
10 egg yolks

For the plum ripple
500g (1lb 2 oz) plums, halved
  and stoned
150g (5½oz) golden caster
  sugar
juice of 1 lemon

For the crumble
3 Granny Smith apples
150g (5½oz) golden caster
  sugar, plus a little extra
  for coating
200g (7oz) butter, plus a
  little extra for pan-frying
150g (5½oz) plain flour
50g (1¼oz) hazelnuts,
  chopped

Apple plum crumble with hazelnuts

Traditional crumble featuring seasonal fruit and set off by plum ripple ice cream

1 To make the ice cream, scald the cream, milk, vanilla pod and 1 tablespoon of the caster sugar in a pan; do not allow to boil.

2 Using an electric whisk, whisk together the egg yolks and remaining sugar, then slowly whisk in the hot milk mixture. Strain the ice-cream mixture into a clean pan and heat gently until it coats the back of a spoon. Transfer to a bowl and chill for 30 minutes.

3 To make the plum ripple for the ice cream, heat the plums with the sugar, lemon juice and 100ml (3½fl oz) water until the fruit breaks down. Using a hand-held blender, purée the hot plum mixture until smooth. Pour half of the mixture into a bowl and chill for 20 minutes. Tip the other half into another bowl, and leave to stand at room temperature. Set aside.

4 Pour the ice-cream mixture into an ice-cream machine and churn for 20 minutes according to the manufacturer's instructions. Stir the chilled plum ripple into the ice-cream mixture and churn again briefly. Transfer to the freezer.

5 Meanwhile, to make the crumble, preheat the oven to 180°C (350°F/Gas 4). Peel, core and dice the apples and coat them in a little caster sugar. Pan-fry the diced apples in a little butter until just starting to caramelize.

6 To make the crumble topping, blend together the 200g (7oz) butter, 150g (5½oz) caster sugar and flour in a food processor until the mixture forms a crumble; be careful not to overwork.

7 Add the pan-fried apples to the bowl of unchilled ripple sauce and divide the mixture equally among 4 ramekins. Top with the crumble mixture. Bake in the oven for 20 minutes. Sprinkle the hazelnuts over the crumbles and return to the oven for a further 5 minutes.

8 Serve the hot crumbles in their ramekins, with a spoonful of the plum ripple ice cream on the side.

Cloutie dumpling

A very Scottish suet pudding packed
with the flavours of dried fruit and spices

Prep time 10–15 minutes
Cooking time 3 hours
Difficulty Easy–medium

1 Soak a pudding cloth or square of muslin in boiling water.

2 To make the dumpling, sift the flour into a bowl and rub in the suet. Add the breadcrumbs, bicarbonate of soda, spices, sultanas, raisins and sugar and mix with a wooden spoon. Make a well in the centre and add the treacle or golden syrup and pour in the milk. Mix together to form a fairly soft batter.

3 Remove the cloth from the water, wring out and lay out flat. Dredge well with flour. Smooth the flour over the cloth with your hands so that it is evenly spread. Put the dumpling batter in the centre of the floured cloth and draw the cloth together evenly around the batter, leaving a little room for the pudding to expand; tie the top of the cloth with kitchen string.

4 Put a plate in the bottom of a large pot (you will need one big enough to cover the dumpling generously with water, so that there is no need to top up the water level during cooking). Sit the cloth-wrapped dumpling on the plate and cover completely with boiling water. Simmer the dumpling for 2–3 hours.

5 Remove from the pot and put in a colander in the sink. Untie the string and gently pull the corners of the cloth apart. Put a plate over the dumpling while in the colander and turn over. Carefully pull the cloth off the dumpling.

6 To make the custard, use the end of a teaspoon to scrape out the seeds from the vanilla pod. Put the pod and seeds in a small saucepan along with the cream. Place the pan over a gentle heat and heat to just below simmering point.

7 While the cream is heating, whisk together the egg yolks, cornflour and sugar in a bowl. Remove the vanilla pod from the hot cream, then gradually add the hot cream to the egg mixture, whisking all the time.

8 Pour the mixture back into a clean pan and, over a very low heat, continue whisking until the custard is thick and smooth. Pour into a serving jug and serve hot with the dumpling.

For the dumpling
150g (5½oz) self-raising flour
150g (5½oz) suet, shredded
150g (5½oz) brown
  breadcrumbs
1 tsp bicarbonate of soda
2 tsp ground cinnamon
1 tsp ground ginger
1 tsp mixed spice
150g (5½oz) sultanas
110g (4oz) raisins
110g (4oz) soft light brown
  sugar
2 tbsp black treacle or
  golden syrup
375ml (13fl oz) whole milk
plain flour, to dredge

For the custard
1 vanilla pod, split
  lengthways
570ml (18fl oz) single cream
6 large egg yolks
2 tsp cornflour
50g (1¾oz) caster sugar

Chocolate and boozy raspberry puddings

Enticingly decadent, these puddings will satisfy even the most ardent chocoholic

Prep time 30 minutes, plus
20 minutes' marinating time
Cooking time 15 minutes
Difficulty Medium

For the boozy raspberries
200g (7oz) fresh raspberries
100ml (3½fl oz) raspberry
   liqueur such as framboise

For the hot chocolate puddings
125g (4½oz) unsalted butter
   (Welsh if possible)
200g (7oz) Green & Black's
   organic dark chocolate
4 medium organic eggs, plus
   2 extra yolks
100g (3½oz) Fairtrade caster
   sugar
25g (scant 1oz) plain flour

For the chocolate kisses
1 x 100g (3½oz) bar Green
   & Black's organic milk
   chocolate
1 x 100g (3½oz) bar Green
   & Black's organic white
   chocolate

For the raspberry cream
150g (5oz) Fairtrade caster
   sugar
500ml (16fl oz) crème fraîche

To serve
unsweetened cocoa powder,
   to dust
icing sugar, to dust

1 Put the raspberries in a bowl, cover with the liqueur and leave to marinate for about 20 minutes.

2 Preheat the oven to 180°C (350°F/Gas 4). Butter and flour 4 individual pudding moulds.

3 To make the hot chocolate puddings, melt the butter and chocolate in a heatproof bowl set over a pan of simmering water. Stir until smooth and allow to cool slightly.

4 Now make the chocolate kisses. Gently melt the milk chocolate and white chocolate separately, then carefully marble the two together. Pipe crosses onto a tray lined with baking parchment and put in the refrigerator to set.

5 In a clean bowl, whisk the eggs, extra egg yolks and 100g (3½oz) caster sugar until thick, pale and fluffy. Fold the cooled chocolate mixture into the eggs and sugar. Sift in the flour and fold gently until combined.

6 Divide the mixture equally among the prepared moulds and drop 3 boozy raspberries into each one. Place on a baking sheet and bake in the oven for 15 minutes. Allow to cool slightly before turning out to serve.

7 Meanwhile, to make the raspberry cream, whisk the caster sugar and the crème fraîche until thick. Use a spatula to fold most of the remaining liqueur-soaked raspberries (reserve a small handful for the coulis) into the crème fraîche mixture. Chill until needed.

8 Take the last of the boozy raspberries and mash down with a fork to make a coulis. Push through a fine sieve until smooth.

9 To serve, dust each serving plate with a little cocoa powder. Turn out a chocolate pudding onto each plate. Use a stencil to create a heart-shaped dusting of icing sugar on top of each pudding. Place a quenelle of raspberry cream at a jaunty angle on each plate, with a swirl of coulis on the other side. Garnish each pudding with a chocolate kiss and serve.

Lemon tart with margarita ice cream

Tangy citrus and a touch of tequila prevail in this delicious and refreshing dessert

Prep time 45 minutes, plus 30 minutes' chilling time
Cooking time 55 minutes, plus 25 minutes' cooling time
Difficulty **Medium**

1 To make the pastry, sift the flour, salt and icing sugar into a food processor. Pulse with half the butter until the mixture resembles breadcrumbs. Add the rest of the butter; pulse again until mixed. Gradually add enough of the cold egg liquid so that the pastry starts to come together. Knead lightly on a floured work surface until smooth. Wrap in cling film and chill for 30 minutes.

2 Preheat the oven and a baking tray, to 200°C (400°F/Gas 6). Lightly grease 6 individual flan tins with softened butter.

3 Divide the pastry into 6, roll out and use to line the flan tins, leaving some surplus hanging over the edges. Gently press the pastry into the corners; do not trim. Line with greaseproof paper and fill with baking beans. Blind bake in the oven for 10 minutes. Remove the beans and paper and return the tart cases to the oven for 6–7 minutes until lightly coloured. Leave to cool for 5 minutes. Reduce the oven temperature to 120°C (250°F/Gas ½).

4 To make the filling, lightly whisk the eggs to break up the yolks. Gently whisk in the sugar, then add the cream and lemon juice. Pass the mixture through a sieve, then add the zest. Carefully pour the filling into the tart cases. (Any surplus can be poured into ramekins, baked and served as lemon pots.) Bake the tarts in the oven for 30–35 minutes until just set. Trim off the pastry edges to neaten. Leave to cool for 20–25 minutes, then dust with icing sugar.

5 To make the sauce, heat the citrus juices, sugar and 150ml (5fl oz) water until the sugar has dissolved. Add the wine, bring to the boil and simmer for 2 minutes. Briskly stir in the arrowroot paste until glossy. Add the blanched lime zest. Leave to cool.

6 To make the ice cream, put the lime juice, tequila and triple sec in a bowl. Stir in the icing sugar until it has dissolved. Add the cream and whisk until the mixture is thick and smooth. Churn in an ice-cream machine according to the manufacturer's instructions.

7 Dip the rim of 6 martini glasses into the egg white, then the pink sugar. Allow to dry. Serve the tarts with a quenelle of ice cream in a martini glass, a quenelle of crème fraiche on the side and lime sauce drizzled around. Garnish with redcurrants.

181

DESSERTS • LEMON TART WITH MARGARITA ICE CREAM

For the pastry
150g (5½oz) plain flour
¼ tsp salt
25g (scant 1oz) icing sugar
100g (3½oz) chilled butter, cubed
1 egg yolk, mixed with 2 tbsp ice-cold water

For the filling
5 eggs
200g (7oz) caster sugar
250ml (8fl oz) double cream
grated zest of 3 lemons and juice of 5
25g (scant 1oz) icing sugar

For the lime sauce
juice of 2 limes
juice of ½ lemon
75g (2½oz) sugar
150ml (5fl oz) white Zinfandel
1 rounded tsp arrowroot, blended with 1 tbsp cold water to make a paste
thinly pared zest of 1 lime, blanched in boiling water for 1 minute

For the Margarita ice cream
120ml (4fl oz) freshly squeezed lime juice
4 tbsp tequila
4 tbsp triple sec
165g (6oz) icing sugar
500ml (16fl oz) double cream

To decorate
1 egg white, whisked
55g (2oz) caster sugar, coloured pink with a few drops of red food colouring
crème fraiche, to serve
fresh redcurrants, to garnish

Prep time 1 hour, plus cooling and setting time
Cooking time 25 minutes
Difficulty Medium

For the shortbread biscuits
110g (4oz) unsalted butter
50g (1¾oz) caster sugar
175g (6oz) plain flour

For the honeycomb biscuit base
200g (7oz) caster sugar
100g (3½oz) golden syrup
40g (1½oz) butter
½ tsp vinegar
1 tsp bicarbonate of soda
60g (2oz) melted butter
110g (4oz) shortbread
 biscuits, crushed (see above)

For the cheesecake
18g (2 sheets) gelatine
250g (9oz) cream cheese
60g (2oz) caster sugar
200g (7oz) plain yogurt
120g (4½oz) Venezuelan
 dark chocolate (86 per cent
 cocoa solids), melted
1 whole home-grown fresh
 red chilli, finely chopped
120g (4½oz) white chocolate,
 melted

For the whisky ice cream
250ml (8fl oz) single cream
225g (8oz) soft brown sugar
1 x 397g can condensed milk
50ml (2fl oz) whisky

For the raspberry coulis
300g (10oz) fresh raspberries
100g (3½oz) icing sugar
1 tbsp lemon juice

Chocolate and chilli cheesecake

Heavenly chocolate cheesecake with a honeycomb base and a touch of chilli

Shortbread biscuits

1 Preheat the oven to 160°C (325°F/Gas 3).

2 Beat the butter until creamed, then add the sugar and beat until pale and fluffy. Sift in the flour and mix together until smooth.

3 Place the shortbread mixture on a board and roll out until about 1cm (½in) thick. Cut into small pieces. Place on a baking tray and bake in the oven for 25 minutes until golden. Remove from the oven and leave to cool on a wire rack.

Honeycomb biscuit base

1 Line a small baking tin with greaseproof paper.

2 In a heavy pan, heat together the sugar, syrup, butter and 1 tbsp water and stir until all the sugar has dissolved. Bring to the boil and heat until a teaspoon of the syrup becomes a soft ball when dropped into a cup of cold water, or until the temperature of the syrup reaches 120°C/280°F on a sugar thermometer.

3 Remove from the heat and carefully add the vinegar and bicarbonate of soda to the toffee mixture. Stir well with a wooden spoon and pour straight into the baking tin. Allow the honeycomb to set completely.

4 Meanwhile, gently melt the butter in a small saucepan. Using a rolling pin, crush the shortbreads biscuits. Put in a bowl, add the melted butter and stir until well mixed.

5 Once the honeycomb has set, smash into small pieces with a wooden rolling pin and add to the biscuit base. Stir through.

Cheesecake

1 Put the gelatine and 3 tbsp water in a heatproof bowl and place over a pan of simmering water to dissolve the gelatine. Stir well.

2 Put the cream cheese and sugar in a food processor and process until smooth and creamy. Add the yogurt and continue to beat until the mixture is completely smooth. Blend in the dissolved gelatine and mix well.

3 Divide the cream cheese mixture equally between 2 bowls. Add the dark chocolate and chilli to one bowl and the white chocolate to the other.

4 Arrange four 10cm (4in) metal food rings on a plate, fill each with a quarter of the biscuit base and press down firmly. Add a layer of the dark chocolate mixture, then add a layer of the white chocolate mix. Leave to set in the refrigerator for 15–20 minutes.

Whisky ice cream
1 Whisk the single cream with the soft brown sugar until smooth. Add the condensed milk and whisky and mix until well blended.

2 Pour the cream mixture into an ice-cream machine and churn according to the manufacturer's instructions.

Raspberry coulis
1 Put the raspberries, icing sugar, lemon juice and 4 tbsp water in a saucepan and heat gently for 5 minutes

2 Transfer to a food processor and blend until smooth. Push the coulis through a fine sieve. Serve the individual cheesecakes with a spoonful of ice cream and a drizzle of coulis.

Chocolate roulade with passion fruit

Mouth-watering dark chocolate roulade using local eggs, with a dash of brandy

Prep time 10 minutes
Cooking time 30 minutes
Difficulty Medium

1 Preheat the oven to 160°C (325°F/Gas 3). Line a Swiss roll tin with baking parchment.

2 Melt the chocolate in a bowl set over a pan of simmering water. Leave to cool slightly.

3 Meanwhile, beat together the egg yolks and sugar until thick, pale and creamy. Mix in the brandy.

4 Whisk the egg whites until stiff and forming soft peaks.

5 Combine the melted chocolate with the egg and sugar mixture. Add 2 tbsp of the egg whites to the chocolate mixture to slacken it slightly, then carefully fold in the rest of the egg whites.

6 Pour the mixture into the prepared tin and bake in the centre of the oven for 12–18 minutes. Allow to cool in the tin, on a wire rack, for 1 hour, then cover with baking parchment and a damp cloth.

7 When ready to fill, turn the chocolate sponge out onto clean baking parchment covered with a light sprinkling of icing sugar. Spread with the softly whipped cream and drizzle most of the passion fruit over the top. Roll and serve with extra passion fruit and the chilled pouring cream.

200g (7oz) dark chocolate (at least 70% cocoa solids)
5 free-range organic eggs, separated
175g (6oz) golden caster sugar
1 tbsp brandy
about 1 tbsp icing sugar
300ml (10fl oz) fresh organic double cream, softly whipped
4–6 passion fruits, chopped
chilled organic pouring single cream, to serve

"… the three elements together form a really beautiful whole and I think it's a very good dessert."
— John Burton Race

Prep time 10 minutes, plus overnight soaking time
Cooking time 40 minutes
Difficulty Medium

For the tipsy tart
250g (9oz) Medjool dates, pitted and roughly chopped
1 tsp bicarbonate of soda
2 tbsp slightly salted butter
250g (9oz) golden caster sugar
1 large egg
250g (9oz) plain white flour
1 tsp salt
¼ teaspoon baking powder
65g (2oz) pecan nuts, roughly chopped, plus extra, to garnish
65g (2¼oz) undyed glacé cherries, soaked in whisky overnight
thick double cream, to serve

For the whisky sauce
1 tbsp slightly salted butter
250g (9oz) golden caster sugar
a few drops of vanilla extract
125ml (4fl oz) whisky
pinch of salt

Iona's tipsy tart with whisky sauce

Made with traditional ingredients, this gorgeous sticky tart is packed with flavour

1 Preheat the oven to 180°C (350°C/Gas 4). Grease and flour a round or oval ovenproof dish.

2 Pour 250ml (8fl oz) boiling water over the chopped dates, and add the bicarbonate of soda. Leave to cool.

3 Meanwhile, cream together the butter and sugar. Add the egg and beat again. In another bowl, sift together the flour, salt and baking powder, then add to the egg mixture. Beat until combined, then mix in the water from the soaked dates.

4 Stir in the dates, nuts and cherries and mix well. Pour into the prepared dish, scatter some extra chopped nuts over the top and bake in the oven for 30 minutes. Test with a skewer to ensure that the tart is cooked all the way through.

5 To make the whisky sauce, put the butter, sugar and vanilla extract in a saucepan and add 125ml (4fl oz) water. Bring to the boil. Continue to boil for 5 minutes, then add the whisky and a pinch of salt. Bring to the boil again.

6 Prick the pudding in several places with a metal skewer and spoon the sauce all over. Serve warm with thick double cream.

Bread and butter meringue flan

Irresistible dessert with summer fruits, shortcrust pastry and airy meringue

Prep time 10 minutes
Cooking time 50 minutes
Difficulty Medium

1 To make the pastry base, combine the flour and butter in a food processor and pulse until the mixture resembles breadcrumbs. Put in a bowl, making a well in the centre. Add the 1 whole egg and the sugar and work together with a knife, adding a little water to combine into a dough. Wrap in cling film and chill for 30 minutes.

2 Preheat the oven to 200°C (400°C/Gas 6). On a floured work surface, roll out the pastry and use to line a greased tart tin (or use four 10cm (4in) individual tart tins). Line with greaseproof paper, fill with baking beans and blind-bake for 12 minutes. Remove the beans and paper, brush the bottom of the pastry lightly with the egg yolk and bake for a further 2 minutes.

3 To make the filling, heat together the milk, cream and butter over a medium heat until the butter has melted. Remove from the heat and mix in the breadcrumbs and sugar. Leave to cool for 10 minutes, then add the egg yolks, vanilla and sultanas. Pour the mixture into the pastry case or cases and bake in the centre of the oven for 15 minutes until set. Do not turn off the oven.

4 In a saucepan, gently heat the summer fruits, red wine and sugar for 10 minutes until the sugar has dissolved. Remove from the heat.

5 To make the meringue topping, whisk the egg whites with an electric whisk until soft peaks form. Add the sugar, vanilla essence and cornflour and whisk again until stiff and glossy.

6 To finish the flan, spread the summer fruits over the bread-and-butter filling, then pipe the meringue over the fruit. Bake in the oven for 10 minutes until the meringue is lightly golden. Serve warm, cut into wedges.

For the pastry base
200g (7oz) plain flour
100g (3½oz) butter
1 egg plus 1 egg yolk
50g (1¾oz) caster sugar

For the bread and butter filling
250ml (8fl oz) milk
125ml (4fl oz) cream
1 tbsp butter
60g (2oz) brioche breadcrumbs
25g (scant 1oz) caster sugar
2 egg yolks
1 vanilla pod, split lengthways
50g (1¾oz) sultanas

For the summer fruits
250g (9oz) summer fruits such as raspberries, strawberries and blackcurrants
2½ tbsp medium red wine
35g (1¼oz) caster sugar

For the meringue topping
3 egg whites
75g (2½oz) caster sugar
1 tsp vanilla essence
1 tsp cornflour

"A very, very good pudding and if I wasn't so full I could probably finish it off."

— Ed Baines

English apple strudel

Local produce and East Anglian white wine make this a very British incarnation

Prep time 30 minutes, plus resting time for pastry
Cooking time 25 minutes
Difficulty Medium–hard

For the strudel pastry
250g (9oz) strong white flour
175ml (6fl oz) lukewarm water
2–3 tbsp vegetable oil
about 100g (3½oz) butter, melted

For the strudel filling
about 400g (14oz) eating apples
50g (1¾oz) icing sugar
1 tsp ground cinnamon
50g (1¾oz) dried breadcrumbs
50g (1¾oz) nuts such as hazelnuts or Brazil nuts, chopped

For the East Anglian white wine mousse
1 vanilla pod, split lengthways
70ml (2½fl oz) apple juice
70ml (2½fl oz) East Anglian white wine
2 eggs, separated
1 tbsp cornflour
2 tbsp runny honey

To decorate
some caster sugar, to make caramel threads
icing sugar, to dust

1 To make the strudel pastry, sift the flour into a bowl and add the lukewarm water and oil. Knead briefly to combine into a dough. Brush the dough with oil and leave to rest for 30 minutes.

2 To make the apple filling, peel, core and chop the apples. Put in a large bowl and mix with the icing sugar and cinnamon. Leave to marinate for 5 minutes. Combine the breadcrumbs and nuts in another bowl.

3 Once the pastry has rested, cut the dough into 8 equal portions. Roll into a rectangle shape on a floured work surface, then lift the pastry rectangle onto a floured tea towel. Using your hands, carefully start pulling and stretching the pastry from each of the edges until it is about 30 x 30cm (12 x 12 in) and as thin as possible, but still comfortable to work with. Be careful not to make it too thin, as it tears easily. Trim the edges to make a neat rectangle once again.

4 With a short edge facing you, brush the pastry with melted butter. Spread a quarter of the breadcrumb and nut mixture evenly on the front third closest to you, then cover with a quarter of the apples, keeping a border of pastry clear of filling.

5 Lift the towel, roll up the strudel away from you – remembering to fold in the edges – and transfer it to a greased baking tray. Brush with a little more melted butter and place in the refrigerator to rest. Repeat the process to produce 8 individual strudels.

6 To make the mousse, using the end of a teaspoon, scrape out the seeds from the vanilla pod into a small bowl. Add the apple juice and wine and leave to marinate for 5 minutes.

7 In a clean bowl, cream together the egg yolks, a little of the wine and apple juice mixture and the cornflour. Add the remaining liquid and the honey and whisk well. Pour the mixture into a saucepan and thicken over a low heat, whisking all the time. Remove from the heat and transfer to a bowl to cool.

8 Whisk the egg whites until stiff and fold gently into the wine mousse. Place the bowl in the refrigerator until ready to serve.

9 Preheat the oven to 200°C (400°F/Gas 6). Bake the strudels for 15 minutes, brushing with melted butter twice during cooking.

10 Meanwhile, prepare the caramel threads: take extra care when handling hot sugar. Dissolve the sugar in a pan over a medium heat until caramelized. Using a metal spoon, carefully drizzle the molten sugar onto a non-stick baking tray and allow to cool. When cool enough to handle, gently shape into balls.

11 To serve, halve each strudel and arrange 2 halves on each serving plate, with 1 slice pointing upwards. Dust with a little icing sugar. Make a quenelle of about 1 tbsp of the mousse for each serving and place next to the strudel, then arrange the caramel threads on each plate. Serve immediately.

"I love the balance of the tastes and the contrasts, with the nuts and the apples together. Great texture. The pastry's heavenly."
— John Burton Race

Cranachan panna cotta

A celebration of creamy subtlety, enlivened with tart raspberries and oatmeal tuiles

Prep time 30 minutes, plus setting and chilling time
Cooking time 30 minutes
Difficulty Medium–hard

For the sauce
150g (5½oz) raspberries for sauce, plus extra 15–20g (½–¾oz), to garnish
50–65g (1¾–2oz) caster sugar
juice of 1 lemon

For the panna cotta
400ml (14fl oz) double cream
100ml (3½fl oz) milk
2–3 leaves gelatine, soaked in a little cold water
about 100g (3½oz) caster sugar
about 3 tbsp clear honey (the sugar–honey split depends on taste – it should be at least half and half, but up to three-quarters honey works, depending on how strongly flavoured the honey is)
3–4 tbsp malt whisky, to taste

For the oatmeal tuiles
25g (scant 1oz) rolled oats, plus a little extra, to garnish
50g (1¾oz) unsalted butter, softened
50g (1¾oz) caster sugar
pinch of ground cinnamon
¼ tsp salt
1 egg white, lightly whisked
30g (1oz) sifted plain flour

1 Rinse and drain the raspberries in a sieve. Reserve the largest and best-shaped fruits to garnish, leaving 150g (5½oz) in the sieve.

2 Set the sieve over a saucepan and, using a ladle, squeeze the raspberries through the sieve to extract all the juice. There should be about 100g (3½oz) juice, but you need to weigh it so that you know how much sugar to cook it with.

3 Return the weighed raspberry juice to the saucepan and add between 50% and 60% sugar (by weight of the raspberry juice) and the lemon juice. You need the sauce to soft-set, but do not want it too sweet, so do not add too much sugar.

4 Heat gently until the sugar has dissolved, then bring to the boil and boil rapidly for a few minutes until just set into a very soft jelly. To test, take out a teaspoon of the jelly every minute or so, place it on a cold plate and, when fairly cold, prod it with a finger – it is ready when it just starts to crinkle. Remove the pan from the heat while testing to ensure that you do not overset the sauce. If not ready, return the pan to the heat and keep testing.

5 When the sauce is ready, skim off any scum. Decant the sauce into a cold bowl or jug, cover with cling film and allow to cool.

6 When cool, check for consistency – you want it to be very soft-set so that it oozes out when the panna cotta is opened: remember that the panna cotta will be served chilled, so the sauce will be at its coldest/thickest. If the sauce is too thick, add a little water and/or whisky and stir to loosen it slightly.

7 To make the panna cotta, gently heat the cream and milk in a pan until bubbles just start to form around the edge of the pan. Reduce the heat and simmer slowly until reduced by a quarter to a third. Remove the pan from the heat.

8 Gently squeeze out the excess water from the gelatine. Mix together the sugar and honey to taste, depending on the sweetness desired. Add the gelatine to the cream and milk mixture, together with the honey/sugar mixture. Stir until the gelatine and sugar have dissolved. Leave to cool, but not set.

continued...

192

DESSERTS • CRANACHAN PANNA COTTA

...continued from p.190

9 Add the whisky to taste (it should be noticeable, but not overpowering). Pour the mixture into 4 lightly oiled dariole moulds until about two-thirds full. Sit the moulds on a baking tray and put the tray in the freezer to chill rapidly for 10–15 minutes until set.

10 Remove the moulds from the freezer and, with a teaspoon, scoop out a hollow in each panna cotta large enough to take a large raspberry and a good helping of raspberry sauce. Place a raspberry, pointed end down in each hollow and carefully spoon in some of the cooled raspberry sauce until full. Return the moulds to the freezer for 5–10 minutes until the sauce is firm enough to support the remaining panna cotta mixture. Fill with the remaining mixture and chill in the refrigerator until set, but still a little wobbly.

11 To make the oatmeal tuiles, preheat the oven to 220°C (425°/Gas 7). Lightly toast the rolled oats in a dry frying pan; set aside all but 25g (scant 1oz). Lightly chop the 25g (1oz) toasted oats.

12 Put the softened butter, sugar, cinnamon and salt in a small bowl. Cream with a wooden spoon until smooth. Add the egg white and whisk lightly until smooth, then stir in the flour and chopped oatmeal until well mixed.

13 Evenly spread small quantities (about a rounded teaspoon) of the mixture on a non stick silicone sheet into small flat rounds of about 6cm (2½in) diameter. Set the silicone sheet on a baking sheet. Bake in the centre of the oven for 7–9 minutes; you may need to turn the tray a few times to ensure even colouring.

14 Remove from the oven, leave to cool for a few seconds, then carefully remove from the silicone sheet with a metal spatula and place on a flat surface. Using a 6cm (2½in) cutter, press firmly on each tuile, then allow to cool completely and crisp. Carefully break off the dark brown edges around the cut mark. If you like, you can also shape them around a rolling pin or similar as they cool.

15 To serve, toss the remaining raspberries in the remaining sauce. Turn out the panna cottas onto 4 plates. Sprinkle with the reserved oatmeal and serve with the tuiles and glazed raspberries.

Chilli and chocolate deep-fried ice cream

A delicious and unusual deep-fried ice cream, served with a chilli chocolate cake

1 To make the ice cream, beat together the egg yolks and sugar until pale and fluffy. Scrape out the vanilla seeds into the milk and bring slowly to the boil in a small saucepan. Pour into the egg mixture, whisking constantly. Return the mixture to the pan and stir constantly until it coats the back of a spoon; do not allow to boil. Leave to cool for 1 hour.

2 Whip the cream to soft peaks, add to the custard mixture, then pour the mixture into the ice-cream machine bowl and churn to the desired consistency. Place in the freezer to set further.

3 For the ice-cream balls, take a freezer bag and make a ball of ice cream as quickly as possible. Immediately place back in the freezer for 2 hours. Remove, dip in the beaten egg, crumb with the breadcrumbs and coconut quickly and put back in the freezer for an hour. Repeat the crumbling and freeze again for 1 hour.

4 Melt the 15g (½oz) grated chilli chocolate in a bain-marie and paint onto greaseproof paper. Leave to harden.

5 For the cake, preheat the oven to 150°C (300°F/Gas 2). Grease and line a Swiss roll tin. Whisk the egg whites to stiff peaks. In a separate bowl, cream the butter and sugar well and add the egg yolks one at a time. Double-sift the flour and cocoa power and add to the mixture. Melt the grated chilli chocolate and stir through the mixture with the chilli flakes and 3 tbsp water to make a batter. Gently fold the egg whites into the batter, then pour into the tin. Bake in the oven for 17 minutes.

6 For the chilli chocolate sauce, slowly melt the chocolate, butter and cream in a heatproof bowl set over simmering water. Smear a layer of chocolate sauce over the top of the cake, reserving any leftover sauce and roll up while still warm. Cut into 4 slices each about 2 fingers thick. Place the hardened chocolate on top.

7 In a deep, heavy saucepan, heat enough oil for deep-frying to 175°C (350°F). Coat the ice cream balls one last time in the egg and crumb mixture; deep-fry for 10–20 seconds. Remove with a slotted spoon. Place straight onto the chocolate cake slices, pour over any leftover sauce and garnish with the strawberries. Serve.

Prep time 20 minutes, plus 4 hours' cooling and freezing time
Cooking time 25 minutes
Difficulty **Medium**

For the vanilla ice cream
3 egg yolks
75g (2½oz) caster sugar
1 vanilla pod, split lengthways
225ml (8fl oz) milk
225ml (8fl oz) double cream

For the ice cream balls
4 eggs, beaten
125g (4½oz) white breadcrumbs
125g (4½oz) desiccated coconut

15g (½oz) chilli chocolate, grated

For the chilli chocolate cake
2 medium organic eggs, separated
50g (1¾oz) softened unsalted butter
50g (1¾oz) caster sugar
60g (2oz) self-raising flour
2 tbsp cocoa powder
100g (3½oz) chilli chocolate, grated
½ tsp dried red chilli flakes

For the chilli chocolate sauce
100g (3½oz) chilli chocolate, grated
knob of unsalted butter
50ml (1¾fl oz) cream

vegetable oil for deep-frying
handful of strawberries, sliced and fanned, to garnish

Prep time 30 minutes, plus overnight chilling time
Cooking time 35 minutes
Difficulty Medium–hard

For the rhubarb compote
500g (1lb 2oz) rhubarb, chopped into 2cm (¾in) chunks
50g (1¾oz) caster sugar
2cm (¾in) piece of fresh root ginger, grated

For the rhubarb and ginger beer jelly
250g (9oz) rhubarb compote (see above)
6 sheets gelatine, softened in a little cold water for about 5 minutes
250ml (8fl oz) Old Jamaica ginger beer

For the rhubarb and ginger crumble
300g (10oz) rhubarb, chopped into 2cm (¾in) chunks
25g (scant 1oz) caster sugar
250g (9oz) strawberries
100g (3½oz) plain flour
pinch of salt
1 tbsp ground ginger
100g (3½oz) demerara sugar
100g (3½oz) ground almonds
100g (3½oz) unsalted butter, softened

For the rhubarb ripple ice cream
1 vanilla pod, split lengthways
200ml (7fl oz) single cream
200ml (7fl oz) whole milk
4 egg yolks, beaten
90g (3oz) vanilla sugar
200ml (7fl oz) double cream

Rhubarb renaissance

A veritable celebration of humble rhubarb, with rhubarb jelly, ice cream and crumble

1 To make the rhubarb compote, gently cook the rhubarb, sugar and ginger in a pan for 10–15 minutes until softened. Allow to cool.

2 To make the rhubarb and ginger beer jelly, push about half of the cooled rhubarb compote through a sieve into a bowl to obtain a syrup (reserve several large chunks of the cooked rhubarb). Squeeze out any excess water from the gelatine. Mix with 100ml (3½fl oz) of the ginger beer, stirring until dissolved. Combine the rest of the ginger beer with 100ml (3½fl oz) water and the rhubarb syrup, then stir through the gelatine mixture. Pour into 4 dariole moulds and leave to set in the refrigerator overnight. Add a chunk of the cooked rhubarb once the jelly has set enough to hold its weight. Turn the set jellies out onto a board and carefully transfer to a plate.

3 To make the rhubarb and ginger crumble, preheat the oven to 180°C (350°F/Gas 4). Put the rhubarb in a saucepan and add the caster sugar and a splash of water. Gently cook for about 10 minutes until just soft, then place into 4 individual ramekins with a handful of chopped strawberries. To make the crumble topping, sift the flour into a large bowl. Add the pinch of salt, ginger, sugar, ground almonds and butter. Crumble until the right consistency is achieved. Layer the crumble mixture over the fruit. Cook for about 10–15 minutes in the hot oven. Cool slightly before serving.

4 To make the rhubarb ripple ice cream, scrape out the vanilla seeds into a pan with the single cream and milk. Bring just to boiling point, remove from the heat and leave to infuse for 10–15 minutes. Pour the cream mixture onto the egg yolks, whisk well to blend, then return to the pan. Continue whisking over a low heat until the mixture thickens. Add the vanilla sugar and leave to cool.

5 Whisk the double cream until stiff. Gently but thoroughly fold in the vanilla mixture. Churn in an ice-cream machine according to the manufacturer's instructions. For the rhubarb ripple effect, add 2–3 tbsp rhubarb compote at the last stages of churning.

6 Serve the ramekins of crumble on plates, with the jellies on the side. Put a scoop of ice cream in each of 4 small serving dishes and sit on the plate with the other desserts.

Almond tarts with Amaretto ice cream

The ultimate almond indulgence,
right down to the Amaretto ice cream

Prep time 45 minutes,
plus 1¾ hours' resting time
and churning time
Cooking time 15 minutes
Difficulty Medium

1 First make the pastry. Whizz the flour, butter, sugar and almond extract in a food processor until the mixture resembles large breadcrumbs. Add the egg yolk to bind together into a dough. Wrap the pastry in cling film and leave to rest at room temperature for 45 minutes.

2 Preheat the oven to 190°C (375°F/Gas 5).

3 Roll out the pastry to about 3mm (⅛in) thick and cut out circles about 7.5cm (3in) in diameter. Grease a 12-hole Yorkshire pudding tin sitting on a piece of kitchen paper with olive oil, then line the holes with the pastry. Put a dab of raspberry jam in the bottom of each pastry case.

4 To make the filling, whisk the egg whites until stiff, then fold in the sugar, ground almonds and almond extract. Beat for 2 minutes, then spoon the mixture into the pastry cases. Place a split almond on top of each tart and bake in the oven for 15 minutes.

5 To make the Amaretto ice cream, whisk the egg yolks and caster sugar together with the salt until pale and creamy. Heat the milk and cream to just below boiling point, then slowly pour the hot mixture into the egg and sugar mixture, stirring constantly. Pour the mixture back into the pan and stir over a low heat until thickened. Add the Amaretto.

6 Churn in an ice-cream machine for 45–60 minutes or according to the manufacturer's instructions.

7 To make the raspberry coulis, whizz together the ingredients in a blender, then push through a sieve. Chill until ready to serve.

8 To serve, place 2 tarts on each serving plate with 2 scoops of the ice cream on one side and the raspberry coulis on the other. Arrange 3 raspberries at the side of the ice cream and serve.

195

For the pastry
170g (6oz) plain flour
115g (4oz) butter, as cold
  as possible, cubed
30g (1oz) caster sugar
a few drops of almond
  extract
1 egg yolk
2 tbsp raspberry jam

For the filling
2 egg whites
230g (8oz) caster sugar
170g (6oz) ground almonds
a few drops of almond
  extract
split blanched almonds,
  to decorate

For the Amaretto ice cream
4 egg yolks
110g (4oz) caster sugar
pinch of salt
285ml (9fl oz) whole milk
285ml (9fl oz) double cream
1 tbsp Amaretto liqueur

For the raspberry coulis
250g (9oz) raspberries
2 tsp clear honey
1 tsp freshly squeezed
  lemon juice
grated zest of ½ lemon

handful of raspberries,
  to decorate

Trio of lavender and orange desserts

Orange almond cake, crème brûlée and ice cream are laced with fruits and flowers

Prep time 1 hour, plus overnight chilling time
Cooking time 40–60 minutes
Difficulty Medium–hard

Orange almond cake

1 Preheat the oven to 180°C (350°F/Gas 4). Butter a 18cm (6in) round cake or pie tin, lining the bottom with greaseproof paper.

2 Beat the egg yolks with a wooden spoon, gradually adding 130g (4½oz) of the sugar, until pale and creamy. Fold in the almonds, zest, juice and cinnamon to make a stiff paste.

3 Whisk the egg whites until they form soft peaks, then gradually beat in the remaining sugar. Keep whisking until the mixture is glossy and the peaks are stiff when you remove the whisk.

4 Stir one-third of the whisked whites into the almond mixture to loosen it slightly, then, using a metal spoon, fold in the remaining mixture in two batches.

5 Pour the mixture into the prepared tin and bake in the oven for 35 minutes. It should be slightly risen, with a chewy crust, but still soft in the inside. Leave to cool slightly before turning out. Remove the greaseproof paper and flip the cake onto the plate so that the brown side faces upwards. Sift some icing sugar over the top and serve while still slightly warm.

Lavender crème brûlée

1 Heat the cream to boiling point.

2 While the cream is heating, in a bowl, blend together the egg yolks, cornflour and lavender sugar. Pour in the hot cream, stirring all the time with a wooden spoon.

3 Return the mixture to the saucepan. Heat very gently, stirring all the time, until the custard has thickened. It is ready when the mixture coats the back of a spoon. Divide the custard between 6 ramekins or espresso coffee cups and leave to cool. Cover with cling film and chill for 2 hours or preferably overnight until set.

continued...

For the orange almond cake

3 medium eggs, separated
150g (5½oz) golden caster sugar
160g (5½oz) ground almonds
zest and juice of 1 small unwaxed orange, plus extra 1½ tbsp freshly squeezed juice
¼–½ tsp ground cinnamon
icing sugar, to dust

For the lavender crème brûlée

570ml (17fl oz) double cream
6 medium free-range egg yolks
4 level tbsp cornflour
2 tbsp lavender sugar
110g (4oz) granulated sugar
unsprayed lavender flower, to decorate

For the lavender ice cream

600ml (1 pint) double cream
10 g (1¼oz) unsprayed lavender flowers, plus extra, to garnish (optional) (if flowers are not available, use unsprayed leaves)
4 tbsp Scottish runny honey

...continued from p.197

4 To make the caramel, put the granulated sugar in a heavy pan over a very low heat and allow the sugar to dissolve gently and caramelize, without stirring. When the sugar has completely dissolved, remove the pan from the heat and pour immediately over the set custards, covering the surface of each one. Leave for a few minutes for the caramel to harden.

5 Alternatively, if a thinner caramel is preferred, dust the crème brûlées with icing sugar and caramelize using a blowtorch or put under a hot grill for 2–3 minutes. Decorate with lavender flowers.

Lavender ice cream

1 Bring half the cream slowly to the boil. When the cream starts to bubble, remove from the heat.

2 Put the 10g (¼oz) lavender flowers or leaves in a wide jug, and pour the cream over them. Allow to cool, stirring often.

3 Once cooled, strain into a bowl and refrigerate the cream until very cold. Add the remaining cream to the lavender cream and whisk together until soft peaks form. Gently fold in the honey.

4 Either pour into a shallow freezer container without stirring, seal and freeze for 4–5 hours until firm, or churn in an ice-cream machine for 40 minutes, then freeze for 20 minutes. Soften slightly in the refrigerator, before serving with a sprinkling of extra flowers or leaves (if using).

Chocolate mud cakes with truffles

Rich, moist cake, alcohol-laced truffles and creamy mousse – a recipe for sinners

Prep time 1 hour, plus overnight chilling time
Cooking time 40 minutes
Difficulty Medium

1 To make the truffles, heat the double cream in a heatproof bowl set over a pan of simmering water, until the cream is almost boiling. Divide the cream into three smaller bowls. Add the milk, dark and white chocolates separately to each bowl. Stir until thickened.

2 Add the Tia Maria to the dark chocolate ganache, the Baileys to the milk chocolate and the raspberry liqueur to the white chocolate. Leave all three in the refrigerator overnight to chill.

3 To make the mud cakes, preheat the oven to 160°C (325°F/Gas 3). Lightly grease a 6-hole muffin tin.

4 In a heatproof bowl set over a pan of simmering water, melt together the butter, dark chocolate, coffee and 170ml (6fl oz) hot water. In a jug, whisk together the buttermilk, eggs and oil.

5 In a separate bowl, mix together the flours, cocoa powder, bicarbonate of soda and sugar. Make a well in the centre and pour the contents of the jug into it. Stir to combine. Now add the melted chocolate mixture and stir to combine. Pour the mixture into the holes of the muffin tin. Bake in the oven for 30 minutes.

6 To make the chocolate mousse, in a heatproof bowl set over a pan of simmering water, gently heat the sugar, egg yolks, whipping cream and cocoa powder until the sugar has dissolved. Add the butter and chocolate and stir until the mixture looks like mud. Beat the egg whites to soft peaks and gently stir into the mixture. Chill until ready to assemble the cakes.

7 To make the chocolate topping, place a clean bowl over a pan of simmering water. Melt together the extra 140g (5oz) butter and 140g (5oz) chocolate, then leave to cool until the mixture thickens.

8 When the truffle mixtures have firmed, roll each one out into balls. Roll in cocoa powder and/or grated chocolate and chill until needed. Whisk together the double cream and crème fraîche.

9 When the cakes are cool, slice each one through the middle horizontally. Spread the chocolate mousse on the lower halves, and sandwich together again. Smooth the topping over the top and sides of the cakes and decorate with the truffles.

For the truffles
180ml (6fl oz) double cream
200g (7oz) milk chocolate
200g (7oz) dark chocolate
200g (7oz) white chocolate
2 tbsp Tia Maria
2 tbsp Baileys
2 tbsp raspberry liqueur
cocoa powder and/or grated chocolate, to decorate

For the mud cakes
225g (8oz) butter, plus extra 140g (5oz) for topping
225g (8oz) dark chocolate (70% cocoa solids), plus extra 140g (5oz) for topping
2 tbsp freeze-dried coffee granules
115ml (4fl oz) buttermilk
4 eggs
2 tbsp light olive oil
140g (5oz) self-raising flour
140g (5oz) plain flour
55g (2oz) dark cocoa powder
½ tsp bicarbonate of soda
500g (1lb 2oz) sugar

For the mousse
55g (2oz) sugar
6 egg yolks
200ml (7fl oz) whipping cream
1 tbsp dark cocoa powder
100g (3½oz) butter
250g (9oz) dark chocolate
3 egg whites
100g (3½oz) sugar

To serve
125ml (4fl oz) double cream
2 tbsp crème fraîche

Traditional English trifle

A pretty and delectable version from the pantheon of traditional British puds

Prep Time 1 hour, plus drying time for rose petals
Cooking Time 40 minutes
Difficulty Medium–hard

For the crystallized rose petals
unsprayed rose petals
1 large egg (white only)
55g (2oz) caster sugar

For the rhubarb and Earl Grey jam
450g (1lb) rhubarb
450g (1lb) caster sugar
zest and juice of 1 lemon
125ml (4fl oz) Earl Grey tea
½ vanilla pod, split and
 seeds scraped out

For the strawberry jelly
125g (4½oz) caster sugar
325ml (12fl oz) rosé sparkling
 wine, preferably English
4 leaves gelatine
350g (12oz) ripe English
 strawberries, hulled

For the sponge
115g (4oz) unsalted butter
115g (4oz) golden caster
 sugar
2 large free-range eggs
a few drops of vanilla extract
115g (4oz) flour
splash of milk

For the custard
570ml (1 pint) whole milk
55ml (2fl oz) single cream
4 large free-range egg yolks
30g (1oz) golden caster sugar
a few drops of vanilla extract
2 level tsp cornflour

1 glass of Rutherglen Muscat
300ml (10fl oz) double cream

Crystallized rose petals

1 To crystallize the rose (or other flower) petals, lightly whisk together the egg white and 1 tbsp water until a few air bubbles start to appear. Put the caster sugar into a small dish.

2 Dip a paintbrush into the egg white and gently paint the petals until they are completely covered (make sure the petals are scupulously dry first). Holding the petals over the sugar dish, gently sprinkle sugar evenly over both sides.

3 Place the petals on baking parchment or waxed paper to dry. (You can put them in a low oven to accelerate the drying process.)

Rhubarb and Earl Grey jam

1 Slice the rhubarb into 2cm (¾in) pieces and put in a heavy saucepan. Sprinkle over the sugar, lemon juice, Earl Grey tea, and vanilla seeds. Cook over a gentle heat, stirring continuously, until the sugar has dissolved. Stir in the lemon zest.

2 Increase the heat and boil the jam for 10 minutes, then remove the pan from the heat. Spoon the jam into a bowl and allow to cool. Alternatively, pot straight into hot sterilized jars with tight-fitting lids, seal and leave on a wire rack to cool. Store in a cool, dark place and keep refrigerated once opened.

Strawberry jelly

1 Prepare a sugar syrup base. Put the caster sugar and half of the wine in a saucepan and place over a gentle heat to dissolve the sugar. Simmer gently for 2 minutes. Leave to cool.

2 Soften the gelatine leaves in a dish of cold water for 5 minutes. Remove the softened leaves, squeeze out the excess water, then stir the gelatine into the still-hot sugar syrup. Allow to cool at room temperature, until just beginning to set, then continue with the second stage of the jelly method.

3 Tip the strawberries into the setting jelly mix. Stir to disperse the fruit evenly without breaking up the fruit, then gently stir in the remaining sparkling wine. Put the jelly layer into a bowl, and carefullly sit the bowl in iced water. Allow to set.

Sponge

1 Preheat the oven to 180°C (350°F/Gas 4). Grease a 20cm (8in) sponge tin and line with baking parchment.

2 Using an electric mixer, cream together the butter and sugar until pale and fluffy. With the mixer running on a slow speed, add the eggs one at a time, beating well between after each addition until well blended. Add the vanilla extract and flour and a touch of milk and blend until smooth and creamy.

3 Pour the sponge mixture into the prepared tin and bake in the oven for about 20 minutes until golden and slightly springy to the touch. Leave in the tin for 5 minutes, then turn out onto a wire rack to cool completely.

Custard

1 In a saucepan, slowly bring the milk and cream to simmering point over a low heat.

2 Meanwhile, in a bowl, whisk together the egg yolks, sugar and cornflour until smooth and creamy.

3 Pour the hot milk and cream mixture onto the eggs and sugar, whisking all the time. Return the custard to the pan, add the vanilla extract and keep stirring over a very low heat until thick.

4 Cover the surface of the custard with cling film to prevent a skin forming and leave to cool over a bowl of iced water.

To assemble

1 Once the sponge has cooled, cut out rounds using a small pastry cutter. Spread the rounds thickly with the cooled rhubarb and Earl Grey jam, arrange in the bottom of the serving dish (or individual dishes) and drizzle with the Muscat.

2 Arrange the jelly fruit layer over the sponge layer, then pour the cooled custard over the top. Chill for 10 minutes.

3 Whisk the double cream to soft peaks and carefully spread over the custard layer. Decorate with sprinklings of the crystallized rose petals and serve.

Chocolate brownie with crème caramel

Gooey brownie temptation to the max, with silky caramel and soft summer fruits

Prep time 20 minutes
Cooking time 45 minutes,
plus 2 hours chilling
Difficulty Medium

For the chocolate brownies
250g (9oz) unsalted butter
250g (9oz) dark chocolate
  (at least 70% cocoa solids),
  broken into pieces
4 large eggs
350g (12oz) granulated sugar
1 tsp vanilla extract
175g (6oz) plain flour
pinch of salt

For the crème caramels
350g (12oz) caster sugar
840ml (28fl oz) double cream
1 vanilla pod, split
  lengthways
4 free-range eggs
100g (3½oz) caster sugar

For the blueberry and strawberry coulis
200g (7oz) blueberries
200g (7oz) strawberries
juice of 1 lemon
4 tbsp icing sugar

To finish
400ml (14fl oz) double cream
4 tbsp cocoa powder
4 tbsp icing sugar
4 sprigs of fresh mint,
  to garnish

Chocolate brownies

1 Preheat the oven to 180°C (350°F/Gas 4). Line a 4-hole Yorkshire pudding tart pie tin with greaseproof paper.

2 Melt the butter and chocolate together in a heatproof bowl set over a pan of barely simmering water.

3 Beat together the eggs, sugar and vanilla extract until the mixture is thick and creamy and coats the back of a spoon.

4 Once the butter and chocolate have melted, remove from the heat and beat into the egg mixture.

5 Sift together the flour and salt, add to the egg mixture and continue to beat until smooth.

6 Pour the mixture into the holes of the prepared tin and bake for 20–25 minutes until the top has formed a light brown crust that has started to crack. The brownies should not wobble, but remain a little gooey on the inside. Leave in the tin to cool completely. Do not turn off the oven.

Crème caramels

1 Meanwhile, to make the crème caramels, put the sugar and 90ml (3fl oz) water in a pan and bring to the boil. Cook for 4–5 minutes until the sugar has dissolved and turned a caramel colour. Be careful not to burn.

2 Pour a little of the caramel into the bottom of each of 4 ovenproof ramekins, carefully swirling the caramel up the sides.

3 Put the cream and split vanilla pod into the pan that the caramel was made in and bring to a simmer.

4 In a bowl, whisk together the eggs and sugar until smooth, then pour the hot cream over the egg mixture, whisking all the time. Strain into the caramel-lined ramekins.

5 Sit the ramekins in a deep roasting tin. Carefully fill the roasting tin with hot water until it comes two-thirds of the way up the sides of the ramekins. Bake in the oven for 15–20 minutes until just set.

continued…

...continued from p.202

6 Remove from the oven and lift the crème caramels out of the roasting tin. Allow to cool completely before leaving to chill in the refrigerator for 1–2 hours.

Blueberry and strawberry coulis

1 Purée all the ingredients in a blender or food processor for about 30 seconds until smooth.

2 Sieve into a bowl and set aside.

To finish

1 Whip the double cream with the cocoa powder and icing sugar until smooth.

2 Remove the brownies from the tin and place one in the middle of each of 4 serving plates. Spread some of the chocolate cream over the top of each brownie.

3 Carefully turn out a crème caramel on top of each of the cream-covered brownies and liberally pour the coulis around the edges, trying to avoid touching it.

4 Garnish each crème caramel with a sprig of fresh mint. Serve.

Apple batter cake

Old-fashioned apple batter cake, served hot, warm, or cold – perfect comfort food

1 Preheat the oven to 180°C (350°F/Gas 4). Line the bottom of a 20cm (8in) round cake tin with greaseproof paper. Butter the sides, dust with flour and shake off the excess.

2 To make the apple batter cake, take out half of 1 egg yolk and beat the eggs until fluffy. Add the sugar and whisk for about 3 minutes until pale and creamy. Scrape the seeds from the vanilla pod into the egg and sugar mixture and put the pod in the melted butter to infuse. Peel, core and slice the apples very thinly.

3 Remove the vanilla pod from the butter and stir the butter into the egg and sugar mixture. Sift the flour, baking powder and salt into the batter, adding alternately with the milk and stir until it is all combined. Pop the apples into the batter, ensuring that every piece is well coated. Pour the batter into the prepared tin and bake in the oven for 50 minutes, turning once halfway through. Test with a skewer to check whether it is cooked; if it comes out clean, it's ready. Remove from the oven and leave to sit for 20 minutes.

4 To make the cinnamon ice cream, put the milk and cinnamon stick in a pan and bring just to the boil. Whisk together the egg yolks, sugar and ground cinnamon until pale and fluffy. Discard the cinnamon stick and strain the milk onto the yolk mixture, whisking as you go. Pour the mixture back into the pan and cook over a low heat, stirring constantly, for about 8 minutes until thickened. Whisk the custard into the cream, cool and churn in an ice-cream machine according to the manufacturer's instructions.

5 To make the tuiles, turn up the oven to 200°C (400°F/Gas 6). Mix together all the tuile ingredients in a bowl. Spread very thinly in the shape of circles on a baking tray lined with non-stick baking parchment. Bake in the oven for 5–7 minutes until the edges are golden. Quickly drape on an upturned glass or rolling pin, pushing the edges of each tuile over to form a curve. Leave to cool.

6 To make the coulis, bring the rhubarb, sugar and 1 tbsp water to a simmer in a pan. If it's not pink enough, add a drop of cochineal. Simmer for 3–4 minutes until soft, then pass through a sieve. Serves slices of the cake, dusted with icing sugar, with a scoop of ice cream and a tuile, surrounded by a little of the coulis.

Prep time 20 minutes
Cooking time 1 hour
15 minutes
Difficulty Medium

For the apple batter cake
2 medium eggs
70g (2½oz) caster sugar
1 vanilla pod, split lengthways
100g (3½oz) unsalted butter, melted
600g (1lb 5oz) eating apples (whatever is in season)
25g (scant 1oz) plain flour
2 tsp baking powder
¼ tsp salt
125ml (4fl oz) whole milk

For the cinnamon ice cream
225ml (8fl oz) whole milk
1 cinnamon stick
2 egg yolks
65g (2oz) caster sugar
1 tsp ground cinnamon
300ml (10fl oz) double cream

For the tuiles
55g (2oz) plain flour
55g (2oz) unsalted butter
110g (4oz) caster sugar
2 egg whites, lightly whisked
½ tsp vanilla extract

For the rhubarb coulis
100g (3½oz) rhubarb, cut into small chunks
1 tbsp caster sugar
a drop of cochineal

Trio of afternoon tea desserts

Lemon Victoria sponge, fruity tea bread ice cream and strawberry tarts, anyone?

Prep time 1 hour, plus 2 hours' soaking time
Cooking time 2 hours
Difficulty Medium

For the tea bread
200g (7oz) mixed dried fruit
50g (1¾oz) crystallized ginger
50g (1¾oz) dates
450ml (15fl oz) strong black tea
75g (2½oz) soft light brown sugar
75g (2½oz) caster sugar
1 tsp ground cinnamon
1 tsp ground nutmeg
250g (9oz) self-raising flour
2 eggs
1 tbsp clear honey
1 tbsp golden syrup
grated zest of 1 orange

For the lemon curd
1 egg
grated zest and juice of 1 lemon
40g (1½oz) caster sugar
25g (scant 1oz) butter
1 tsp cornflour

For the ice cream
80ml (2½fl oz) semi-skimmed milk
300ml (10fl oz) double cream
½ tsp vanilla essence
2 egg yolks
60g (2oz) caster sugar
1 tsp cornflour

1 To make the tea bread, soak the dried fruit, ginger and dates in the tea for at least an hour, preferably much longer.

2 Add the different sugars and spices and leave for another hour.

3 Preheat the oven to 150°C (300°F/Gas 2). Add the spiced fruit and sugar to the flour, eggs, honey, golden syrup and orange zest and mix thoroughly. Spoon the mixture into a loaf tin and bake in the oven for 1½ hours.

4 To make the lemon curd, whisk the egg in a medium saucepan. Add the remaining ingredients. Cook over a low heat, whisking continuously. Let the mixture simmer for about a minute or so on the lowest heat. Once it starts to thicken, whisk constantly until about the consistency of home-made mayonaisse. Set aside to cool to room temperature, then chill for at least 10 minutes.

5 To make the tea bread ice cream, heat the milk, cream and vanilla essence over a medium heat, but not to boiling point. Whisk the egg yolks with the sugar and cornflour until pale and fluffy.

6 Slowly add the hot milk to the egg mixture, whisking continusouly, until combined. Return the mixture to the pan and heat slowly until it thickens to the consistency of thick double cream. Remove from the heat and leave to cool completely.

7 Churn in an ice-cream machine according to the manufacturer's instructions until the ice cream is nearly ready and set.

8 To make the Victoria sponge, preheat the oven to 180°C (350°F/Gas 4). Beat together the margarine, butter and caster sugar until light and fluffy. Gradually add the eggs, flour and baking powder until everything is combined, but remains as light as possible. Pour the mixture into a greased mini sponge tin and bake in the oven for about 20 minutes until cooked through. Leave to cool completely before turning out of the tin.

9 For the butter icing, beat the butter until soft. Gradually mix in the icing sugar until combined, keeping it as light as possible. Add the honey to taste. Chill until 30 minutes before needed. Remove from the refrigerator to allow it to return to room temperature.

10 To make the pastry for the strawberry tarts, put the flour in a bowl and rub in the butter with your fingertips until the mixture resembles breadcrumbs. Add half the caster sugar, then the egg yolk, then gradually add the cold water, a very little at a time, until the mixture just comes together into a dough. Leave to rest in the refrigerator for at least 30 minutes, preferably longer.

11 To finish the ice cream, remove the nearly ready ice cream mixture from the machine and mix in the crumbled tea bread until evenly distributed. Transfer to a freezerproof container and keep in the freezer until needed.

12 To finish the tart, preheat the oven to 190°C (375°F/Gas 5). Hull all of the strawberries to remove the stalks. Cut off the bottom of 10 or 12 of the strawberries, so that they are all of the same level, then cut the rest of them into small pieces. Mix together all of the strawberries with the remaining 25g (scant 1oz) sugar and leave to marinate for about 10 minutes.

13 Take the pastry out of the refrigerator and roll out with a dusting of icing sugar to prevent it sticking to the board. Use to line in four 10cm (4in) individual tart tins.

14 Mix together the whole egg and milk and brush over the pastry, then blind-bake in the oven for about 20 minutes until golden brown and cooked through. Leave to cool.

15 Spread the clotted cream onto the base of the pastry cases and arrange the chopped strawberries over the top, with the uniform-height strawberries arranged neatly with points upwards.

16 To finish the sponge, trim the sponge to a neat and dainty size using a 5cm (2in) diameter pastry cutter. Slice the cake in half and spread over the lemon curd and some of the butter icing. Sandwich the sponge back together. Dust with some icing sugar.

17 Serve the desserts on a single round plate, with each of the components of the dish set as a trio in a triangle. Serve the ice cream will be served in 4 small bone-china cups, as a way of continuing the afternoon tea theme of the dish.

For the lemon Victoria sponge
50g (1¾oz) margarine
50g (1¾oz) unsalted butter
100g (3½oz) caster sugar
2 eggs, beaten with a couple of drops of vanilla extract
100g (3½fl oz) self-raising flour
1 tsp baking powder
2 tbsp home-made lemon curd (see opposite)
icing sugar, to dust

For the butter icing
50g (1¾oz) unsalted butter
100g (3½oz) icing sugar
1 tbsp clear honey

For the strawberry tart
100g (3½oz) plain flour
50g (1¾oz) butter, diced
50g (1¾oz) caster sugar
1 egg yolk
3 tbsp cold water
100g (3½oz) small, ripe strawberries
1 egg
3 tbsp whole milk
1 tbsp clotted cream
icing sugar, for rolling out the pastry

Steamed kumquat marmalade pudding

Fruity sponge pudding with a duo of ice creams, biscuit curls and citrus sauce

Prep time 50 minutes, plus
freezing and soaking time
Cooking time 1 hour
45 minutes
Difficulty Medium–hard

For the kumquat marmalade
900g (2lb) kumquats
1 litre (1¾ pints) water
juice of 1 lemon
900g (2lb) granulated sugar
225g (8oz) pectin sugar

For the marmalade whim wham ice cream
284ml (9fl oz) Channel Island milk
4 egg yolks (reserve whites for the cigarette biscuits)
110g (4oz) caster sugar
204ml (9fl oz) double cream
½ tsp vanilla extract
120ml (4fl oz) warmed marmalade

For the Cointreau ice cream
115g (4oz) caster sugar
115g (4oz) Cointreau or to taste
570ml (17fl oz) whipping cream
2 tbsp clotted cream or to taste

For the kumquat marmalade pudding
115g (4oz) unsalted butter
115g (4oz) caster sugar
2 free-range eggs, lightly beaten
a few drops of vanilla extract or grated zest of 1 orange
about 140g (5oz) self-raising flour
about 2 tbsp kumquat marmalade
milk (if needed)

1 To make the marmalade, slice the kumquats into rounds and remove all the pips. Put the pips in a bowl with some of the water.

2 Put the kumquats, lemon juice and the rest of the water in a large bowl and leave overnight.

3 The next day, boil the pips in the water for a few minutes, then strain, pushing the pectin that has formed through the sieve. Add this to the kumquats and put in a large stainless-steel pan. Let the fruit simmer for about 30 minutes until the peel feels soft.

4 Warm the sugar in a low oven, then add to the fruit, ensuring that it has dissolved completely. Now boil rapidly and start testing for setting point after about 10 minutes.

5 When the setting point is reached, pot the marmalade into hot sterilized jars, seal and cover with wax so that it seals immediately. Allow to cool on a wire rack and label. The marmalade will keep for up to 6 months; refrigerate once opened.

6 To make the marmalade whim wham ice cream, gently heat the milk in a pan until just below boiling point. In a bowl, whisk together the egg yolks and sugar until pale and creamy, then gradually add the hot milk, whisking constantly. Pour the mixture into a clean pan and heat gently, stirring, until the mixture coats the back of a spoon. Transfer to a bowl and allow to cool. Stir in the cream and vanilla and leave to chill in the refrigerator. Churn in an ice-cream machine for about 10 minutes or according to the manufacturer's instructions. When the ice cream has thickened, swirl through the warmed marmalade. Transfer the ice cream to a freezerproof container and put in the freezer to firm.

7 To make the Cointreau ice cream, put the sugar and Cointreau in a saucepan and heat gently until the sugar has dissolved; allow to cool. Pour the sugar syrup and whipping cream into a bowl and whisk until the mix starts to thicken. Add the clotted cream and churn in the ice-cream machine for about 30 minutes until thick. Transfer to a freezerproof container and place in the freezer.

continued…

For the cigarette biscuits

2 egg whites
115g (4oz) caster sugar
1 tsp vanilla extract or grated zest of 1 orange (optional)
55g (2oz) unsalted butter, melted
55g (2oz) plain flour, sifted (or a mixture of flour and cocoa powder)

For the marmalade sauce

2 tbsp kumquat marmalade
about 200ml (7fl oz) water
zest of 1 lemon
arrowroot, to thicken

...continued from p.208

...continued from p.208

8 To make the kumquat pudding, lightly grease a 600ml (1-pint) pudding basin or four 150ml (5fl oz) pudding basins.

9 Cream together the butter and sugar until light and fluffy. Add the beaten eggs, a little at a time. Now add the vanilla extract or orange zest and fold in the flour. If the mixture is too stiff, use a little milk.

10 Spoon the marmalade into the prepared basin(s) and spread over the bottom. Fill the basin(s) with the pudding mixture and cover with greaseproof paper and foil with a pleat. Tie with kitchen string and steam for about 1¼ hours for a large pudding or about 40 minutes if making 4 individual puddings.

11 Meanwhile, to make the cigarette biscuits, preheat the oven to 200°C (400°C/Gas 6). Line a baking sheet with silicone paper, or grease and flour a baking sheet.

12 Whisk the egg whites until stiff, add the caster sugar and whisk until the mixture is smooth. Add the vanilla now, if using, then add the melted butter to the mixture with the sifted flour (or sifted flour and cocoa). For an orange alternative, fold in the orange zest.

13 Spread the mixture in long oval shapes onto the prepared baking sheet and bake in the oven for 5–6 minutes. When cooked, remove carefully from the baking sheet and wrap around the handle of a wooden spoon to shape.

14 To make the marmalade sauce, put the marmalade, water, and lemon zest in a pan. Bring slowly to the boil and taste. Adjust the flavour, adding arrowroot if necessary to thicken.

15 Serve the hot steamed pudding with the sauce and a scoop of each ice cream on the side with a cigarette biscuit.

Trio of Scottish profiteroles

Another delicious melding, with French pastry meeting Scottish ingenuity

Prep time 35 minutes
Cooking time 1 hour
Difficulty Medium–hard

1 Preheat the oven to 200°C (400°F/Gas 6). Grease a mini muffin tin well and wet with a little water.

2 To make the profiteroles, bring the butter and 150ml (5fl oz) water to the boil in a saucepan. Remove from the heat and add the sifted flour all in one go. Beat for a minute or so, leave to cool for about 5 minutes, then beat in the eggs. Beat in the vanilla extract.

3 Put teaspoons of the pastry mix in the muffin tin. Bake for 7 minutes. Increase the temperature to 220°C (425°F/Gas 7) and bake for a further 12 minutes until puffy and golden brown. Leave to cool on a wire rack – prick a hole in each to let steam escape.

4 To make the cranachan filling, fold the toasted oatmeal, raspberries and Drambuie into one-third of the whipped cream.

5 To make the tablet filling, put butter, milk and sugar in a pan over a low heat. Once the sugar has dissolved, bring to the boil for 10 minutes. Add the condensed milk and bring to the boil again until just under 118°C (244°F), stirring all the time. Remove from the heat, add the vanilla essence and beat until very thick. Pour into a greased baking tray. Once set, cut or crumble some tablet into small pieces; fold through one-third of the whipped cream.

6 To make the Athol Brose filling, mix the oatmeal and 150ml (5fl oz) water to form a paste. Leave to stand for 30 minutes, then strain through a fine sieve, squeezing out as much liquid as possible. Discard the oatmeal. Mix the oatmeal liquid with honey, orange zest and whisky in a small pan. Bring to the boil and simmer for 2–3 minutes until thick. Leave to cool. Fold the thickened Athol Brose into the remaining whipped cream.

7 To make the chocolate sauces, melt the milk and white chocolates separately, each with 1 tsp of the cream, in heatproof bowls set over pans of simmering water. Mix thoroughly until smooth and leave to cool slightly.

8 Fill the profiteroles with each of the different fillings. Serve one of each type of profiterole on each plate, with the white chocolate sauce poured over the Cranachan profiteroles and the milk chocolate sauce over the other two variations.

For the profiteroles
50g (1¾oz) unsalted butter
60g (2oz) plain flour
2 free-range eggs
½ tsp vanilla extract
300ml (10fl oz) whipping cream, whipped until soft peaks form

For the Cranachan filling
3 tbsp pinhead oatmeal, otasted in a dry frying pan
100g (3½oz) fresh raspberries, plus a few extra, to decorate
about 1 tbsp Drambuie, or to taste

For the tablet filling
110g (4oz) unsalted butter
285ml (9fl oz) whole milk
1kg (2¼lb) granulated sugar
450g (1lb) condensed milk
2 tsp vanilla essence

For the Athol Brose filling
3–4 tbsp Alford pinhead oatmeal
3–4 tsp heather honey
1 tsp grated orange zest, plus extra grated or strips of zest, to decorate
3 tbsp whisky
1 tbsp granulated sugar

For the chocolate sauces
100g (3½oz) good-quality milk chocolate
100g (3½oz) good-quality white chocolate
2 tsp double cream

Chocolate stout ice cream

Moreish ice cream with zesty shortbread –
pair with chocolate stout of the liquid kind

Prep time 10 minutes
Cooking time 30 minutes
Difficulty Easy–medium

For the ice cream
1 vanilla pod, split
  lengthways
250ml (8fl oz) double cream
1½ tbsp dark cocoa powder
  or grated dark chocolate
4 egg yolks
175g (6oz) granulated sugar
250ml (8fl oz) Titanic stout

For the orange shortbread
125g (4½oz) plain flour
40g (1½oz) caster sugar
zest of 1 orange
90g (3oz) unsalted butter,
  softened

strips of orange zest,
  to decorate

1 To make the ice cream, using the end of a teaspoon, scrape out the seeds from the vanilla pod. Add to a pan with the double cream and bring to the boil.

2 In a large bowl, mix together the cocoa powder or grated chocolate and the egg yolks and sugar, blending thoroughly. Add a small amount of the cream, whisking quickly to temper the eggs. Add the egg mixture to the pan and cook until thick, whisking constantly. Mix in the stout. Allow to cool, then churn in an ice-cream machine according to the manufacturer's instructions.

3 To make the shortbread, preheat the oven to 180°C (350°F/Gas 4). Mix together the flour, sugar and orange zest in a bowl. Rub in the butter until the mixture resembles fine breadcrumbs, then knead together until it forms a dough. Roll out the dough and cut into shapes. Bake in the oven for about 20 minutes.

4 Serve scoops of the ice cream decorated with fine strips of orange zest and a couple of pieces of the shortbread alongside.

Sticky toffee and date pudding

This may be the ultimate in sticky toffee puddings – light as air but fondly familiar

1 Preheat the oven to 180°F (350°F/Gas 4). In a small bowl, soak the dates in the boiling water and vanilla extract for 5 minutes, then drain and mash.

2 Cream together the butter and demerara sugar until light and fluffy. Add the egg to the butter mixture and beat thoroughly, then beat in the black treacle.

3 Fold in a third of the flour and all the bicarbonate of soda. Add half the milk, then repeat, adding the milk and the rest of the flour in batches. Stir in the mashed dates.

4 Spoon the date and treacle mixture into 4 ramekins and bake in the oven for 20–25 minutes.

5 To make the sauce, heat the butter, sugar and half the cream in a pan until the butter has melted. Bring to the boil, reduce the heat slightly and simmer for about 5 minutes until the sugar has dissolved completely.

6 Stir in the black treacle, increase the heat and allow the mixture to simmer for 2–3 minutes, stirring occasionally. Remove from the heat and stir in the rest of the cream.

7 For the triangle drizzle, dissolve the granulated sugar in a little cold water and boil for 4 minutes until golden in colour. Drizzle 4 triangle shapes onto a Bake-O-Glide or other non-stick silicone sheet and leave for about 10 seconds to set.

8 To serve, turn the puddings out onto a plate, pour the toffee sauce over the top and serve with a dollop of frozen crème fraîche and a triangle drizzle to garnish.

Prep time 20 minutes
Cooking time 35 minutes
Difficulty Easy–medium

For the pudding
100g (3½oz) chopped dates
90ml (3fl oz) boiling water
½ tsp vanilla extract
35g (1oz) softened butter
65g (2oz) demerara sugar
1 egg, lightly beaten
1 tsp black treacle
75g (2½oz) self-raising flour
½ tsp bicarbonate of soda
60ml (2fl oz) milk

For the toffee sauce
25g (scant 1 oz) butter
75g (2½oz) soft dark brown sugar
120ml (4fl oz) double cream
1 tbsp black treacle

For the triangle drizzle
2 tbsp granulated sugar

To serve
crème fraîche, frozen

"It's a real sort-of nursery-time treat … The flavours are very good … It's perfect. What a great dessert."

— Ed Baines

Prep time 15 minutes, plus overnight chilling time
Cooking time 45 minutes
Difficulty Medium

For the pastry
25g (1oz) icing sugar
100g (3½oz) plain flour
60g (2oz) salted butter, chopped into cubes
1 egg yolk

For the lemon filling
finely grated zest and juice of 3 lemons
100g (3½oz) salted butter
175g (6oz) caster sugar
2 eggs plus 2 egg yolks
4 tbsp double cream

For the meringue
6 egg whites
100g (3½oz) caster sugar

Lemon meringue pie

Gorgeous lemon filling topped with fluffy meringue – little bites of heaven

1 Preheat the oven to 180°C (350°F/Gas 4). Lightly grease four 10cm (4in) individual tart tins.

2 To make the pastry, put the icing sugar and flour into a large bowl. Add the butter and rub together with your fingertips, squeezing the mixture together, until the mixture resembles breadcrumbs. Make a well in the centre, add the egg yolk and continue to mix with your fingers until a smooth pastry forms. Leave to chill for as long as possible, preferably overnight.

3 To make the lemon filling, put all the ingredients except the double cream in a saucepan, heating slowly over a low heat until the butter has melted. Remove from the heat and set aside for a minute to cool, before adding the cream.

4 Roll out the pastry to the required thickness, about 3mm (⅛in), and use to line the individual tart tins. Line the pastry cases with greaseproof paper and fill with baking beans. Blind-bake in the oven for 4 minutes, then remove the beans and paper and bake the pastry cases for a further 4 minutes or until golden.

5 To finish the lemon filling, push the lemon mixture through a sieve; return to the pan and heat slowly until it thickens. Sieve the mixture again, then pour into the pastry cases to set.

6 To make the meringue, put the egg whites in a clean, dry bowl. Using an electric mixer, whisk the egg whites on a low to medium speed until they start to turn white, then increase the speed to high. While the egg whites are whisking, put the sugar and 4 tsp cold water in a saucepan over a low heat and heat until the mixture reaches a temperature of 110°C (225°F) on a cook's thermometer. Carefully swirl an extra 1 tbsp cold water around the edge of the saucepan to prevent sugar crystals forming.

7 Slowly pour the sugar syrup into the egg whites while they are whisking. Keep whisking until the mixture cools and soft peaks form. Place the meringue on top of the lemon tarts, using a chef's blowtorch to crisp the outer shell (or lightly brown the tops under a hot grill). Decorate with sifted icing sugar if desired.

8 These tarts are best served cold, but can also be enjoyed warm.

Prep time 1 hour, plus
cooling time for conserve
and overnight drying time
Cooking time 50 minutes
Difficulty Medium

**For the crystallized
rose petals**
1 unsprayed red or pink rose
1 egg white
100g (3½oz) caster sugar

**For the strawberry
conserve**
1kg (2¼lb) strawberries
1kg (2¼lb) jam sugar
juice of 2 lemons

**For the vanilla and
strawberry ripple
ice cream**
250ml (8fl oz) Jersey whole
    milk
250ml (8fl oz) Jersey cream
2 vanilla pods, split
    lengthways
1 tsp vanilla paste
4 egg yolks
75g (2½oz) sugar
2 tbsp liquid glucose
200g (7oz) home-made
    strawberry conserve
    (see above)

Strawberry and rose tart

Summertime flavours and floral aromas temptingly combine in this luscious tart

Crystallized rose petals

1 Make the crystallised rose petals the day before. Carefully peel off the rose petals and choose the best-shaped ones for crystallizing. They should not be damaged and must be dry.

2 Dip a petal in the egg white and use a clean paintbrush to spread the egg white evenly all over it. Now dip the petal straight into the sugar and make sure that it is well coated on both sides. Place on a sheet of baking parchment. Continue until all the petals have been coated and leave to dry overnight.

3 The crystallized rose petals will keep stored in an airtight tin for 3–4 days. Do not store them in the refrigerator or leave them in a humid place, as they will go soggy.

Strawberry conserve

1 Wash and hull the strawberries, then pat dry with kitchen paper.

2 Put in a dish and cover with the sugar. Cover the dish with cling film and leave to steep overnight. The sugar will extract the juice from the strawberries.

3 Strain off the juice and sugar and put in a saucepan; reserve the strawberries. Boil until the liquid has reduced by half.

4 Add the reserved strawberries and the lemon juice. Simmer for 10–15 minutes until the fruit is soft and has reached setting point. To check for setting point, have a cold saucer ready in the refrigerator. Take out and place a little of the jam onto the cold saucer. Return to the refrigerator for a few seconds. A wrinkly skin should form on the top when setting point has been reached.

5 Cool a little, then pour into hot sterilized jars with tight-fitting lids. Seal and leave to cool completely. (Sterilize the jars and lids on a baking tray in a very low oven for 15 minutes, or run through a hot cycle on the dishwasher.)

Vanilla and strawberry ripple ice cream

1 In a heavy saucepan, heat the milk and cream with the vanilla pods and vanilla paste. Simmer gently for 3 minutes.

2 In a bowl, whisk together the egg yolks, sugar and liquid glucose until thick and glossy.

3 Gradually add the hot milk and cream mixture to the egg mixture, stirring constantly. Mix well. Pour this custard mixture back into the saucepan and gently heat, stirring, until the custard coats the back of a spoon. Strain through a sieve into a bowl, cover with cling film and cool rapidly in the freezer for 10 minutes.

4 Pour the cooled custard into an ice-cream machine and churn according to the manufacturer's instructions for 40–60 minutes.

5 Using a food processor, whizz the strawberry conserve until almost smooth, but still with a few pieces of strawberry throughout. Fold the puréed conserve through the churned vanilla ice cream just before the ice cream has set completely. Freeze until needed.

Strawberry and rose tart

1 Preheat the oven to 180°C (350°F/Gas 4).

2 To make shortcrust pastry, pulse the butter, vegetable fat, flour and icing sugar in a food processor until the mixture resembles breadcrumbs. Add just enough cold water to form a dough.

3 Roll out the pastry to around 3mm (⅛in) thick and use it to line four 10cm (4in) individual fluted tart tins. Line the pastry cases with greaseproof paper and fill with baking beans. Blind-bake in the oven for 15 minutes. Take out of the oven and remove the beans and paper. Do not turn off the oven.

4 To make the filling, beat the butter, sugar, ground almonds, flour, whole egg and rose water until creamy. In a separate, clean bowl, whisk the egg white until stiff; fold into the cake mixture.

5 Spread strawberry conserve over the bottom of each tart case. Spoon over the cake mixture and bake for 10–15 minutes. Remove from the oven and dust with icing sugar and rose-scented sugar.

6 To serve, place a tart on each of 4 plates. Decorate each tart with crystallized rose petals and a strawberry fan and serve with a scoop of strawberry ripple ice cream on the side.

For the strawberry and rose tart

90g (3oz) cold unsalted butter
40g (1½oz) white vegetable fat such as Flora White
250g (9oz) plain flour
2 tbsp icing sugar
55g (2oz) soft unsalted butter
55g (2oz) caster sugar
25g (scant 1oz) ground almonds
30g (1oz) self-raising flour
1 large egg, plus 1 egg white
4 tsp rose water
120ml (4fl oz) fresh strawberry conserve (see opposite)

To decorate

2 tbsp icing sugar
2 tbsp rose-scented sugar
crystallized rose petals
4 small strawberries, sliced and shaped into fans

Traditional apple pie with whipped cream

The pastry for this apple pie is simply extraordinary and well worth the effort

Prep time 20 minutes
Cooking time 35 minutes
Difficulty Medium

For the filling
900g (2lb) Bramley apples
  (or use other old varieties
  such as Bascombe Mystery
  and Lane's Prince Albert)
2 tsp quince marmalade,
  or to taste
freshly squeezed lemon
  juice, to taste
caster sugar, to taste for
  the filling, plus a little more
  to sprinkle over the pie

For the pastry
175g (6oz) self-raising flour
85g (3oz) hard margarine
  such as Stork, plus a little
  extra for rolling pastry lid
85g (3oz) lard
pinch of salt
300ml (10fl oz) soured milk
  (leave out fresh milk for
  2–3 days in a warm kitchen)

To serve
300ml (10fl oz) double cream,
  whisked with a little caster
  sugar, to serve

1 For best results, all ingredients and equipment, including the rolling pin, should be well chilled in the refrigerator before use. Quantities of quince marmalade, sugar and lemon juice will depend on the apples used, so make sure that you taste the filling before putting it in the pie.

2 Preheat the oven to 200°C (400°F/Gas 6). Peel, core and chop the apples. Put in a pan of salted water until to ready to use, to prevent them turning brown. When ready, drain off the salted water and put the apples in a pan over a medium heat. Add the quince marmalade and part-cook for about 10 minutes, then add the lemon juice and sugar to taste. Drain and set aside to cool.

3 To make the pastry, sift the flour into a bowl. Add the margarine, lard and salt. Cut the mixture with a knife until it combines, then gradually add about 200ml (7fl oz) of the soured milk until the mixture just comes together into a dough; do not use your hands. The dough should be elastic and not be too wet or too dry.

4 On a floured work surface, roll out two-thirds of the pastry into a rectangle. Fold in three by folding the ends into the middle. Turn the pastry 90 degrees and repeat the process twice more. Keep your rolling movements very light. Roll out the pastry again and use to line a greased pie plate. Cut off the trimmings and set aside for the lid. Arrange the apple over the bottom of the pastry case, leaving a clear edge around and brush with soured milk.

5 For the lid, roll out the remaining third of pastry (but not the trimmings). Fold in the ends and turn 90 degrees. Cut a little extra margarine into small pieces and dot onto the pastry. Roll out the trimmings and place on top of the rolled-out dough. Dot more margarine on two-thirds of the pastry. Fold the non-margarine-dotted end into the middle; fold the other end over it. Turn and repeat twice more. Roll out and place on top of the pie. Cut a vent hole in the top and work around the edges, lifting and pinching together to seal. Glaze with soured milk and sprinkle with sugar.

6 Bake in the oven for 20–25 minutes until the pastry is a rich golden brown – it is important not to undercook it. Serve the warm pie cut into slices, with a dollop of the whipped cream.

Plum and blueberry upside-down cake

Caramelized plums and blueberries make a fine pairing in this warm pudding cake

Prep time 30 minutes
Cooking time 1¼ hour
Difficulty Medium

Honey ice cream

1 Put the cream and milk in a pan and heat until almost boiling. At the same time, whisk together the egg yolks and caster sugar until thick, pale and creamy.

2 Slowly add the hot cream mixture to the egg mixture, whisking all the time. Pour the mixture back into the pan, stirring constantly until it is thick enough to coat the back of a spoon. Add the honey.

3 Pour the custard into an ice-cream machine and churn according to the manufacturer's instructions until frozen.

Upside-down cake

1 Preheat the oven to 180°C (350°F/Gas 4). Grease a 20cm (8in) round cake tin.

2 To make the caramelized topping for the upside-down cake, put the sugar, whisky and 150ml (5fl oz) water in a heavy pan and slowly bring to the boil. Continue cooking until the sugar has dissolved and is starting to caramelize; this usually takes 10–15 minutes.

3 Meanwhile, prepare the fruit by cutting the plums in half and removing the stones. When the caramel is ready, transfer to the cake tin and carefully arrange the plums cut-side down in the caramel, in a circle around the edge of the tin. Fill the centre and any gaps with the blueberries.

4 Next, make the sponge. In a bowl, cream together the sugar and margarine until light and fluffy. Add the eggs, one at a time, beating well after each addition. Add the flour and a little milk alternately and mix until well combined. Pour the sponge mixture over the caramel fruit and spread evenly. Bake in the oven for 40–45 minutes until a skewer inserted into the centre of the cake comes out clean. Leave to cool in the tin for a minute or so, then run a knife around the edge of the tin. Sit an inverted serving plate on top of the cake, carefully flip over and remove the tin.

5 Serve the cake, cut into slices, as a warm pudding, accompanied by the honey ice cream. It also works well cold as a tea cake.

For the honey ice cream
300ml (10fl oz) clotted cream
150ml (5fl oz) semi-skimmed milk
5 egg yolks
75g (2½fl oz) caster sugar
3 tsp clear honey

For the caramelized fruit topping
150g (5½oz) caster sugar
90ml (3fl oz) Dalwhinnie whisky
4 large plums
100g (3½oz) blueberries

For the sponge
100g (3½oz) caster sugar
100g (3½oz) hard baking margarine, softened
2 medium eggs
100g (3½oz) self-raising flour
a little milk

Index

INDEX

Acknowledgements

Britain's Best Dish

This is the ITV series that aims to track down the best cookery happening in the UK today. One hundred and sixty-eight hopeful chefs are selected from regional auditions to appear in studio heats, before a tense final week in which twenty-one finalists are whittled down to three to see who can win the votes of celebrity judges and the audience.

The Judges

Ed Baines is a classically trained chef and owner of a string of exclusive restaurants. He began his career at The Dorchester, moved on to The River Café, and now runs champagne and oyster bar Randall & Aubin, with branches in Soho and Chelsea. He makes regular appearances on TV and contributes to a number of food and cookery magazines.

John Burton Race describes himself as "mad as a hatter, sharp as a knife, a culinary genius and a big softie at heart". A Michelin-starred chef, he has founded esteemed eateries such as L'Ortolan, and now manages The New Angel in Devon. His TV credits include French Leave, which documented his move from a hectic London career to a slower pace of life in the French countryside.

Wine expert **Jilly Goolden** presented TV programme *Food and Drink* for 18 years, and has made numerous appearances on other TV shows, including *I'm A Celebrity… Get Me Out Of Here*. She is a prolific author and journalist.

Publisher's Acknowledgements

DK would like to thank Emma-Jane Frost for food styling, Helen Finch for food styling assistance, Jim Smith, Saskia Janssen and Kat Mead for photography direction, Naomi Waters for proofreading and Susan Bosanko for indexing. Thanks also to Kevin Morgan and his team at ITV.

ITV would like to thank Mike Harris, Juliet Leith, Tim Miller, Jeanette Moffat, Jo Scarratt and Putul Verma.